A QUICK
LOOK
AT
CHRISTIAN
HISTORY

GEORGE THOMAS KURIAN

HARVEST HOUSE PUBLISHERS
EUGENE, OREGON

Cover by Dugan Design Group, Bloomington, Minnesota

All cover photos © Fotolia and iStock

A QUICK LOOK AT CHRISTIAN HISTORY

Copyright © 2015 by George Thomas Kurian
Published by Harvest House Publishers
Eugene, Oregon 97402
www.harvesthousepublishers.com

Library of Congress Cataloging-in-Publication Data
 Kurian, George Thomas.
 A quick look at Christian history / George Kurian.
  pages cm
 ISBN 978-0-7369-5378-8 (pbk.)
 ISBN 978-0-7369-5379-5 (eBook)
 1. Church history. I. Title.
 BR145.3.K865 2014
 270—dc23

                2013043583

Printed in the United States of America

     15 16 17 18 19 20 21 22 23 / VP-JH / 10 9 8 7 6 5 4 3 2 1

Contents

Introduction

"History," the German existentialist philosopher Martin Heidegger said, "is a river in which human beings float, driven by its currents." *A Quick Look at Christian History* traces the river of Christian history and its tributaries as it meanders over the course of 2000 years.

A Quick Look at Christian History belongs to a genre known as timelines. It is a horizontal linkage of people and events, ideas and institutions. Timelines are different from narrative history, but both are included in a branch of historiography known as chronology. In the early centuries, the church had as many chronologers as historians. One of the earliest was James Usher, who wrote a chronology of the world starting with creation. Then there was the 13-volume *Magdeburg Centuries*, a chronology of the church divided by centuries. Written by seven authors called Centuriators led by M. Flacius Illyricus, it was published in Basel between 1559 and 1674. New divisions of time were sometimes devised, such as age, era, and dispensation, to illustrate patterns of growth and the waxing and waning of civilizations.

But the greatest triumph of Christian chronology came from the work of a little-known monk named Dionysius Exiguus, who, on orders of the pope, devised a dividing line across human history known as *Anno Domini*, or Year of the Lord. This revolution was as influencial and consequential as Copernicus's heliocentric theory. The birth of Christ became the central event in history. Later the term "before Christ" (BC) was devised to cover the centuries that ended with the birth of Christ.

A Quick Look at Christian History may be called (to borrow from John Bunyan) the Pilgrim Church's Progress. It is a story of growth and expansion and the efforts of the gates of hell to thwart it. The church grew on three fronts. First, it grew territorially from a room in Jerusalem to the uttermost parts of the earth. Second, it grew numerically from 12 illiterate men to more than two-thirds of the human race to become the first truly universal faith. But the greatest transformation was institutional and structural. That the church is not of human origin; it is actually an institution alien to the earth system. As a result, it has to adopt the protocols, rubrics, and modalities that undergird it as a universal institution. This process took centuries and is perhaps even now incomplete.

For decades the church and its members did not even have a name. They were called the Way or the Nazarenes or some such words of insult. Finally, the name Christians was used at Antioch, and then only in derision. Similarly, Christ's divinity did not become dogma until centuries after His resurrection. During the same period, hymns had to be composed, the canon of the Scriptures established, the

Eucharist incorporated into the worship services, dates set for fasts and feasts, liturgies written, churches built, and the sacerdotal hierarchy set up. The church's institutional infrastructure is the most brilliant and well-ordered in the world and has contributed to the church's success.

The great advantage of timelines over narrative history is that while the latter travels along the highways, the former can explore the byways and side roads of history. What may appear as inconsequential to the great historians may be fascinating to the lay student. Timelines are a serendipitist's delight.

The most enjoyable part of completing a manuscript is acknowledging help in its compilation. In this, as in my 65 books that preceded it, I drew from the wellsprings of love, encouragement, and support of my wife, Annie. My daughter Sarah was the laboring oar in many of these projects, and her cheerful disposition made her an ideal coworker, troubleshooter, and problem solver. At Harvest House Publishers, Terry Glaspey was in at the creation and worked on it closely every step of the way. Gene Skinner handled the editing with professional skill and brought in imaginative ideas and resources.

George Thomas Kurian
Yorktown Heights, New York
June 10, 2014

The Age of the Apostles

THE STATUS OF THE CHRISTIAN CHURCH

On the Day of Pentecost, the church begins with about 4000 members. By the end of the first century, 28 percent of the then-known world has heard the gospel, and 0.6 percent of the population is Christian. The church is 70 percent nonwhite, and Scriptures are available in six languages.

INFLUENTIAL CHRISTIANS

Apostles Paul, John, and Matthew; Gospel writers Mark and Luke; Stephen (the first martyr)

SIGNIFICANT EVENTS AND INFLUENCES

- The birth of Christ is the great watershed in human history. This cosmic event did not explode on the scene like a supernova, but arrived in secret with the gentle cry of an infant in the Judean night. It would reverberate through the corridors of time and change human lives as no other event before or since.

- When Christ was born, Octavian (later Emperor Caesar Augustus) was at the zenith of his power, and his army enforced peace throughout the largest empire history had known. It extended to Armenia and Arabia in the east, to Nubia and Carthage in the south, to Gaul in the north, and to Spain in the west. The other two great powers, China and India, were outside the pale of known civilization.

- Christianity began not with the birth of Christ, but with His resurrection. The New Testament, like all testaments, became effective only with the death of the testator. It is not so much Christ's message that forms the foundation stone of Christianity as His atoning sacrifice and His resurrection.

- Pentecost transformed the small band of apostles and their immediate followers into the largest missionary enterprise the world had known. On this day the Holy Spirit was poured out on this motley crowd of believers and emboldened them to challenge the established religions of Greece and Rome.

- Christianity spread like a fire from heaven, consuming the pagan cultures of the day. Within two decades of Calvary, Christianity had spread to three continents. Paul, Peter, and possibly James took it to Europe. Mark took it to Africa, Thomas took it to India, and the other apostles took it to some of the smaller countries in the Middle East. By the end of the first century, there were Christians in Egypt, Nubia, Armenia, France, Italy, Spain, Greece,

Cyprus, Germany, Britain, Mesopotamia, Persia, India, Illyria, Dalmatia, Asia Minor, Albania, Libya, and all of North Africa.

- Seven years after Calvary, Christ's followers were called Christians for the first time in Antioch. In Roman usage, the suffix "-ian" implied "the property of," and the term "Christian" originally pointed to one who belonged to Christ rather than someone who simply believed in Him.

- The three decades after Calvary were dominated by a man who was not even one of the 12 apostles—Paul, formerly Saul, the learned Jew from Cilicia. Paul was a towering figure in all except the physical sense, a brilliant intellect, a gifted writer, and a tireless worker. Half of the New Testament books came from his pen. His elegiac epistles form the foundation of Christian theology. Known as the apostle of the Gentiles, Paul almost single-handedly took the gospel to the non-Jewish world and made it a global rather than an ethnic religion.

- Within a few years of Calvary, Christianity had its first martyr—Stephen. He set the pattern that would last through the centuries. The blood of the martyrs would become the seeds of the church as millions of Christian martyrs gave their lives that their faith might live.

- Open persecution of Christians began in Palestine under King Herod Agrippa, who beheaded James, one of the original apostles, in Jerusalem. The spread of Christianity to other provinces of the Roman Empire incurred imperial wrath. In the first century, both Nero and Domitian proscribed the new religion and put tens of thousands to the sword or exposed them to lions.

- By the end of the first century, Christianity had cut its umbilical cord to Judaism. Christians were ousted from all synagogues. The temple in Jerusalem was destroyed by the Romans as Jesus had predicted, and the Jews were expelled from their native land after the suppression of their final revolt against Rome in AD 70. For the next 19 centuries, Jews and Christians would remain hostile to one another.

- All the documents eventually included in the New Testament were written by the end of the first century.

CHRONOLOGY

30 Jesus commissions the 12 apostles (and later 70 other disciples) to preach the good news.

Jesus is crucified and resurrected, and He ascends to heaven.

Jesus gives the Great Commission: "Go and make disciples of all nations."

The church in Jerusalem is founded on the Day of Pentecost in Jerusalem as the disciples are filled with the Spirit in an upper room and 3000 others are converted.

31 The apostles begin evangelizing widely. Some remain in Jerusalem, where they evangelize only Jews. The church remains Jewish.

34 Stephen, one of the first deacons, becomes the first martyr.

Saul, a Jew from Tarsus, is directed by the high priest to suppress Christianity. On the road to Damascus, Saul encounters a blinding light and receives a vision of the risen Christ, who asks him, "Why do you persecute me?" Saul departs to Arabia and later to Jerusalem. He eventually becomes well known by the Greek version of his name, Paul.

Philip extends the mission to Samaritans. He baptizes the Ethiopian eunuch, who takes the gospel to Nubia (present-day Sudan).

35 According to tradition, Thaddeus and Bartholomew evangelize in Armenia.

Christians multiply throughout Judea, Samaria, and Galilee.

36 Peter ministers at Caesarea, and many Italians are converted.

37 The wider mission to the Gentiles is launched.

Peter preaches in Samaria and the coastal cities of Palestine.

Emperor Tiberius dies, and Caligula becomes emperor.

40 Believers are first called Christians in Antioch, perhaps derisively. The suffix "-ian" indicates that they belong to Christ.

The first Christians are reported in Greece and the city of Rome.

42 Claudius becomes emperor.

Mark the Evangelist arrives in Alexandria and plants the seeds of the Coptic Church.

44 King Agrippa executes James, the brother of John. Peter is imprisoned but miraculously escapes.

45 Paul begins his first missionary journey, which lasts three years. He travels with Barnabas to Antioch, Cyprus, Pamphilia, Pisidia, and Lystra.

The church in Antioch sends famine relief to Jerusalem.

48 The apostles and elders of the church meet in Jerusalem for the first apostolic council. They discuss whether Christians need to follow Jewish rites, such as circumcision.

49 Peter and Paul fall out over whether Jewish and Gentile Christians should follow the *kashruth*, or Jewish dietary laws, especially those banning pork. The apostles decide that Gentiles are exempt from these restrictions. Paul is recognized as the apostle to non-Jews.

50 Jews and Christians are banished from Rome.

The first Christians are reported in Persia. Assyrian Christians form the Church of the East.

Paul begins his second missionary journey, which lasts two years. He visits Phrygia, Galatia, and Greece. He enlists Timothy and Silas and plants many churches.

51 Paul writes 1 Thessalonians from Corinth.

52 The apostle Thomas sails to an ancient Jewish colony in India. He evangelizes Hindus and establishes seven churches. He is eventually martyred in Mylapore, and his body is buried in San Thome.

Paul writes 1 Corinthians and 2 Thessalonians.

53 Paul writes to the Philippians, the first church he founded, while he is in prison.

Paul embarks on his third missionary journey, which lasts five years. He visits Ephesus, Corinth, Macedonia, Philippi, Phrygia, Galatia, and Caesarea. He is arrested during Pentecost at Jerusalem, taken before Governor Felix at Caesarea, and imprisoned there from 58 to 60.
In 60 he appears before Festus, appeals to Caesar, is brought before Agrippa and Berenice, and sails to Rome as a prisoner. He remains in Rome until 63.

54 Nero becomes emperor and launches the first imperial persecution of Christians.

55 The Roman province of Asia, which includes 500 cities, is evangelized from Ephesus, its capital. Acts reports that all residents of Asia hear the word of God.

56 The 12 apostles cover the known world with the good news. Paul and Peter preach in Roman provinces, James in Spain, Bartholomew in Armenia, and Thomas in India.

57 Paul's epistle to the Romans is sent out to 3000 Christians in five Roman congregations. Paul reports that the word of God has reached the ends of the earth as far as Illyricum.

60 The apostle Andrew, brother of Peter, is crucified in Achaia.

James, a brother of Jesus, writes his epistle.

The first Christians are reported in Malta following Paul's shipwreck on the island.

61   Paul arrives in Rome as a prisoner. He reports that the good news has been preached to "every creature under heaven."

The first Christians are reported in England.

In Jerusalem, James (the brother of Jesus) is stoned to death by order of the high priest, Annas. Simeon, son of Cleophas and Mary, succeeds James.

63   Paul is freed in Rome. He later visits Spain.

The apostle Mark is martyred in Alexandria.

64   Peter writes his first epistle.

Paul sends his pastoral epistles to Timothy and Titus.

Fire breaks out in Rome, and Christians are blamed. Peter is crucified upside down.

Paul is executed with thousands of other Christians.

66   Luke concludes the book of Acts.

69   Ignatius becomes bishop of Antioch.

Polycarp (69–155), bishop of Smyrna and martyr, is born.

70   The Gospel of Mark, the earliest of the synoptic Gospels, is completed.

Titus destroys Jerusalem with four Roman legions, killing 10,000 Jews and taking 90,000 more to Rome as prisoners.

Antioch becomes the center of Christianity in the eastern half of the Roman Empire.

75   Luke and Matthew complete their Gospels.

Christians are expelled from Jewish synagogues.

80   The first Christians are reported in France and in North Africa.

81   Christians refuse to offer incense to Emperor Domitian and suffer their second imperial persecution.

85   Barnabas, Clement, Hermas, Ignatius, Papias, and Polycarp compose the earliest writings of the Apostolic Fathers.

90   Gnosticism, a dualistic heresy, arises.

The Gospel of John is completed.

93 Jewish historian Flavius Josephus mentions Jesus in *Antiquities of the Jews*.

95 Ignatius of Antioch writes *Letters*, seven letters written to his friends before his martyrdom.

The Eucharist is widely celebrated on Sunday, which becomes the Christian Sabbath.

John, the aged and sole surviving apostle, is exiled to the island of Patmos in the Aegean Sea.

96 Clement writes his first epistle to the Corinthians, the oldest of the extracanonical epistles.

"*Sanctus*," an early hymn of praise, is first used. Clement mentions singing of psalms during service.

Timothy is killed by a mob while opposing a pagan festival.

98 Christians suffer their third imperial persecution under Trajan.

The Second Century (100–200)

The Age of the Church Fathers

THE STATUS OF THE CHRISTIAN CHURCH

At the end of the second century, 32 percent of the known world has heard the gospel, and 3.4 percent of the population is Christian. The church is 68 percent nonwhite, and Scriptures are available in seven languages.

INFLUENTIAL CHRISTIANS

Ignatius, Polycarp, Tertullian, Justin Martyr, Hermas, Tatian

SIGNIFICANT EVENTS AND INFLUENCES

- At the turn of the first century, the last of the surviving apostles, John, is an exile on the island of Patmos, where the angel of the Lord parted the veil of the future and revealed to him the mysteries of things to be. His Apocalypse is couched in enigmatic language that speaks of cosmic cataclysms that defy human understanding. The Apocalypse was to become the last chapter of the New Testament, and he ended the great drama of which he had been such a faithful witness with the words, "Amen. Come, Lord Jesus."

- A new generation of saints and martyrs took up the torch of faith even as the last of the apostles passed from the scene. The greatest among these were Ignatius of Antioch and Polycarp, bishop of Smyrna, who was burned at the stake. Other church fathers were defining the faith that had been handed down from the apostles, creating a *consensus patrum* that was to develop later. Irenaeus of Lyons, a student of Polycarp, emerged as one of the earliest Christian theologians. His *Against Heresies* was the first attempt to defend orthodoxy.

- The fledgling church was already being beset by heretics by the beginning of the second century. The most formidable of these heretics was Marcion of Sinope, who was a brilliant theologian. He was the first to realize the radical nature of the Christian revelation and to break away completely from Judaism. He considered the Jehovah of the Old Testament as a Demiurge who was not only inferior to the Father of Jesus Christ, but in fact, evil. Marcion rejected most of the Old Testament and accepted only the Pauline epistles in the New Testament. By doing so, he prompted the church to determine the authenticity of each of the books of the Bible.

- The Gnostics also emerged as a serious threat to orthodoxy. They followed a form of Manichaeism that posited a struggle between a god of light and a god of darkness and offered knowledge (*gnosis*) as the path of salvation.

- By the end of the second century, the church recognized 23 of the 27 books of the New Testament as canonical. At this time, these books came to be called Scripture. Other New Testament writings were received more slowly. Doubts persisted about Hebrews, Jude, 2 Peter, 2 and 3 John, and Revelation. Certain books, not included in the modern New Testament, were considered canonical by some churches but rejected by others. These included the Epistle of Barnabas and the *Shepherd of Hermas*.

- By the second century, two of the seven major sacraments of the church—baptism and the Eucharist—had been accepted as the defining marks of a Christian life. The other five sacraments—extreme unction, confirmation, ordination, marriage, and monastic consecration—were being incorporated as divine services. Baptism was originally only for adults, but the baptism of infants was becoming increasingly the norm. The Eucharist was being celebrated on Sundays, as prescribed by Paul, rather than on the Sabbath, as the earliest Christians did.

- By the end of the second century, Christianity was sweeping the empire, posing a threat to the imperial religion. Tertullian wrote, "There is no nation indeed which is not Christian." Hermas wrote, "The Son of God has been preached to the ends of the earth." And Justin Martyr wrote that "Christ has been proclaimed to every race of men." Christianity spread to present-day Morocco, Bulgaria, Portugal, Romania, Arabia, and Austria.

- The second century witnessed the birth of Christian literature. Among the notable works was the Didache, an important document describing Christian beliefs, practices, and church government. Justin Martyr wrote his *Apology*, introducing the branch of theology known as apologetics. Another classic is the *Shepherd of Hermas* by the subapostolic writer Hermas.

- In 132 the Jews revolted again under Bar Kokhba, leading to the second destruction of Jerusalem by the Romans in 134. Almost all the Jews in Palestine were either killed or exiled, and the nation was not to return to its native land until modern times.

- The second century witnessed even more brutal persecutions of Christians under Septimus Severus and Marcus Aurelius. The number of martyrs throughout the Roman Empire was in the tens of thousands. The church was planted in blood, and it was being watered with blood.

CHRONOLOGY

100 Justin Martyr (100–165), an early Christian apologist, is born.

The age of the apostles comes to a close when apostle John dies at Ephesus.

Christianity is predominantly urban, spreading from city to city along Roman trade routes.

Saudi Arabians become Christians. (Christianity will be eradicated in the seventh century by Islam.)

Sri Lanka (then Ceylon) receives the gospel from Christians who had been evangelized by Thomas in India.

105 Ignatius of Antioch applies the term "catholic" to the church for the first time in his letter to the Smyrnaeans.

110 This is the earliest plausible date for the Old Roman Creed, a precursor to the Apostles' Creed.

Ignatius writes his seven *Letters* during his journey to Rome.

112 Ignatius is martyred at Rome.

120 Tatian (120–180), author of *Diatessarion*, a harmony of the four Gospels, is born.

The Didache, an early manual of church life, is written as early as 65 or as late as 150. It includes teaching that baptism is administered both by triple immersion and by pouring, and it mentions regular fasting on Wednesday and Friday.

Shepherd of Hermas, a series of eschatological and prophetic tracts, is written sometime between 120 and 155.

128 The Latin hymn "*Gloria in Excelsis Deo*" ("Glory to God on High") is written. The authorship is probably Greek.

130 Irenaeus (130–202), an early Church Father and apologist, is born.

135 Polycarp writes his Epistle to the Philippians.

144 Marcion of Pontus is excommunicated and forms a separate Christian community. He rejects the Old Testament, whose God he contrasts with the God of Jesus. His radical selection of New Testament books prompts the church to be more specific about what books it believes to be part of the Bible.

Aristides of Athens writes the earliest surviving *apologia* for (defence of) Christianity, much influenced by Judaism.

150 *Marcion's Canon*, a collection of New Testament books, is compiled according to Gnostic criteria. It is the first known New Testament canon. Though the text is not extant, it has been reconstructed from the writings of Marcion's critics.

The Roman provinces of Moesia and Thracia (modern Bulgaria) are evangelized. The first churches are formed at Anchialos (modern Pomorie) and Debeltum (modern Burgas) along the Black Sea.

The Roman province of Lusitania (modern Portugal) is evangelized.

Justin Martyr founds a catechetical school in Rome and documents signs and wonders among the faithful.

A shrine is constructed over the tomb of the apostle Peter on Vatican Hill in Rome.

Clement of Alexandria (150–215), a Church Father, is born.

155 Justin Martyr describes worship in Rome. It includes Old and New Testament readings, a sermon, an offering of bread and wine, a prayer of the faithful, the kiss of peace, a eucharistic prayer, and communion. He writes his *First Apology*, reconciling faith and reason, outlining doctrine, and responding to charges of immorality.

156 Montanism begins. Tertullian will be its most famous member. Persecuted by the established church, it goes underground.

160 Tertullian of Carthage (160–220), a brilliant Christian apologist, expositor, and Church Father, is born.

Clement of Alexandria (150–215), a Greek theologian and philosopher, is born.

161 Christians suffer the fourth imperial Roman persecution under Marcus Aurelius.

170 Hippolytus (170–235), an important theologian, is born.

Tatian, a Gnostic apologist, writes his *Address to the Greeks* and also the *Diatessaron*, a harmony of the four Gospels in Old Syriac.

175 The earliest references to incense being used in Christian worship date from this time.

Hegesippus writes his list of apostolic succession. It is the oldest record of the names of the early bishops of Rome.

Athenagoras writes his *Apology* and *On the Resurrection*.

177 Christianity is introduced to Britain.

180 Christians are now found in all provinces of the Roman Empire and in Mesopotamia.

The first Christian commentary on the beginning of Genesis is written. The existence of the invisible God is argued from His visible works in creation. It includes the first usage of the word "Trinity."

The churches of Rome and Alexandria celebrate Easter on the Sunday after the first full moon of spring, but the churches of Asia Minor observe it on the fourteenth of the month Nisan.

Celsus writes his *True Speech* against the Christians.

The Scillitan Martyrs are executed at Carthage. The *Acts of the Scillitan Martyrs* is considered the earliest document of the church of Africa.

182 Origen (182–254), an influential Christian thinker and writer, is born.

185 Irenaeus writes *Against Heresies*. It is a detailed attack on Gnosticism, especially that of Valentinus, and is eventually regarded as a classic formulation of orthodoxy.

188 Church Fathers allow chant in the liturgy but warn against polyphony, chromatic music, dance, and the use of some instruments.

Clement of Alexandria writes *Miscellaneous Studies*, *An Exhortation to the Greeks* (*Protrepticus*), and *On Christian Life and Manners*. These three works contain the most thorough synthesis of Christian doctrine and Greek philosophy at the time.

190 Parts of the Bible are translated into Latin for the first time, perhaps by a Christian community in Africa.

193 Christians suffer the fifth imperial Roman persecution under Septimius Severus.

194 The *Muratorian Canon* of Scripture is compiled. It is the oldest extant list of New Testament writings and is somewhat different from the modern one.

195 The threefold hierarchy of bishop, presbyter, and deacon is widespread by this time.

197 Tertullian writes his *Apology*, appealing for state toleration of Christianity. He also writes *On the Lord's Prayer* and *On Baptism*. He writes, "The blood of the martyrs is seed," and "There is no nation indeed which is not Christian."

199 Christian catacombs are constructed in the suburban area of Rome. They consist of several underground chambers, usually laid out in a grid. Recesses in the walls, one above another, contain the bodies, grouped by family.

The Montanist movement is officially condemned.

200 Tertullian is among the first to mention various Daily Office hours. He notes that Vigils, Lauds, and Vespers are said in Carthage and that Terce, Sext, and None are recognized as private prayer hours.

The Great Persecutions

THE STATUS OF THE CHRISTIAN CHURCH

At the end of the third century, 36 percent of the world is evangelized, and 10.4 percent of the population is Christian. The church is 65.7 percent nonwhite, and Scriptures are available in ten languages.

INFUENTIAL CHRISTIANS

Anthony the Great, Clement of Alexandria, Origen, Gregory the Illuminator, Cyprian of Carthage, Gregory Thaumaturgus

SIGNIFICANT EVENTS AND INFLUENCES

* By 200 the Scriptures were translated into seven languages, including Syriac and Coptic. The edition of the four Gospels in a continuous narrative, compiled by Tatian in about 170, began to circulate widely in Syriac-speaking churches. It became the standard text until the fifth century, when it was replaced by the four separate Gospels we have today.

* The third century saw the birth of Christian monasticism in Egypt. Anthony the Great (251–356) was the first Desert Father to go into the Wadi El Natrun as a hermit to launch the great wave of asceticism that would blossom in the fourth century.

* Christian theology was taken to new heights in the early third century by two theologians based in Alexandria. Clement of Alexandria was the head of a school of catechumens there. He was an authority on Greek philosophy and was able to fashion a theology rooted in the best Hellenic traditions. After Clement came Origen, the greatest of the Alexandrian theologians. He taught in Alexandria for 28 years. He wrote some 2000 works, about which Jerome wrote, "Who could ever read all that Origen wrote?" Origen's writings included commentaries on most books of the New Testament. Origen was killed in the Decian persecution.

* The Decian persecution began in the middle of the century. Emperor Decius decreed that all citizens were required to sacrifice to an image of the emperor and obtain a certificate called a *libellus* attesting to their obedience. Those who failed to obtain a *libellus* were tortured and beheaded, a fate that befell most of the bishops and church leaders. Valerian succeeded Decius as emperor and issued another decree in 257: "The most sacred emperors Valerian and his son Gallienus command that there shall be no meetings of Christians in any place, and that they shall not frequent the cemeteries. If

anyone fails to observe this beneficial precept, he shall be beheaded." Those who were killed included Cyprian of Carthage, one of the greatest Christian theologians. The persecution ended in 261 when Emperor Gallienus issued his edict of toleration.

- The end of the third century marked the bloodiest persecutions against Christians. In 298 pagan priests accused Christians of disrupting sacrifices at a pagan temple in Antioch. Roman troops were called in, and they unleashed a persecution that lasted more than seven years and left hundreds of thousands dead. Diocletian, the senior emperor, had been tolerant of Christians during the first 20 years of his reign, as his wife and daughter were probably Christians. But Galerius, the junior emperor, was opposed to the new religion. In 300, as some Christians refused to serve in the imperial army, Galerius ordered all Roman soldiers to offer sacrifices to the pagan gods. Three years later, further edicts ordered the destruction of churches, the confiscation of Scriptures, and the arrest of bishops and theologians. In 304 the edict was extended to all Christians in the empire. As Galerius redoubled his efforts to stamp out Christianity, Lactantius wrote, "There is another cause why God permits persecutions to be carried out against us, that the people of God may be increased."

- In the third century, North Africa in general and Carthage in particular were among the most heavily Christianized areas of the Roman Empire. The first Latin-speaking church was there, and it produced some of the greatest of the Church Fathers, including Tertullian and Augustine.

- In the third century, the first church buildings began to take shape as rectangular basilicas. Previously Christians met in homes or in underground hiding places. Archeological excavations in the city of Dura-Europos, on the eastern frontier of the Roman Empire, discovered the remains of the earliest surviving Christian church. It had an altar, a chair, a baptistery, and room for some 60 people.

- The third century saw the establishment of the first Christian kingdom and the first national church. Gregory the Illuminator (257–332) went to Armenia and persuaded King Tiridates, who was then persecuting the church, to embrace Christianity. The king then encouraged all his people to follow him—the first time such a national conversion had taken place. Armenia is the oldest Christian nation in the world.

CHRONOLOGY

200 Clement of Alexandria writes *Stromata*. Minucius Felix writes *Octavius*. Irenaeus writes *Demonstration of Apostolic Teaching*.
Most of the New Testament is available in Coptic.
Thousands of Christians are martyred in vicious persecutions in Egypt.

Switzerland and Belgium are evangelized.

The New Testament in Latin is completed.

The first permanent church buildings are constructed.

202 Septimius Severus issues an edict against Jews and Christians, forbidding any form of proselytism.

Clement flees Alexandria.

Tertullian refers to making the sign of the cross at various times during the day. The sign is made with the finger or thumb on the forehead.

203 Perpetua, a 22-year-old noblewoman and nursing mother, and Felicity, an expectant mother, are martyred at Carthage. The account of their deaths, *Passio Perpetuae et Felicitatis*, becomes the prototype of acts of Christian martyrs.

205 Cyprian of Carthage (205–258), an African bishop, theologian, and martyr, is born.

206 Tertullian includes the first explicit mention of infant baptism in *On Baptism*. He also distinguishes baptism, unction, and the laying on of hands in the initiation rite—the first time all three are mentioned together. Baptism involves elaborate preparation, including confession of sin, renunciation of the devil, fasting, vigil, and anointing.

Tertullian writes *On the Soul*.

215 The custom of saying grace before meals is common by this time.

Clement of Alexandria is the first to refer to the fish as a Christian symbol.

220 Origen writes *On First Principles*, his most systematic and speculative work.

225 *Didascalia Apostolorum*, an early treatise on church life and order, is written, probably in Syriac.

230 Sextus Julius Africanus writes his *History of the World*. His estimate that the creation took place 5499 years before the birth of Christ is later adopted by many Eastern churches.

235 Christians suffer the sixth imperial Roman persecution under Maximinus.

Hippolytus writes *Refutation of All the Heresies*.

240 Lucian of Antioch (240–312), teacher of Arius and of Eusebius of Nicomedia, is born.

Origen writes his commentary on the Song of Songs.

Gregory Thaumaturgus becomes bishop in Pontus, a mostly pagan diocese. Ninety-five percent of the population is converted before his death in 270.

The earliest known baptistry is found in a house-church at Dura-Europos. Prior to this time, baptism was probably carried out in natural water sources.

245 Origen compiles *Hexapla*, a parallel edition of six Old Testament Greek translations.

248 Origen writes his eight-volume *Against Celsus*, an apologetic work against the pagan philosopher who objected to Christianity's supernatural and exclusivist claims.

249 Christians suffer the seventh imperial Roman persecution under Decius. The Roman state systematically attempts to destroy Christianity.

250 Gregory Thaumaturgus writes his *Statement of Faith*, which includes the earliest known record of an appearance of Mary.

Novatian writes *On the Trinity*, a completely orthodox doctrine of the Trinity by a man later condemned as a rigorist.

The Caesarean Creed is developed. It is a catechetical and baptismal creed of the Caesarean episcopate and later becomes the basis for the Nicene Creed at the Council of Nicaea.

The first known hermit, Paul of Thebes, goes into seclusion. According to legend, he lives as a hermit for more than a hundred years. He is known through Jerome's biography of him.

Pope Fabian sends Dionysius of Paris (Saint Denys) to be a missionary in Paris and the first bishop there.

Emperor Decius orders the arrest of the bishops of Rome, Antioch, and Jerusalem. The bishops of Carthage and Alexandria go into hiding. Alexander, bishop of Jerusalem, dies in prison. Fabian, bishop of Rome, is also martyred.

The Roman provinces of Pannonia and Valeria (modern Hungary) are evangelized.

251 The city of Rome includes 30,000 Christians (5 percent of the population), 46 presbyters, 7 deacons, 42 acolytes, 52 exorcists, and 1500 widows and persons in distress.

Anthony of Egypt, a desert hermit, is born.

Cyprian writes *On the Unity of the Catholic Church*.

252 A catastrophic plague epidemic strikes the Mediterranean world, killing 25 percent of the entire population of the Roman Empire over 20 years. Fifty percent of the population dies in Alexandria. In Carthage, bishop Cyprian organizes medical aid.

253 Christians suffer the eighth imperial Roman persecution under Valerian. Christians are no longer allowed to assemble for worship, and their property is confiscated.

255 The Council of Carthage addresses the rebaptism of heretics.

256 Arius (256–336), an Egyptian heretic, is born.

257 Gregory the Illuminator (257–331), the apostle to Armenia, is born.

260 Some Christians of Pentapolis denounce Dionysius, the bishop of Alexandria, for Christological errors. The Synod of Rome upholds the doctrine of the Trinity and condemns both Sabellianism (modalism) and tritheism.

Emperor Gallienus issues an edict of religious tolerance and restores confiscated goods.

According to some calculations, there are about six million Christians in the Roman Empire.

261 The first basilicas (rectangular churches) are built.

263 Eusebius (263–339), bishop of Caesarea, scholar, and father of church history, is born.

268 Rome is regarded as the senior bishopric at the Council of Antioch.

About 40 percent of the Roman Empire is Christian, and the number is increasing rapidly.

270 Antony of Egypt establishes himself in the desert.

Christians suffer the ninth imperial Roman persecution under Aurelian.

Manicheism arises. It is a dualistic hierarchical rival religion to Christianity.

Monasticism begins in Egypt.

Nicholas (270–343), bishop of Myra, is born. Many people today associate him with Santa Claus.

272 Dionysius, bishop of Paris, and two of his companions are beheaded on a hill called *Montreartre* (Martyrs' Mound).

Constantine the Great (272–337) is born. He became a Byzantine emperor and ended the persecution of Christianity.

290 The Roman Empire is reorganized by Emperor Diocletian into 4 prefectures, 15 (secular) dioceses, and 120 provinces.

Pachomius (290–346), a hermit and monastic founder in Egypt, is born.

291 Hilarion (291–371), the founder of Anchoritic monasticism in Palestine, is born.

296 Athanasius the Great of Alexandria (296–373), a Church Father, chief defender of Tinitarianism, and father of Orthodoxy, is born.

298–302 Christians in the Roman army are forced to resign.

Imperial Conversion

THE STATUS OF THE CHRISTIAN CHURCH

At the end of the fourth century, 12 generations after Christ, 39 percent of the known world is evangelized, and 17.1 percent of the population is Christian. The church is 64 percent nonwhite, and Scriptures are available in 11 languages.

INFLUENTIAL CHRISTIANS

Eusebius of Caesaria, Constantine the Great, Ambrose of Milan, Jerome, Basil the Great, John Chrysostom, Pachomius

SIGNIFICANT EVENTS AND INFLUENCES

- In the fourth century, the church emerged from its catacombs and became an established religion in the Roman Empire. The central event in the century took place not in a church or a palace, but on Milvian Bridge outside of Rome, where Emperor Constantine the Great defeated his rival, Maxentius, in 312. At that battle, following instructions received in a dream the previous night, Constantine fought under the sign of the cross, which was subsequently modified into the labarum military standard. Although he was baptized only near his death in 337, Constantine favored Christianity for the rest of his life. He built several basilicas (including Saint Peter's), used Christian symbols on his coinage, and declared Sunday the official rest day. In 313 he and fellow-emperor Licinius issued the Edict of Milan, ending the persecution against Christians.

- However, Christianity did not become the state religion until much later. In the interim, Julian the Apostate, who came to power in 361, tried to restore paganism and renewed the persecution of Christians. He was killed in battle in the third year of his reign. According to tradition, on his deathbed he acknowledged the triumph of Christianity by saying, "Thou hast conquered, Pale Galilean." His successors, Jovian and Flavius Theodosius, favored Christianity. In 380 Theodosius made Christianity the official religion of the empire, and in 391 he closed all pagan temples. "It is our will," he decreed, "that all the peoples we rule shall practice that religion that Peter the apostle transmitted to the Romans."

- Almost at the same time Christianity succeeded in overcoming the pagan empire, the first of the many serious theological dissensions that were to plague the church in the succeeding centuries broke out. In 319 Arius began to preach a heresy that denied the divinity of Christ, the cardinal tenet on which Christianity is founded. Arius was silenced and exiled, but the heresy gained support in Antioch and other places. The celebrated opponent of Arianism was Athanasius the Great, who had succeeded Alexander as bishop of Alexandria in 328. He became known as the chief defender of trinitarianism and the champion of orthodoxy.

- The rise of the Arian heresy led to one of the defining events in Christian history, the First Ecumenical Council. It was convened by Constantine, who ordered 1800 bishops to meet in Nicaea (modern-day Iznik in Turkey). Between 220 and 250 bishops actually attended under the presidency of Hosius, the venerable bishop of Cordoba. The council not only condemned Arius but also drew up the central statement of the Christian faith, now known as the Nicene Creed. The creed defined the Trinity and affirmed that Jesus was of one substance with the Father—true God of true God. Arianism, however, survived in pockets of the empire, especially among the Goths. In the sixth century, the Second Ecumenical Council of Constantinople (the Fifth Ecumenical Council) reaffirmed the Nicene Creed.

- The fourth century also saw the birth of Christian history. Eusebius of Caesaria, known as the father of church history, wrote his ten-volume *Ecclesiastical History*, the first major historical work on Christianity.

- The fourth century was the golden age of Egyptian monasticism. At this time, the Egyptian desert contained history's largest concentration of monks. They lived as hermits or in monasteries. Pachomius (called Abba, from which we get the word "Abbot") established Tabenna, the first cenobitic monastery between 318 and 323 on an island of the Nile in Upper Egypt.

- Christianity continued to expand into all parts of the known world. By the end of the fourth century, it had spread to Belgium, Switzerland, Edessa, Hungary, Ethiopia, and Luxembourg. Missionaries from Eastern churches carried the gospel to parts of Northern India and Afghanistan as a step toward their eventual evangelization of Central Asia and China. The first Christians arrived in Ireland.

- In the fourth century, Christian liturgy and the special vestments associated with it began to take shape. Bishops began to wear purple, and the clergy began to wear a cloak of fine material when celebrating the Eucharist.

- Constantine moved the capital of the Roman Empire to Byzantium and renamed it Constantinople in 330.

- The canon of the New Testament was finally agreed upon in 367. The present 27 books were listed both in the *Easter Letter* of Athanasius in the East and the Synod of Carthage in the West.

CHRONOLOGY

300 Rome has more than 40 churches in the city limits. In the empire, the areas of strongest Christian development are Syria, Asia Minor, Egypt,

North Africa, and the cities of Rome and Lyons. The chief numerical strength is in the East, but every area in the empire is at least partially evangelized.

301 Gregory the Illuminator converts King Tiridates III of Armenia to the Christian faith. Armenia becomes the first country to adopt Christianity.

303 Christians suffer the tenth and last imperial Roman persecution under Diocletian, who orders the destruction of all church buildings and Scriptures. Government officials arrest bishops and church leaders (and later laity) and force them to sacrifice to Roman gods. Approximately 500,000 Christians are executed in ten years. This is the most extensive repression of Christianity up to that time. Numerous Christian leaders are martyred, including Agnes, Cosmas, Damian, Maurice, and Genesius.

304 Alban of Britain is martyred. He is traditionally considered the protomartyr of Britain.

305 Sebastian, a Roman soldier who aided Christians marked for death, is ordered to be executed by being shot with arrows and then beaten to death.

306 Christ's nativity begins to be celebrated on the winter solstice.

Lactantius completes his six-volume *Divinae Institutiones* (306–313). Between 318 and 321, he composes *De Mortibus Persecutorum* to testify to future generations the vengeful justice of God, who punishes all the main persecutors of the Christians.

Meletius causes a schism when he calls for the expulsion of Christians who abandoned the faith during persecutions.

311 Ulfilas (311–383) is born. He is eventually consecrated bishop at Constantinople by Eusebius of Nicomedia and starts to propagate Arian Christianity among the Goths.

Galerius issues his edict of toleration.

Donatists (named for a bishop named Donatus Magnus) cause a schism in North Africa. As rigorists, they oppose leniency toward those who lapsed under persecution.

Constantine introduces a series of measures in favor of the church.

312 Constantine is victorious in battle at the Milvian Bridge and becomes Augustus of the Western Empire. He attributes the victory to his inscribing *XP*, the first two letters of the Greek word for "Christ," on the shields of his troops.

313 Constantine and Licinius issue the the Edict of Milan. The document provides freedom of worship and restitution of the goods confiscated from the Christian communities.

Bishops from Italy and Gaul take part in a council at Rome regarding the Donatist question.

Eusebius of Caesarea writes his two apologetic works, *Praeparatio evangelica* and *Demonstrario evangelica*. The former is addressed to pagans, and the latter to Jews. They are also aimed at a Neoplatonic philosopher named Porphyry of Tyre.

314 The dedication of the cathedral at Tyre is the earliest recorded instance of a church building being dedicated.

Constantine calls the Council of Arles to consider the Donatist controversy. Churches from as far away as Britain send bishops.

315 Cyril (315–387), bishop of Jerusalem, is born.

Hilary of Poitiers (315–367), known as "Athanasius of the West," is born.

316 Emperor Licinius begins persecuting Eastern Christians.

Martin of Tours (316–397), a monk and bishop who pioneered Western monasticism, is born.

318 Athanasius writes *The Incarnation of the Word of God*.

319 Pagan sacrifices are prohibited throughout the Roman Empire.

320 The Forty Martyrs, a group of Christian soldiers, are killed in Sebaste, Lesser Armenia.

Pachomius (292–347), a converted Egyptian soldier, founds the monastary of Tabennisi, initiating cenobitic monasticism. He founds another monastery at Pabau in 328.

Constantine builds Old Saint Peter's Basilica on Vatican Hill, the traditional site of Peter's crucifixion.

321 Constantine adopts a policy of tolerance toward Donatists after trying unsuccessfully to suppress them by force.

Sunday becomes the official day of rest for the Roman Empire.

Constantine allows unlimited bequests to churches.

323 Eusebius of Caesarea writes *Ecclesiastical History*. It includes numerous otherwise unknown documents. Its apologetic intention is evident.

325   The First Council of Nicaea, the First Ecumenical Council, declares the
          Father and the Son are consubstantial—one being (*homoousion*). The
          council condemns Arius and drafts the Nicene Creed.

          The custom of giving the Eucharist to the dying is well established. It is
          considered *viaticum* (sustenance for a long journey). Pagans also pro-
          vided a last meal for the dying.

326   Constantine orders the building of the Church of the Holy Sepulchre in
          Jerusalem. A Roman temple to Aphrodite and a grove to Jupiter and
          Venus have to be removed to clear the site.

327   Constantine and his mother, Helena, commission the building of the
          Church of the Nativity in Jerusalem.

328   Athanasius succeeds Alexander as bishop of Alexandria.

329   Gregory of Nazianzus (329–389), also called "the Theologian," is born.
          He, Basil of Caesaria (330–379), and Basil's younger brother Gregory
          of Nyssa (332–395) are known as the Cappadocian Fathers.

330   The feast of Christmas is celebrated at Rome on December 25.

          Juvencus composes the first Christian poetical work, *Evangeliorum Libri
          IV*, a life of Christ based on the Gospels.

          Constantine moves the capital of the empire to Byzantium, "the New
          Rome," which he renames Constantinople. Pagan rites play no part in
          the dedication ceremony.

333   The anonymous "Pilgrim of Bordeaux," the earliest known pilgrim from
          Western Europe to Jerusalem, begins his journey. He also visits Con-
          stantinople and ends his journey in Milan.

335   Constantine makes bishops a part of the political structure of the empire
          by granting them judicial power.

336   Martin of Tours (336–397), a bishop and monk, is born.

338   Ambrose (338–397), bishop of Milan, is born.

339   Christians suffer severe persecution in Persia from 339 to 379. Intermit-
          tent vicious persecution by Sassanian rulers follow until the Muslim
          conquest of Persia in 640.

340   Ulfilas converts a flock of his fellow Goths.

          Ephrem the Syrian of Edessa takes over melodies from Bardaisan's docetic hymns, writes orthodox lyrics, and employs them in the fight against heresy.

341 The Synod of Antioch is held *in encaeniis*—"in dedication"—of the basilica there.

343 The Council of Sardica is summoned in Sofia to settle disputes between Eastern and Western bishops over the Arian controversy. It is continued by the Westerners alone, who approve various disciplinary canons and a doctrinal document without the *homoousios*—a statement that Jesus is of the same substance as the Father.

345 Evagrius Ponticus (345–399), a Greek Orthodox monk, preacher, and writer, is born.

346 Theodosius I (346–395), a Roman emperor, is born.

347 Jerome (347–420), who wrote the Vulgate (a Latin translation of the Bible), is born. His Latin name is Eusebius Hieronymus.

Bands of roving marauders use violence to enforce Donatist principles. The state steps in and begins to suppress and exile them.

348 Council of Carthage records gratitude for the effective official repression of the Donatists.

349 John Chrysostom (349–407) is born. He becomes a Greek preacher (known as the golden-tongued) and a doctor of the church.

350 Christianity reaches Geneva. A thriving community grows into a diocese with a cathedral in less than 50 years.

The Sanctus is a part of the Eucharistic liturgy in many Eastern and some Western churches.

Isaac the Great (350–438), patriarch of the Armenian church, is born.

The anonymous Apostolic Constitutions, collection of ecclesiastical law, are compiled.

Hibernia (modern Ireland) is evangelized by monks from Crete.

The entire Eastern Church is now Arian.

Ulfilas translates the Bible into Visigothic, a work that proves to be of great importance not just religiously but also culturally.

354 Augustine (354–430), bishop of Hippo and one of the most important Church Fathers in the history of the Western Church, is born.

Pelagius (354–420), a heretic, is born.

357   Basil of Caesaria, having visited Palestine and Egypt, retires to Annesi and propagates monastic life and rules.

Athanasius writes *Life of Antony*. Basil of Caesarea writes *Letters*.

358   Church music undergoes radical changes. Beginning in monasteries in Antioch, responsive (alternation between a cantor and the congregation) and antiphonal (alternation between two groups) psalms are introduced.

Basil of Caesarea and Gregory of Nazianzus compile an anthology of the works of Origen called *Philocalia*.

Basil of Caesarea begins writing his monastic rule, also called the *Rule of Saint Basil*. It becomes the basis for subsequent Eastern monasticism.

359   The sarcophagus of the 42-year-old Junius Bassus, a prefect of Rome, is created. It is a masterpiece of the classic Christian sculpture of the fourth century.

Constantius II calls the Council of Rimini, where Restitutus of Carthage presides over 400 bishops. The Nicene Creed is confirmed, but the bishops, constrained by the emperor, accept a formula of pro-Arian compromise.

360   Athanasius writes *Discourses Against the Arians*.

Ephraem the Syrian (306–373) compiles his *Hymns Against Heresies*.

John Cassian (360–435), a monk, is born.

The first Latin hymns are sung during the tenure of the French prelate Hilary of Poitiers.

The church of *Hagia Sophia* is built in Constantinople.

Ligugé Abbey, the first monastery north of the Alps, is founded.

361   Julian the Apostate becomes emperor. He attempts to restore paganism throughout the Roman Empire but fails. On his deathbed, he conceded, "Thou hast conquered, O pale Galilean."

364   Athanasius writes *Against Eunomius*. Hilary of Poitiers writes *Treatise on the Mysteries*.

367   The canon of the New Testament is finally agreed on. The 27 books are listed in Athanasius's *Easter Letter* (367) for the East and by the Synod of Carthage (397) for the West.

370   The Coptic texts of the Nag Hammadi library are assembled.

Christians create beautiful paintings on the walls of the Via Latina catacomb.

370–419   Jerome writes his *Pastoral Epistles*.

373   All Saints' Day (called the feast of All Martyrs) is first mentioned in Ephraem the Syrian's writings.

374   Basil of Caesarea speaks of antiphonal and responsive singing of psalms throughout Eastern Christianity.

Ambrose of Milan (337–397), a layman, is acclaimed bishop by crowds.

375   The anonymous *Apostolic Constitutions* indicate that the Gloria in Excelsis Deo is used as a canticle of morning prayer, the Kyrie Eleison ("Lord, have mercy") is beginning to be used, and the Nunc Dimittis ("now dismiss," or the Song of Simeon), is a part of daily prayers.

Basil of Caesaria writes *Treatise on the Holy Spirit*.

378   Goths and northern barbarians begin their conquest of the Roman Empire.

Jerome estimates that 1.9 million Christians have been martyred up to this time.

Cyril of Alexandria (378–444), an Alexandrian bishop and writer who opposed Nestorius, is born.

379   Theodosius the Great becomes Roman emperor.

Latin becomes the liturgical language at Rome.

Ambrose writes *On the Christian Faith*.

380   Theodosius makes Christianity the religion of the empire with the edict of Thessalonica. The faith of Damasus of Rome and Peter of Alexandria is deemed orthodox. Those who are not in communion with them are heretics. The emperor decrees that all imperial subjects must become Christians.

Gregory of Nazianzus preaches at Constantinople his five *Theological Orations*, a coherent treatise on the mystery of God as Father, Son, and Holy Spirit.

Gregory of Nyssa writes his commentary on the Lord's Prayer.

381   Theodosius the Great convenes the First Council of Constantinople (the Second Ecumenical Council) to resolve the Arian controversy, which Nicaea had not settled. It endorsed the teaching of the Council of Nicaea, affirmed the divinity of the Holy Spirit, and issued the classic Nicene Creed.

John Chrysostom writes *Discourses on the Priesthood*.

382   Pope Damasus issues the official canon of scriptural books.

Theodosius the Great declares heresy to be a capital crime.

383 Jerome begins revising the *Vetus Itala*—a collection of Latin manuscripts based on the Septuagint Old Testament and Greek manuscripts of the New Testament. He did not initially intend to create a new version of the whole Bible. However, over time, he produced the Vulgate, the definitive Latin translation of the Bible.

384 During the pontificate of Pope Damasus, the term "apostolic see" is first used to refer to Rome.

Pope Siricius adopts the imperial title Pontifex Maximus.

385 Priscillian, a bishop and theologian and the first heretic to be condemned to death, is executed at Trier.

Jerome leaves Rome for the East.

Gregory of Nyssa completes *Great Catechesis*, a classic outline of Orthodox theology that examines the place of the sacraments in the church.

386 Augustine of Hippo converts to Christianity.

Ambrose of Milan writes *De Sacramentis* (*Concerning the Sacraments*), six Easter addresses to the newly baptized on baptism, confirmation, and the Eucharist.

Nestorius (386–451) is born. He became a patriarch of Constantinople but was deposed because of his heretical teaching.

387 Augustine of Hippo is baptized by Ambrose.

Patrick, an Irish saint and the apostle of Ireland, is born about this time or a little later.

390 Simeon Stylites (390–459), the first of the pillar ascetics, is born. He lived for 37 years on a small platform on top of a pillar near Aleppo, Syria.

Arianism collapses throughout the Roman Empire but continues among some German tribes until about 700.

391 The Edict of Theodosius prohibits pagan worship under any form.

Augustine is ordained a priest at Hippo.

392 Good Friday begins to be observed separately from Easter.

Jerome produces the Gallican Psalter, the basis of Gregorian chant.

393 The Synod of Hippo publishes the first complete list of canonical New Testament books, forbids the practice of giving Holy Communion to the dead, and provides the first mention of Maundy Thursday and of the Eucharistic fast, which typically starts on midnight before one receives Holy Communion.

Epiphanius visits Jerusalem and insists on the condemnation of Origen. Jerome distances himself from Origen's teaching.

395   The Roman Empire is permanently divided. The Western empire is ruled from Rome (sacked in 410, 455, and 476). The Eastern region is ruled from Constantinople.

Ambrose writes *On the Duties of the Clergy*.

Augustine becomes bishop of Hippo.

John Chrysostom writes *Homilies on the Statutes*.

397   Augustine writes *Confessions*, an autobiography.

398   John Chrysostom publishes more of his *Homilies*.

399   Sulpicius Severus writes *Dialogues*.

400   Origen is condemned by a papal synod.

Paulinus of Nola introduces bells in churches.

The Fifth Century (400–500)

The Great Councils

THE STATUS OF THE CHRISTIAN CHURCH

At the end of the fifth century, 16 generations after Christ, 42 percent of the world is evangelized, and 22.4 percent of the population is Christian. The church is 61.9 percent nonwhite, and Scriptures are available in 13 languages.

INFLUENTIAL CHRISTIANS

Augustine of Hippo, Patrick

SIGNIFICANT EVENTS AND INFLUENCES

- The fifth century is known to the church as the Post-Nicene Age. In the Council of Nicaea, the church had passed another landmark. Christianity had become the established religion of the empire, but the lands outside the imperial borders still beckoned Christian missionaries. The church had successfully defused the first challenge to orthodoxy posed by Arius, but it still had to contend with many more heresies before the century ended.
- The first of these heresies was Nestorianism. Nestorius, a patriarch of Constantinople, taught that Jesus Christ had two distinct natures, the divine and the human, and that Mary, the mother of the human Jesus, was not entitled to the title *Theotokos*, or Mother of God. This was opposed to the orthodox teaching that the incarnate Christ was a single person, at once God and man. Emperor Theodosius II summoned the Council of Ephesus (the Third Ecumenical Council) in 431 to condemn Nestorianism. This council also condemned Pelagianism, a heresy formulated by the British-born Pelagius and his associate Celestius. Pelagianism denied the doctrine of original sin and held that man can achieve salvation through his own efforts.
- The next great heresy to trouble the church was Monophysitism, also called Eutychianism, after its founder, Eutyches. Monophysitism was a reaction to Nestorianism and held that Jesus Christ had only a divine nature and not a human nature. Many variations of this heresy developed over the centuries. To condemn this heresy, the Council of Chalcedon was held in 451 in Chalcedon, a city in Asia Minor. Its statement of faith, the Definition of Chalcedon, affirmed the Tome of Pope Leo. However, it proved unacceptable to the churches of Alexandria and Antioch, both of which to this day uphold a moderate form of Monophysitism.
- The towering figure of the fifth century was Augustine, bishop of Hippo, whose *City of God* and *Confessions* are theological and literary classics.

Augustine's ideas dominated Christian theology for centuries, just as Aristotle dominated Greek philosophy. Augustine introduced the term "predestination" into the currency of Christian thought, and it passed through Roman Catholic Scholasticism to influence John Calvin and the Reformers of the sixteenth century. During his struggle against Pelagianism and the doctrine of human free will, Augustine wrote a massive vindication of Christianity against its pagan critics. The 22 books of the *City of God* appeared in installments and portrayed Christianity as the heavenly city whose gates are open to all believers. Augustine wrote more than 1000 works in all, including 242 books.

- Meanwhile, in Jerusalem; the monk and scholar Jerome (Eusebius Hieronymous) completed the translation of the Old and New Testaments into Latin after working on it for 22 years. The Vulgate, as his work came to be known, was the only Bible used in the Latin Church for the next 1000 years. Jerome was a prolific writer. In addition to translating the Bible, he was active in many of the controversies of the day.

- Christianity continued to spread to the farthest corners of the known world. In the fifth century, many more countries and reigons were added to those evangelized earlier, including Western North Africa, Isle of Man, San Marino, Liechtenstein, Caucasia, and Ireland. The gospel was brought to the Irish by Patrick, whose work as the apostle of Ireland spanned 30 years. The Franks became part of the Christian world when Clovis, their king, was converted and baptized in 496.

- The fifth century is particularly significant for the Roman Catholic Church, as it marked the consolidation of its influence. Leo I, also known as Leo the Great, became pope in 440. A great defender of orthodoxy, his Tome was accepted by the Council of Chalcedon. He also increased the power of his office by persuading Attila the Hun to spare Rome and by securing concessions when the Vandals took Rome. He was the first to use the title *Pontifex Maximus* (Supreme Pontiff), once reserved for the emperors.

- In 404 the imperial residence was moved from Rome to Ravenna in northeast Italy. The city provided a safe haven for the Western emperor and grew in wealth and importance until it fell to the Goths in 492.

- In the East, the Nestorian Church was growing by leaps and bounds in Persia, Arabia, and Central Asia.

CHRONOLOGY

400   Ursula and her companions are martyred by the Huns near Cologne. Most likely her companions include eight to ten young women. A medieval typographical error, however, later expands the number to 11,000 virgin martyrs.

The Liturgy of Chrysostom is developed. It is still in use (in modified form) throughout the Eastern church today.

The *Gloria Patri* ("Glory to the Father") becomes the first phrase of a prayer of praise to the Trinity. Also known as the Lesser Doxology, it becomes the most common formulaic close for recitation of the Psalms—"Glory be to the Father, and to the Son, and to the Holy Spirit. As it was in the beginning, is now, and will be forever. Amen."

John Chrysostom founds a training school for native Gothic evangelists. He writes, "'Go and make disciples of all nations' was not said for the Apostles only, but for us also."

Persia is 25 percent Christian. The people speak Syriac but have no Persian liturgy or Scriptures.

Several million Christians have been buried in catacombs near Rome over three centuries by this date.

Scriptures are being translated into Ethiopic by monks from Egypt.

Augustine writes *On the Trinity* and *First Catechetical Instruction* around this time and completes *Confessions*, an autobiographical, philosophical, theological, and mystical work that is rich in poetry.

Narsai (400–500), head of the School of Edessa and the most important writer of the Nestorian Church, is born.

403 John Chrysostom is deposed as patriarch of Constantinople and sent into exile.

405 An imperial edict is issued against the Donatists. Rebaptism is prohibited.

406 *Codex Alexandrinus*, the Greek Bible, is written on vellum, probably of Byzantine origin. It contains the earliest extant Greek text of the Gloria in Excelsis Deo, an expanded paraphrase of Psalm 148.

409 King Yazdegerd I of Persia legalizes Christianity.

410 Mesrop Mashtots completes the Armenian alphabet and eventually translates the Scriptures.
North Africa has 1200 bishops.

411 The Council of Carthage condemns Donatism.

415 Pagans are excluded from the imperial army and from public functions.
The Synod of Diospolis (present-day Lydda in Palestine) condemns Pelagius.
John Cassian founds two abbeys of Saint Victor in Marseilles. He later writes *Institutes of Monastic Life*.

416 Orosius writes *Historiae Adversus Paganos*, the earliest Christian universal history, spanning from the flood to 416.

418 The Council of Carthage upholds the Augustinian doctrine of original sin and condemns Pelagianism.

420 Jerome writes his *Letters*.

421 Augustine writes *Faith, Hope, and Charity* and *Enchiridion on Faith*.

422 Augustine completes *City of God*, a treatise on the special place of Christianity in history.

428 The Athanasian Creed is formed, dealing mainly with the Trinity, the incarnation, and redemption. It also contains anathemas, which are not found in other major early creeds.

430 Augustine writes *On Christian Doctrine*. It contains the most complete treatment of the principles of biblical interpretation written to date. He dies shortly after.

431 The council of Ephesus addresses controversies surrounding Nestorius, who was thought to teach that there were two separate persons in the incarnate Christ, and Cyril, bishop of Alexandria. It gave formal approval to the title *Theotokos* (Mother of God) for Mary.
Christianity is introduced into Ireland.

439 The practice of confirmation is first mentioned, and Epiphany begins being celebrated.

440 Pope Sixtus III introduces the Sanctus into the Western liturgy.

445 The first Irish episcopol see is established at Armagh, where Patrick builds a stone church.

448 A synod held by Flavian, patriarch of Constantinople, condemns Eutyches. Porphyry's writings against the Christians are burned.

449 Leo the Great writes *Tomus ad Flavianum*, an important Christological document.

450 Vincent of Lérins writes that orthodoxy is "what has been believed everywhere, always, and by all."

451 The Council of Chalcedon (the Fourth Ecumenical Council) includes

500 bishops. It issues the Definition of Chalcedon and condemns Docetism.

Brigid of Kildare founds several monasteries.

452 Pope Leo I persuades Attila the Hun to withdraw from Rome.

458 The consecration of nuns is permitted only for women who have reached the age of 40.

460 Confirmation begins to emerge as a separate rite from baptism.

461 Pope Leo the Great writes *Sacramentarium*, one of the oldest extant collections of liturgical prayers and chants. He also fosters the Roman Rite, founds a Schola Cantorum in Rome, popularizes the term "Mass," and institutes a cycle of chants for the church year.

466 Theodoret of Cyrrhus dies. His *Graecarum Affectionum Curario* is the last patristic apology preserved in its entirety.

480 Benedict of Nursia is born. He will become the father of Western monasticism and writes *The Rule of Benedict*.

482 The East–West split over Monophysitism begins.

Henoticon is written by the patriarchs of Alexandria and Constantinople and is sponsored by the emperor. It asserts the Nicene Creed and Cyril's *Twelve Anathemas* but never actually takes a stand on the number of Christ's natures. It is widely accepted in the East but rejected in the West.

485 The Feast of the Holy Innocents is celebrated in Rome.

492 Gelasius I becomes first pope to use the title Vicar of Christ.

499 The task of translating Jesus's message into Greek and Latin is virtually completed after 16 generations.

The Sixth Century (500–600)

The Golden Age of the Eastern Church

THE STATUS OF THE CHRISTIAN CHURCH

At the end of the sixth century, 19 generations after Christ, 39 percent of the world is evangelized, and 21 percent of the population is Christian. The church is 59 percent nonwhite, and Scriptures are available in 14 languages.

INFLUENTIAL CHRISTIANS

Columba, Benedict of Nursia, Dionysius Exiguus, Emperor Justinian, Augustine of Canterbury

SIGNIFICANT EVENTS AND INFLUENCES

- The Middle Ages (500–1000) have been called the Dark Ages, but for the Christian church, the sixth century was anything but dark. The cloud of Roman persecution had just lifted. This century was specially significant for the Eastern churches, for this would be the last full century of free growth before the dark night of Islam would envelop them, seemingly forever.

- For both the Nestorian Church, an outcast church after the Council of Ephesus, and the Monophysite churches of Egypt, Syria, Ethiopia, and Armenia, outcasts after the Council of Chalcedon, this was a century of growth. Shut out of the West, all these churches grew in the only direction they could—east and south. Nestorians gained hundreds of thousands of converts in Central Asia. The Monophysites spread throughout the Middle East and across the Arabian Sea into Malankara in India, where the Saint Thomas Christians formed a Christian beachhead. Jacob Baradaeus is reported to have ordained 100,000 priests to minister to the expanding number of Christians in Syria and Mesopotamia, and Justinian sent missionaries to Nubia, converting its king. Nestorians sent missionaries to the Huns. In Egypt the number of bishoprics grew to 168.

- The church also grew in the West, although less conspicuously. Scotland was evangelized by Columba. His celebrated Iona Monastery in the Inner Hebrides became famous for its learning and was a popular center for pilgrimage until the Reformation.

- Monasticism spread in this century to the West, thanks in large part to Benedict of Nursia, the father of Western monasticism. Repelled by the licentiousness of the society of his day, he withdrew from the world and retired to a cave at Subiaco. He lived as a hermit for some years, but as a community of monks gathered around him, he moved to Monte Cassino, where he founded Benedictine Order and composed the *Rule* named after him.

- In 574, Gregory, a high-ranking Roman official, resigned his post, gave all his wealth to the poor, and entered the holy orders. In 590 he was elected pope. Known as Gregory the Great, he instituted reforms in the church and sent Augustine of Canterbury, who became known as the apostle to the English, to reevangelize England after the invasion of the Anglo-Saxons. Gregory also fostered the growth of monasticism and promoted liturgical music. His name is so closely linked with plainsong that it is commonly known as the Gregorian chant. The fourth and the last of the traditional doctors of the church, he was canonized immediately after his death. His many reforms included the institution of the Gregorian calendar, which established the leap year.

- The Christian era, which firmly established the birth of Christ as the great dividing line of history, was named in this century. The Christianization of the calendar was an achievement of a humble Scythian monk, Dionysius Exiguus, whose somewhat inaccurate arithmetic does not diminish the epic nature of his work. Called *Anno Domini* (the Year of Our Lord), this Christian era eventually became universal.

- The Second Council of Constantinople (the Fifth Ecumenical Council) was held in 553. It was convened by Emperor Justinian to resolve the so-called Three Chapters controversy and thus bring the Monophysite churches back into the mainstream.

- Justinian was one of the greatest of the Roman emperors. He and Queen Theodora worked tirelessly to advance orthodox Christianity. He closed the ancient schools of philosophy in Athens, had 70,000 persons baptized in Asia Minor, built the *Hagia Sophia* in Constantinople and the magnificent Basilica of San Vitale in Ravenna, Italy, and established a legal system now known as the Code of Justinian.

- The Arian Visigoths of Spain were converted to Catholicism, which was then declared the state religion.

- Cosmas Indicopleustes, a Nestorian geographer, completed his 12-volume *Topographia Christiana*.

CHRONOLOGY

500 The Nine Saints establish an Orthodox monastery in northern Ethiopia and secure the Monophysite character of the Ethiopian church.

Dionysius the Pseudo-Areopagite writes *Mystical Theology* and *Divine Names*, two of the earliest works of Christian mysticism. They attempt to blend Neoplatonic thought with Christian doctrine.

Julianus Pomerius writes *Contemplative Life*.

The *Gelasian Sacramentary* arranges the feasts in order of the church year.

Jacob Baradeus (500–578) is born. He becomes one of the great champions of Monophysitism and an organizer of the Syrian Orthodox Church, which is thus known as the Jacobite Church.

The use of incense in worship becomes common.

510 Irish *Peregrini* (exiles) or *Exultantes Christi* embark as wandering hermit-preachers, converting most of Europe during the next 400 years.

512 The West Syrian Church becomes formally Monophysite under Patriarch Severus.

514 Bishops introduce the Agnus Dei in Rome as part of the Gloria in Excelsis Deo in the Mass.

517 The *Hagia Sophia* (Church of the Holy Wisdom) in Constantinople is dedicated.

521 Columba (521–597) is born. He becomes an Irish missionary and establishes the abbey of Jona.

523 The Vandals, a Germanic tribe espousing Arian Christianity, gradually become pro-Catholic.

524 Anicius Manlius Severinus Boethius writes *De Consolatione Philosophiae* (*The Consolation of Philosophy*). It adapts Platonic thought to Christian theology. He also writes *On the Holy Trinity*.

525 "AD" (for Anno Domini) is first used by the monk Dionysius Exiguus, who fixes the birth of Christ on December 25 in the year of Rome 753. He also recalculates the date of Easter.

Christianity is firmly established in the Arabian peninsula until Islam conquers it in the seventh century.

526 Benedict writes his *Rule*, which provides administrative and spiritual guidelines for running a communal monastery. It includes structure for prayer, reading, and work and becomes the model for nearly all medieval monasteries.

527 Byzantine emperor Justinian promulgates laws against heresies, including Nestorianism, Eutychianism, Apollinarianism, and Manichaeism.

Justinian builds the Monastery of Saint Catherine on Mount Sinai.

529   The Second Council of Vaison mandates the liturgical use of the Sanctus and Kyrie during Matins, Vespers, and the Mass.

The Council of Orange declares semi-Pelagianism is heretical, and Pelagianism soon disappears. The empire orders all pagans to become Christians.

Justinian I closes ancient schools of philosophy at Athens.

530   Monophysites and Chalcedonians split into two churches with two separate hierarchies.

535   Cosmas Indicopleustes, a Greek monk, sailor, and cartographer, publishes *Topographica Christiana*, which includes one of the earliest maps of the world.

540   Benedict establishes a complete liturgy for Matins, Lauds, Prime, Terce, Sext, None, Vespers, and Compline throughout the church year.

Benedictines begin wearing the scapular, a piece of cloth that hangs from shoulders in front and back. It is a symbol of the yoke of Christ.

542   Jacob Baradaeus begins ordaining 100,000 priests (ending in 578), marking the expansion of the Jacobite (Syrian Orthodox) Church.

545   Celtic missionaries, including Columba and Columbanus, travel widely throughout the sixth century to win souls, reform abuses, and establish monasteries.

550   Johannes Scholasticus writes *Synagoge Canonum*, one of the oldest collections of Greek canon law.

Bells begin to be used in churches in France.

The doctrine of the assumption of Mary begins to finds its way into orthodox Christianity.

The Magnificat becomes the canticle most used during vespers.

551   Babai the Great (551–628), a Syrian scholar, is born.

553   Emperor Justinian I convenes the Second Ecumenical Council of Constantinople (the Fifth Ecumenical Council) to resolve the so-called Three Chapters controversy.

561   The first Council of Braga condemns suicide. Those who commit suicide are denied a normal Christian burial. The condemnation remains in effect throughout the Middle Ages.

563   Scotland is evangelized by Columba from Ireland. The Iona monastery is founded, and its influence eventually spreads to the English, Franks, and Swiss.

567   The Second Council of Tours proclaims the sanctity of the twelve days from Christmas to Epiphany and the duty of fasting before Christmas.

570   John Climacus (570–649), a Greek ascetic and author of *The Ladder*, is born.

572   The Second Council of Braga forbids fasting on Christmas Day and decrees hymns must take their texts from Scripture. It requires fasting before celebration of the Eucharist and forbids charging of fees. It issues regulations on clerical conduct.

575   Gregory of Tours begins writing his *History of the Franks*.

580   The Lombards destroy the monastery at Monte Cassino. The monks flee to Rome and thereby introduce the Benedictine Rule into that city. Maximus the Confessor (580–662), a Byzantine theologian, is born.

581   The earliest authentic record of the season of Advent states that Advent starts on the feast of Saint Martin—November 11. This timing is still observed in the Orthodox Church.

589   King Reccared convenes the Third Council of Toledo, which celebrates the conversion of the Visigothic people to Catholicism and puts the Nicene Creed into its final form, indicating that the Holy Spirit proceeds from the Father "and the Son."

590   The greater part of Armenia passes under the rule of the Byzantines, who try to impose the regulations of the Council of Chalcedon.
Pope Gregory the Great introduces Ash Wednesday ashes.
The term "canonical hours" comes into popular usage. It refers to the seven formally appointed times for recitation of the Divine Office (Daily Prayer)—Matins, Lauds, Prime, Terce, Sext, None, Vespers, and Compline.
Pope Gregory the Great writes *Pastoral Care*.

593   Pope Gregory writes *Dialogues*. He negotiates peace with the Lombards by buying them off with civil and church funds. He teaches that the sins of individuals who have died might be purged in purgatory.

595   John the Faster, the Eastern Orthodox archbishop (or patriarch) of

Constantinople, first uses the title Ecumenical Patriarch. It is a Greek title meaning "patriarch of the entire inhabited world."

596 Pope Gregory sends Augustine of Canterbury and 40 monks as missionaries to Britain.

597 Augustine of Canterbury baptizes Ethelbert of Kent, the Anglo-Saxon king, and 10,000 others at Canterbury, and parliament adopts the faith. Augustine founds a Benedictine monastery and becomes the first archbishop of Canterbury.

599 The Te Deum becomes a part of the Roman liturgy. Gregorian chant, a specific form of plainsong, begins to take form during the tenure of Pope Gregory. Under his direction, the Schola Cantorum in Rome is reorganized, and a cycle of chants is organized for the entire church year.

The Rise of Islam

THE STATUS OF THE CHRISTIAN CHURCH

At the end of the seventh century, 23 generations after Christ, the world is 31 percent evangelized, and 22 percent of the population is Christian. The church is 54 percent nonwhite, and Scriptures are available in 15 languages.

INFLUENTIAL CHRISTIANS

Aidan, Alopen

SIGNIFICANT EVENTS AND INFLUENCES

- Muhammad was an illiterate Bedouin who, toward the beginning of the century, reported receiving visions from the angel Gabriel (or possibly a Jew named Gabriel), who also dictated the book known as the Koran. The theology that the Koran outlines is heavily borrowed from Judaism, adamantly monotheistic, and extraordinarily rigid. But it was well suited to the genius of the desert, and it inspired his band of Arabians to embark on the jihad, one of history's most enduring and brutal proselytization missions by the sword. Through the next several centuries, that sword would decimate most of the Christian world in Asia, Africa, and the Iberian Peninsula. The rest of Europe would escape—at least until the fifteenth century.

- Muslims, as the followers of Mohammad came to be known, swept across Palestine, Syria, Egypt, Libya, North Africa, and the Iberian Peninsula in one of the swiftest campaigns in military history. The Arabs, though culturally inferior to the nations they conquered, soon imposed their religion and their language on the conquered peoples. So complete was the Arabization of the peoples of the Middle East and North Africa, that even to this day, Berbers, Egyptians, Libyans, and Phoenicians consider themselves Semitic Arabs.

- Between 688 and 691, Caliph Abd-al Malik desecrated the Temple Mount by building the Dome of the Rock on it. The beautiful columns in the shrine are adorned with crosses, indicating that they were plundered from Christian churches.

- As Christianity entered into its long eclipse in the lands of its origin and early growth, it continued to expand into Europe, China, Mongolia, Indonesia, and Niger. The list of newly Christianized countries included the Netherlands and Andorra. The conversion of England was completed under Wilfrid as Sussex and the Isle of Man, the last strongholds of paganism, fell.

The Synod of Whitby aligned the nascent church with Rome for the next nine centuries.

- The oldest Anglo-Saxon translations and paraphrases of the Bible were made by Caedmon and Aldhelm.

- Eastern and Western churches drifted further apart due to differences in church practices and doctrine. The Eastern Church allows its clergy to be married, as long as they are married before ordination. In the West, clerical celibacy is enforced as an ordinance.

- Nestorians continued their vast missionary enterprise, particularly under Patriarch Yeshuyab, who had moved his capital to Seleucia-Ctesiphon, capital of the Sassanid Empire of Persia. One million Persian Christians now belonged to the Nestorian Church. Alopen, a Nestorian missionary from Syria, traveled to China by foot and reached the capital, Chang'an (modern Xi'an), in 635. The Nestorian bishop of Merv converted some Turkish tribes. Nestorians also reached Mongolia and Indonesia. At this point, the territorial extent of the Nestorian Church was greater than that of the Western Church.

- The Third Council of Constantinople (the Sixth Ecumenical Council) was held in 680 to condemn monothelitism (the view that Jesus Christ has two natures but only one will).

CHRONOLOGY

600 A *Schola Cantorum* (Latin for "school of singers") is founded in Rome.
The modern outline of the Divine Office is completed.
The Jesus prayer ("Lord Jesus Christ, Son of God, have mercy on me") appears in writings.
Alopen is born in Persia. A Nestorian, he eventually becomes the first recorded Christian missionary to China.

603 Bells are first used in churches in Rome.
Augustine of Canterbury orders Celtic churches to submit to the authority and rites of Rome, but they refuse.

608 The first Saint Paul's Cathedral is built in London.

610 All Saints' Day becomes a church festival.
Isidore of Seville is one of the first to use the term "double predestination."
The foundation of Westminster Abbey is laid.

614 Persians destroy the Church of the Holy Sepulchre and remove what was believed to be the cross Jesus died on.

619 John Moschus, a Byzantine monk, and Sophronius, patriarch of Jerusalem, publish the *Pratum Spirituale* (*Spiritual Meadow*), an important collection of monastic narratives.

622 Muhammad flees opposition from merchants in Mecca and moves to Medina (the Hegira), marking the consolidation of the first Muslim community.
The Armenian patriarchate is established in Jerusalem.

625 Portable censors begin to be used. Before this time, incense was burned in stationary vessels.

626 The Church of the Holy Sepulchre is rebuilt after being destroyed by the Persians.

630 Byzantine emperor Heraclius recovers the True Cross from the Persians and brings it back to Jerusalem.
Holy Cross Day is first celebrated.
Isidore of Seville writes *Etymologiae*, and Maximus the Confessor writes *Ascetic Life*.

632 Muslim Arabs sweep across Palestine and Syria. Muhammad dies.

633 Isidore presides over the Council of Toledo, which makes the first unambiguous reference to the *crosier*, the long crook-shaped staff symbolizing the bishop's pastoral authority and responsibility. The council also allows poetic text (rather than strictly biblical texts) to be used in hymns.

634 Wilfrid (634–709) is born. He becomes bishop of York and brings the English church closer to Rome.

635 Alopen, one of the greatest Nestorian missionaries of all time, reaches the Chinese capital and translates the Scriptures into Chinese.

636 At the Battle of the Yarmuk River, Arabs defeat the Byzantine army led by Emperor Heraclius.

638 Arabs capture Damascus and Jerusalem.

639 Arabs (Saracens and Moors) invade Egypt and establish Islam and the Arabic language.

640 John Climacus writes *The Ladder of Divine Ascent*.
Christians in Persia number about one million before the Muslim

conquest of the Sassanid Empire. Egypt has three million Coptic and 200,000 Chalcedonian Christians. The 6.5 million Berbers of North Africa are 80 percent Christian, but by 950, all will be converted to Islam.

645 Arabs conquer part of Armenia.

646 Muslims conquer Mesopotamia (Iraq).

647 Byzantine emperor Constans II issues an imperial edict known as the *Typos*, forbidding anyone to assert either monothelitism or dyothelitism.

649 The Lateran Synod in Rome condemns the *Typos* and monothelitism. Arabs capture Cyprus.

650 Aldhelm, bishop of Sherborne, translates the Psalms into Anglo-Saxon. Nestorian missionaries evangelize Mongolia, but Christianity disappears 300 years later.

657 Hilda of Whitby founds Whitby Monastery, a Celtic-style double monastery in England.

660 Egyptians undergo mass conversions from Christianity to Islam.
Pope Gregory the Great standardizes the use of the Alleluia during the Mass. He decrees that the Advent season begins on the fourth Sunday before Christmas.
Andrew of Crete (660–740), a Greek hymnologist, archbishop, saint, and theologian, is born.

668 Theodore of Canterbury is consecrated bishop and reorganizes the church in England.

673 The Council of Hertford, the first all-England synod, is held.

674 Arabs fail in their naval siege of Constantinople.

675 Boniface (675–754), the apostle of the Germans, patron saint of Germany, and first archbishop of Mainz, is born in Crediton, England.

676 John of Damascus (676–749), a Syrian theologian and writer, is born.

680 Emperor Constantine IV convenes the Third Council of Constantinople—the Sixth Ecumenical Council (also called Trullan)—to deal with monothelitism, the view that Christ had two natures but only one will. It affirmed that there were two wills in Christ and reaffirmed the Chalcedonian Definition.

The Croats are converted.

681   Gloucester Abbey is founded.

Arabs occupy Morocco.

687   The conversion of England is completed under Wilfred. He Christianizes Sussex and the Isle of Wight, the last important centers of Anglo-Saxon paganism.

Pope Sergius I introduces the Agnus Dei into the Mass.

690   Willibrord (raised in the Abbey of Ripon in northern England) evangelizes in the Netherlands. He becomes the first bishop of Utrecht and is known as the apostle to the Frisians.

692   Emperor Justinian II convenes the Quinisext Council (the Council in Trullo) to draw up disciplinary canons, which the Fifth and Sixth Ecumenical Councils had failed to do. It affirms that the see of Constantinople is second after Rome and endowed with equal authority.

The *Codex Amiatinus*, the oldest extant copy of the Latin Vulgate, is copied.

697   Muslims capture Carthage. North Africa is now controlled by Muslims.

698   Monks in Northumberland, England, produce the illuminated *Lindisfarne Gospels* using patterns and mythic creatures of Viking art that become Irish and Anglo-Saxon motifs.

The Eighth Century (700–800)

Frankish Christianity

THE STATUS OF THE CHRISTIAN CHURCH

At the end of the eighth century, 26 generations after Christ, 31 percent of the world is evangelized, and 22.5 of the population is Christian. The church is 51 percent nonwhite, and Scriptures are available in 15 languages.

INFLUENTIAL CHRISTIANS OF THE CENTURY

Bede, Boniface, Charles Martel

SIGNIFICANT EVENTS AND INFLUENCES

- In 711, the Muslim Moors, who had captured Carthage in 697, invaded Spain and Portugal—their first foothold in Europe. But in 732, Charles Martel saved European civilization and the Christian church by defeating the Muslims at the Battle of Tours, the first reversal the Arabs had suffered in almost 100 years.
- The Arab conquests in the Middle East and North Africa were paralleled by the continued expansion of Christianity in Europe. Pepin, the son of Charles Martel, united the Franks and founded the first Christian empire in northern Europe. At the request of Pope Stephen II, Pepin invaded Italy to defend it against the Lombards. Pepin gave the conquered lands to the church (called the Donation of Pepin), establishing the Papal States. Charlemagne, the son of Pepin, extended his empire through military conquests to cover all of present-day France, Germany, and Italy, and forced the German Saxons to convert.
- In 722, Boniface, the apostle of the Germans, felled the Oak of Thor at Geismar, Hesse, marking the end of German paganism. He evangelized south and central Germany.
- Bede the Venerable, known as the father of English history, translated the Gospel of John into English and wrote *Ecclesiastical History*. In 1899, Leo XIII declared him a doctor of the church.
- The eighth century saw the beginning of the iconoclastic controversy that troubled the Eastern church for a century. Emperor Leo III, the Isaurian, condemned the veneration of sacred images and relics as unbiblical and as the chief obstacle to the conversion of Jews and Muslims. Pope Gregory III condemned iconoclasm but supported the veneration of icons. In 754 a council of 300 Byzantine bishops endorsed iconoclasm, but the council was condemned by the Lateran Synod of 769.

- The Second Council of Nicaea (the Seventh Ecumenical Council) was convened in 787. It strongly condemned iconoclasts. This is the last of the Ecumenical Councils accepted by both Western and Eastern churches.
- The Nestorian patriarchal see was moved from Seleucia-Ctesiphon to Baghdad.
- The first missionaries from Ireland reached Iceland.

CHRONOLOGY

700 The monasteries of northern Europe begin to celebrate private Mass.
Lay communion begins to disappear from the Western Church.
The unveiling and adoration of the cross is introduced into the Latin liturgy.
Christians begin to wear black instead of white at funeral services.
The patristic age comes to a close.
Observance of the Feast of the Annunciation of the Blessed Virgin Mary has become universal in the West.

711 Muslim Arabs defeat Arian Visigoths in Portugal and in 715 eliminate them from Spain.
Muslim Arabs capture Tangier, Gibraltar, and cities in Spain—Toledo, Seville, and Granada.

716 Muslims capture Lisbon.

717 Cordoba (Spain) falls to the Muslims and becomes capital of Andalusia.

718 Pope Gregory II sends Boniface as a missionary to Germany.

719 Moors capture Barcelona.

720 Bede, a monk at Jarrow on Tyne, England, translates the Gospel of John in Anglo-Saxon.

724 Boniface fells the pagan sacred Oak of Thor at Geismar in Hesse (Germany), signaling the collapse of German paganism.

725 The modern form of the the Apostles' Creed appears in the writings of Pirminius.
Bede's *De Ratione Temporum* (*On the Reckoning of Time*) introduces AD and BC as chronological markers.

726 Byzantine emperor Leo III declares all religious images and icons to be idols, marking the beginning of the iconoclastic controversy.

730 Bede compiles *Church History of the English People*, describing the conversion of the Anglo-Saxons. Its attention to detail and carefully selected information make it one of the most valuable primary sources for the study of early church history in England.

Relations between Constantinople and Rome deteriorate when Pope Gregory II begins to resist the iconoclastic decrees from Byzantine emperor Leo III.

731 Pope Gregory III excommunicates iconoclasts.

Bede traces the origin of the word "Easter" to *Eastre*, the Anglo-Saxon name of a Teutonic goddess of spring and fertility. Her festival included rabbits and colored eggs.

The first known church organ is installed.

732 At a historic battle at Poitiers, Charles Martel defeats the Arabs, saving Europe from Muslim dominance.

735 The Province of York is created with Egbert as its first archbishop.

740 Irish missionaries arrive in Iceland.

741 A Benedictine monastery is established at Fulda. It eventually becomes a manuscript transmission and pilgrimage hub.

All Saints Day is set at 1 November.

742 John of Damascus writes *Fountain of Wisdom*.

Charlemagne (742–814) is born. He becomes the French king of the Franks and Lombards.

747 The Council of Cloveshoe requires English churches to conform to Roman liturgy and chant.

750 Theodore Abū Qurrah (750–825) is born. He becomes the first Christian writer to write in Arabic.

The Bible is first translated into Arabic.

751 Gregorian chant is introduced to France during the reign of King Pepin. Throughout the eighth century, it spreads through England, France, and Germany.

John of Damascus writes *Dialogue Between a Christian and a Saracen*, one of the earliest apologetic works written against Islam.

753 Emperor Constantine V calls the Synod of Hieria, which mandates the destruction of all icons. The patriarchs of Antioch, Jerusalem, and Alexandria as well as the bishop of Rome were not invited to attend.

754 Boniface is martyred while bringing the gospel to the North Friesians.

760 The Book of Kells, a famous illuminated book containing the four Gospels and other texts, is produced in Ireland.

770 The English scholar Alcuin compiles the first formal catechism manual.

772 Charlemagne subdues the Saxons and converts them to Christianity.

774 Venice is founded.
Charlemagne becomes king of the Lombards.

775 The Nestorian patriarchal see is moved from Seleucia-Ctesiphon to Baghdad.

778 The *Donation of Constantine* is forged, alleging that Emperor Constantine had given the pope full authority over the Western empire.

779 Benedict of Aniane founds the Aniane monastery, which becomes a center of French monastic reform.

780 The entire Saxon race is baptized under the imperial edict of Charlemagne.

787 The Second Council of Nicaea (the Seventh Ecumenical Council) condemns the iconoclasts, declares icons worthy of veneration (*dulia*) but not worship (*latria*), anathematizes those who reject the veneration of relics, and declares no church is to be consecrated without the presence of a relic. This is the last ecumenical council recognized by the Eastern Church.

789 Charlemagne orders that the Roman Rite be used throughout the empire. For the first time, Western liturgy and church music are fairly standardized.

793 Alcuin becomes abbot of Saint Martin of Tours, where he founds a school of calligraphy. The school produces beautiful manuscripts in Carolingian minuscule lettering.

794 Alcuin writes *Concerning Rhetoric and Virtue*.

796 Pepin (son of Charlemagne and king of the Lombards) defeats the Avars (equestrian warrior nomads), leading to their conversion.

798 The Synod of Rome declares adoptionism heretical. According to adoptionism, Christ was truly God's Son only in His spiritual nature, and He was adopted as the Son of God in His human nature.

800 Charlemagne is crowned emperor by Pope Leo III, restoring the title in the West after more than three centuries. Some consider this the founding of the Holy Roman Empire. Others prefer 962, when Otto I was crowned Holy Roman Emperor.

The Carolingian Renaissance

THE STATUS OF THE CHRISTIAN CHURCH

At the end of the ninth century, 28 generations after Christ, 26 percent of the world is evangelized, and 20 percent of the population is Christian. The church is 41 percent nonwhite, and Scriptures are available in 17 languages.

INFLUENTIAL CHRISTIANS OF THE CENTURY

Ansgar, Cyril, Methodius

SIGNIFICANT EVENTS AND INFLUENCES

- In 800 Charlemagne was crowned Roman emperor by Pope Leo III. Charlemagne encouraged all monasteries and churches to teach reading and writing. He appointed Alcuin as his adviser to oversee the founding of schools and scriptoria (rooms for scribes). His advocacy of ecclesiastical reforms and patronage of learning earned for his reign and the following centuries the description of the Carolingian Renaissance. After Charlemagne's death, his empire was split among his three sons.

- Christian missionaries continued to evangelize central and northern Europe. Ansgar, a monk from Flanders, known to later generations as the apostle of the north, took the gospel to Sweden and Denmark. In central Europe, Bavaria and Moravia were evangelized in a two-pronged effort from the East and the West.

- The Slavs, one of the most important peoples of Eastern Europe, had not yet heard the gospel. This was the task that two brothers, Cyril and Methodius (the apostles to the Slavs), undertook in 860 when they went on an imperial diplomatic mission to the Khazars, north of the Caucasus. In 862 Emperor Michael III entrusted them with a mission to the Moravians. Before leaving Constantinople, Cyril invented the Glagolitic alphabet and thus became the founder of Slavic literature. In 1980 the brothers were declared by Pope John Paul II to be the Patrons of Europe.

- In 846 Muslims invaded Italy and sacked Rome. This represented the zenith of their power, which would begin its decline over the next few centuries.

- In 857 communion between the Western and Eastern churches was again suspended following what is known as the Photian Schism. Photius, who is venerated as a saint in the Orthodox Church, had been appointed patriarch of Constantinople in 858, succeeding Ignatius, who had been deposed. Pope Nicholas I convened a synod at Rome, annulled the deposition of Ignatius, and reinstated him as patriarch. This act gave great offense to Photius, who anathematized the pope. The Fourth Council of Constantinople condemned the Photian Schism. Although the dispute became moot after the death of Ignatius when Photius once again became patriarch, it had lasting consequences and contributed to the final break between the two churches.

- The heavy hand of Arab Muslim oppression began to weigh down on the ancient Christian church in Egypt and the rest of North Africa. Christian education was prohibited. The heavy *jiziya* (tax) was levied on all *dhimmis* (Christians, Jews, and Sabians) with the sole purpose of forcibly converting them to Islam. The celebration of Christian festivals, including Sunday worship and Christmas, was banned. No new church buildings were permitted, and old ones were demolished. All Christians were ordered to wear five-pound crosses around their necks.

- In 864, Boris, the king of the Bulgars, was baptized. By 870 all of Bulgaria had been Christianized, and a Bulgar had been consecrated as an archbishop. Meanwhile, the Serbs of Narenta Valley were baptized through the efforts of Emperor Basil I.

- Severe persecutions against the Nestorian Church broke out in China. Thousands of churches and monasteries were destroyed.

CHRONOLOGY

800 Christianity is becoming the dominant religion from the Caspian Sea to Xinjiang (China).

Charlemagne is crowned Roman emperor in Rome by Pope Leo III.

807 The Book of Armagh (the Canon of Patrick) is written in Ireland. It contains early texts about Patrick, some of the oldest surviving specimens of Old Irish, and a nearly complete copy of the New Testament.

814 Byzantine emperor Leo V begins to remove icons from churches. He exiles, imprisons, or executes chief defenders of the use of icons.

815 John Scottus Eriugena (815–877), an Irish philosopher, theologian, and poet, is born.

Methodius (815–885), the apostle of the Slavs, is born.

818 The old Cologne cathedral is completed.

825 Two Nestorian bishops and other Persian Christians emigrate to Malabar in southwest India.

826 Ansgar, a monk from Flanders and the apostle of the North, becomes the first missionary to Denmark.

Methodius (826–885), Cyril's brother and fellow apostle of the Slavs, is born.

827 Cyril (827–869), Methodius's brother and fellow apostle of the Slavs, is born.

828 Franks become the first missionaries to Czechoslovakia.

829 Ansgar first evangelizes in Sweden, and many Swedish noblemen are converted.

831 Arabs capture Sicily.

Paschasius Radbertus publishes *On the Blood and Body of the Lord*, stressing the real presence of Christ in the Eucharist.

832 The Utrecht Psalter, the most valuable manuscript in the Netherlands and including 166 pen illustrations, is published.

835 The Vespasian Psalter is published in England. It contains the oldest extant English translation of any portion of the Bible.

Pope Gregory IV orders universal observance of All Saints' Day.

837 In Egypt, Christian education and the celebration of Christian festivals are prohibited. All new churches are demolished, and Christians are ordered to wear five-pound crosses around their necks.

842 Theodora, widow of Byzantine emperor Theophilos and regent for her young son, Emperor Michael III, brings icons back to the empire.

845 Taoist emperor Wu Tsung severely persecutes Nestorians and Buddhists in China and destroys or closes 44,000 temples and monasteries.

850 The customs of sprinkling the congregation with holy water and incensing the altar, celebrant, and people begin.

Polyphony begins to develop in liturgical chant. The earliest form is *organum*—a single line of chant accompanied by another line sung at an unvarying fourth or fifth below the melody line.

The feast of the Transfiguration of Christ is first mentioned.

First church in Denmark is built.

854 Ansgar converts Erik, king of Jutland (Denmark), to Christianity.

Nestorian Christanity is eradicated in Arabia.

The Scriptures are translated into Norman French.

857 Hincmar, archbishop of Reims, writes *De Praedestinatione*.

858   Photius, patriarch of Constantinople, denies the procession of Holy
          Spirit from the Son and opposes the clause "from the Son" in the
          Nicene Creed.

862   Cyril and Methodius are sent as missionaries to the Slavs. Cyril invents
          the Cyrillic/Glagolitic script to aid in his teaching and worship lead-
          ing in the people's language.

864   Boris, king of the Bulgars, is baptized.

869   The Fourth Council of Constantinople (the Eighth Ecumenical Coun-
          cil) is the first council to be recognized as ecumenical only by the
          Western Church. It was convened by the Emperor Basil I to con-
          demn Photius, patriarch of Constantinople. Photius had clashed with
          the pope, who had refused to recognize him. In return, Photius had
          issued an encyclical against some Roman practices and later instigated
          a council that excommunicated the pope (these events are referred to
          as the Photian Schism). The condemnation of Photius brought only
          temporary peace between the Eastern and Western churches.

870   A Bulgar is consecrated as archbishop.
          Basil I, emperor from 866 to 886, forces baptism on Serbs of Narenta
          Valley.

879   The Pope and the patriarch of Constantinople excommunicate each
          other.

880   Methodius translates a Slavonic Bible.
          King Alfred of England translates the Psalms into Anglo-Saxon.

Slavic Christianity

THE STATUS OF THE CHRISTIAN CHURCH

At the end of the first millennium, 32 generations after Christ, 25 percent of the world is evangelized, and 18.7 percent of the population is Christian. The church is 39 percent nonwhite, and Scriptures are available in 17 languages.

INFLUENTIAL CHRISTIANS OF THE CENTURY

Vladimir of Kiev, Abbot Odo, Stephen of Hungary

SIGNIFICANT EVENTS AND INFLUENCES

- The tenth century was a landmark in the history of Christianity. At this point more than half of the original homelands of the Christian faith had been submerged under the flood of Islam. Islam was supreme in all of North Africa and most of the Middle East. As a result, Christianity had become a purely Western or European religion. White Christians had been a minority, but they became a majority in this century and would remain so until the twentieth century.

- As the century began, the first Christian missionaries reached Norway, the northernmost point of the expansion of Christianity in Europe. In 999, Leif Ericson converted to Christianity, and the next year he brought the gospel to his father's colony in Greenland. The conversion of Northmen was also underway in Denmark and Sweden.

- The most significant event of the century was the conversion of Russia. It began in 954 when Olga, the regent of Kiev, was baptized. In 987, Vladimir, the grand duke of Kiev and Olga's grandson, followed suit. Wanting to embrace the purest form of Christianity, he sent emissaries to many countries. Those sent to Constantinople came back with glowing reports of the worship service in *Hagia Sophia*, the great cathedral built by Justinian.

  > We knew not whether we were in heaven or on earth. For on earth there is no such splendor or such beauty, and we are at a loss to describe it. Only we know that God dwells in the church among men, and that their worship surpasses the worship of all other places. We cannot forget their beauty.

- Vladimir was baptized in 988, and the next year he ordered all residents of Kiev to be baptized. In 991 the whole population of Novgorod was baptized by a bishop from Crimea. Within five centuries, Moscow was to become "the third Rome" (after Constantinople).

- In Egypt, Caliph El Hakim began one of the worst persecutions of Christians since Diocletian's reign. He destroyed thousands of churches and forced hundreds of thousands of Christians to convert to Islam. The number of Coptic bishops was reduced to 110. In North Africa, most of the Berbers were forced to apostasize.

- Moravia became a part of the Western Church by the early part of the tenth century, as did Bohemia under Boleslav II. To the north of Moravia, Poland converted to the Latin form of Christianity when Duke Mieszko and his wife were baptized. The first Polish bishopric was established at Poznań. Meanwhile, in Hungary, the Magyars (Hungarians) were converted under the saintly King Stephen I. In 997, as the century drew to a close, Prussians, the last remaining pagans in Europe, were brought into the Christian fold.

- Muslims continued to advance into Europe. Sicily was subjugated after 75 years, as well as some coastal areas in southern Italy.

- Monasticism rose in the West much later than in the East, but by the tenth century it was flourishing in Italy, France, Spain, and England. In France, William I, Duke of Aquitaine, founded the Benedictine Abbey of Cluny, which became the center of monastic resurgence under Abbot Odo. Cluniacs adopted the strict Benedictine Rule, stressing personal spiritual life, long choir offices, and solemn worship. In the next century, the influence of Cluny reached its height with more than 1000 houses spread over Western Europe. The magnificent church at Cluny (which was desecrated during the French Revolution) was the largest church in Europe at that time—more than 555 feet long.

- Otto the Great, the founder of the Holy Roman Empire, was crowned by Pope John XII in 962. This empire would last for another 900 years.

CHRONOLOGY

900 Norway receives its first missionaries (from the Bremen-Hamburg archbishopric). Later, Norwegian kings educated in England return to evangelize their people.

The Magyars (Hungarians) are evangelized.

902 Sicily and the costal areas of southern Italy are subjugated by Muslims after 75 years.

907 Wenceslaus I (907–929), duke of Bohemia, is born. The "Saint Wenceslaus Chorale" is one of the oldest known Czech songs in history.

909 The the monastery at Cluny (France) is formed. The Cluniac Order is formed as a return to the strict Benedictine Rule.

920 Western monasticism is revived under Odo, abbot of Cluny (France).

927 The patriarchate of Bulgaria is founded and the conversion of the Bulgars is completed.

948 Scandinavia is placed under the archdiocese of Hamburg-Bremen.

949 Symeon the New Theologian (949–1022), a Greek Orthodox theologian, is born.

950 Winchester Cathedral installs an organ with 26 bellows and 400 pipes. Previously a secular instrument, the organ begins to appear in other large churches of England.

The conversion of the Scandinavians is underway across Denmark, Norway, and Sweden.

954 Olga, regent of Kiev, is baptized, and the conversion of Russia begins.

958 Prince Vladimir of Kiev (958–1015), a Russian monarch whose baptism spurred the conversion of Russia, is born.

959 Dunstan becomes archbishop of Canterbury. At the time he is the most influential figure in England. He introduces the Benedictine Rule to reform the monastic system. He fosters education and rebuilds churches.

960 Harald "Bluetooth" Gormssom, king of Denmark, unifies his kingdom and accepts Christianity.

961 Athanasius the Athonite founds Great Lavra, the first monastery on Mount Athos.

962 The Holy Roman Empire is founded by Otto I, king of Germany, crowned by Pope John XII. Its population is 10 million by AD 1000, 16 million by 1200, and 29 million by 1800. It is finally abolished in 1806.

966 Duke Mieszko I of Poland is converted to Christianity by his wife. The first Polish bishopric is established at Poznań years later, and the faith expands rapidly.

975 Stephen I (975–1038), the last grand prince of the Hungarians (997–1000) and first king of Hungary (1000–1038), is born.

979 Glassworkers develop a new process for making stained glass. Metallic pigments are fused into the glass, making the painting as durable as the glass itself. It is first used at the Basilica of Saint Denis in Paris.

980 Christianity is introduced in Iceland.

987 Archduke Vladimir of Kiev is converted and baptized by Greek Orthodox evangelists. The mass conversion of Russia is underway.

Muslim rulers in Iraq assume the right to appoint the Nestorian catholicos (church leader).

990 The first Christians arrive in Greenland.

991 The entire population of Novgorod (Russia) is baptized by a bishop from Crimea.

993 Pope John XV canonizes the first saint—Ulrich, bishop of Augsburg.

995 Olaf II (995–1031), king and patron saint of Norway, is born.

996 Caliph El Hakim destroys 3000 Egyptian churches and forcibly converts thousands of Copts to Islam in violent persecution.

997 The Magyars (Hungarians) are converted en masse under Stephen I.

The Prussians, the last remaining heathens in Europe, are evangelized.

Adalbert, bishop of Prague, is martyred.

998 All Souls' Day is first instituted in the monasteries of Cluny, France, as a day for prayers and almsgiving to assist souls in purgatory.

Prince Vladimir establishes Christianity as the state religion of Russia.

999 All of Bohemia is evangelized.

The Eleventh Century (1000–1100)

The Great Schism

THE STATUS OF THE CHRISTIAN CHURCH

At the end of the eleventh century, 35 generations after Christ, 25 percent of the world is evangelized, and 19 percent of the population is Christian. The church is 37 percent nonwhite, and Scriptures are available in 19 languages.

INFLUENTIAL CHRISTIANS OF THE CENTURY

Stephen Harding, Bruno

SIGNIFICANT EVENTS AND INFLUENCES

- On Saturday, July 16, 1054, as afternoon prayers were about to begin, Cardinal Humbert, legate of Pope Leo IX, strode up to the altar in *Hagia Sophia* in Constantinople and placed on it a parchment excommunicating the patriarch of Constantinople, Michael Cerularius. He then marched out of the church, shaking the dust from his feet. This incident marked the beginning of the schism between the Latin (Western) and Greek (Eastern) churches, a division that still persists. The incident was provoked by the fact that Norman rulers of southern Italy, formerly under Byzantine rule, replaced Greek bishops with Latin ones. Patriarch Cerularius retaliated by closing down all Latin churches in Constantinople. However, the break was not complete, and both churches continued negotiations on and off, and the Great Schism would become effective only centuries later.

- In 1096, Pope Urban II issued a call for a Crusade against the Muslim armies. The Crusade, so called because the Crusaders wore crosses, was the first Christian response to four centuries of Muslim assaults against Christianity, the brutal oppression of believers, and the destruction of churches in Asia and Africa. The purpose of the Crusaders was to liberate the Holy Land from the Muslims, reopen Jerusalem to pilgrims, and stem the tide of the Seljuq Turks, who were poised to take over Asia Minor and Constantinople. The Crusades were a series of military expeditions. The First Crusade lasted from 1097 to 1099 and mobilized more than 70,000 people. They captured Jerusalem in 1099 and set up the Latin Kingdom of Jerusalem under Godfrey of Bouillon. In the same year, the Latin patriarchate of Jerusalem was established. Between 1204 and 1291, further expeditions were organized but with diminishing success. The last Latin possessions in the Holy Land fell to the Muslims in 1291.

- In 1073, Hildebrand (Gregory VII) was invested as pope. His papacy lasted 12 years and is noted for his reforms and the moral revival of the church. He opposed simony (paying to receive sacraments), sexual immorality of the clergy and lay leaders, and the practice of lay rulers choosing bishops. After considerable resistance, Henry II of Germany submitted to Hildebrand at Canossa.

- In 1071, Sultan Alp Arslan and the Turks overwhelmed the Byzantines at Manzikert in Anatolia (Asia Minor). This battle marked the darkest chapter in Byzantine history (other than the fall of Constantinople, which would take place in 1453). The Byzantine defeat opened the floodgates to the Turks, who then swept through Asia Minor for the next four centuries.

- Even as the Muslims were strangling the church from Morocco to Afghanistan, the Nestorian Church had become the largest in the world with 250 dioceses stretching across Asia, including such forbidding places as Tibet and Xinjiang. The Arab caliphate included 15 Nestorian metropolitan provinces, and its authority extended as far as Malabar in India and Beijing in China. In northern Mongolia, Nestorians converted more than 200,000 Keraits, including their prince. Nestorians constituted more than 60 percent of the population in Syria, Iraq, and Khorasan (earlier known as Parthia, now Afghanistan and parts of Iran and Turkmenistan).

- The eleventh century saw the ultimate triumph of Christianity in Europe. The Norman conquest of Britain in 1066 brought the British Isles fully into the Christian fold. The Norman reconquest of Sicily from the Arabs was completed in 1091. Iceland, the most western European country, was Christianized, and many monasteries and abbeys were established. The patriarchate of Constantinople had 624 dioceses around the eastern Mediterranean, and the Orthodox Church now included all of Russia. Christian kingdoms emerged in Denmark, England, Hungary, Norway, Poland, Sweden, and Scotland. Nubia (present-day Sudan) was completely Christianized, and the Nubian king erected many churches and monasteries.

- New monastic orders followed the Benedictines. The first was the Carthusians. The ultra strict monastery of Grand Chartreuse was founded near Grenoble in France in 1084. Carthusian houses, called charterhouses, spread throughout Europe. The most popular of the new orders was the Cistercians, which was founded in 1098 in the monastery at Citeaux in Burgundy in eastern France.

CHRONOLOGY

1000 Intinction, or *intinctio panis*, the dipping of the communion bread into the consecrated wine, becomes common in the early eleventh century.

The larger sign of the cross—forehead, chest, shoulders—begins to be used in monasteries.

The Agnus Dei (O Lamb of God) takes its modern form. The formula is repeated three times, the first two followed by "have mercy on us" and the third by "grant us peace."

The Salve Regina (Hail Holy Queen), one of the oldest Marian antiphons, is written.

The Catholic Apostolic Church of the East, also called the Nestorian Church or the East Syrian Church, is now the largest in the world, with 250 bishoprics and 12 million adherents. It is considered outcast by the Western Church.

The conversion of northern Europe by the Latin Church is completed.

Christian kingdoms emerge in Denmark, England, Hungary, Norway, Poland, Sweden, and Scotland.

The end of the first millennium inspires belief in the imminent end of the world.

1007 Peter Damian (1007–1072), an Italian reformer and doctor of the church, is born.

1009 Nestorians convert a prince in northern Mongolia and a tribe of 200,000.

1010 Lief Ericson, a Norse explorer from Greenland, makes the first European and Christian contact with North America.

1014 The Roman Church begins the practice of reciting the Nicence Creed during the Mass.

1015 King Olaf II Haraldsson of Norway Christianizes Norway.

Russia is permanently Christianized. All three bishops and most of the clergy are Greeks. Numerous monasteries have been founded.

1027 The Council of Elne establishes the "Truce of God," prohibiting battle on Sunday. Later rulings also prohibit it during Advent and Lent.

1030 Stanislaus (1030–1079), bishop of Kraków and the patron saint of Poland, is born.

Peter Damian writes *Selected Writings on the Spiritual Life*.

1032 Bruno of Cologne (1032–1101), founder of the Carthusian Order, is born.

1033 Anselm of Canterbury (1033–1109), archbishop of Canterbury, is born.

1035 The Basilica of Constantine in Trier, Germany, is rebuilt.

1036   John Gualbert founds the Order of Vallombrosa, an austere form of the Rule of Benedict, about 18 miles from Florence, Italy.

1038   The term *Cristes Maesse*, Old English for "Christmas," first appears.

1043   Michael Cerularius, patriarch of Constantinople, closes Latin churches in the city because of the Latins' use of unleavened bread in the Eucharist.

1050   The Trisagion ("Holy, Holy, Holy…") is introduced to the Good Friday liturgy as a refrain to be sung during the veneration of the cross.

The Augustinian Canons (also known as the Black Canons or the Canons Regular), a group of priests, begin living communally with vows of poverty, celibacy, and obedience.

Work begins on Saint Sophia Cathedral in Novgorod, the oldest church building in Russia.

Polyphonic singing replaces Gregorian chant.

1052   Building of Westminster Abbey begins.

1054   The Great Schism divides Chalcedonian Christianity into the Western (Latin) and Eastern (Greek) branches. They become known as the Roman Catholic Church (based in Rome) and the Eastern Orthodox Church (based in Constantinople).

1061   Most of Holland is Christianized.

The Norman (Christian) conquest of Sicily begins. It is completed by 1091.

1063   Saint Mark's Basilica in Venice is begun.

1066   The evangelization and conversion of Western Europe is completed with the Normans, Saxons, and Celts.

1070   Lanfranc, archbishop of Canterbury, rebuilds the Canterbury cathedral.

Turkish sultan Alp Arslan overthrows the Byzantine army at Manzikert (modern Malazgirt in Turkey).

1073   The title "pope" is reserved exclusively for the bishop of Rome.

1074   Clerical celibacy is mandated. Married priests are excommunicated.

1075   The Roman Synod condemns simony (the practice of paying for ordination).

Investiture controversy begins as Pope Gregory VII forbids lay people from appointing priests and bishops.

William of Saint Thierry (1075–1148), a French theologian, is born.

1078 Anselm of Canterbury writes *Proslogion*, a reflection on God's existence that included the first known formulation of the ontological argument. He also writes *Monologion*. With Anselm's other writings, it lays the foundation for Scholasticism.

1079 Transsubstantiation receives papal authority during the Berengarian controversy.

Peter Abelard (1079–1142), a French philosopher and theologian, is born.

Work on Winchester Cathedral begins.

1084 Bruno of Cologne founds the Carthusian Order in response to the decadence of his time. He and six companions retreat to a mountain valley north of Grenoble to begin the order.

1085 Christians seize the Arab citadel of Toledo and begin the reconquest of Spain.

1088 The University of Bologna (Italy), Europe's oldest university, is founded.

1090 Bernard of Clairvaux (1090–1153), a French saint and abbot of Clairvaux, is born.

1091 The ceremony of placing ashes on the forehead becomes universal. Ash Wednesday is generally observed by both clergy and laity.

1092 Peter the Venerable (1092–1156), a French Catholic monk, is born.

1093 Anselm is consecrated archbishop of Canterbury.

1095 At the Council of Clermont, Pope Urban II proclaims a remission of all penances for Crusaders. The First Crusade officially begins on Tuesday, November 27. It is declared to repulse Turkish pressure on the Eastern Empire and to make safe pilgrimage to Jerusalem possible. Crusaders take Jerusalem and Antioch, slaughtering Jews and Muslims in the process.

Peter Lombard (1095–1160), a French theologian and author of *The Four Books of Sentences*, is born.

Peter the Hermit leads a band of mostly unarmed rural Crusaders to a Turkish slaughter while he disappears to Constantinople.

1097 The First Crusade arrives in Constantinople.

1098 Hildegard of Bingen (1098–1179), a German abbess and writer, is born.

Anselm of Canterbury writes *Cur Deus Homo* (*Why God Became Human*), a treatise proposing the satisfaction theory of the atonement.

Robert Molesme founds the Cistercian Order in the monastery of Citeaux, south of Dijon, France, as a stricter and more primitive and ascetic Benedictinism.

1099 Crusaders capture Jerusalem.

Robert of Arbrissel, an itinerant preacher, creates the Order of Fontevrault in Anjou, France. Monks and nuns live under a modified Benedictine Rule. The Fontevrault Abbey is now a cultural center.

The Latin patriarchate of Jerusalem established.

The Crusades

THE STATUS OF THE CHRISTIAN CHURCH

At the end of the twelfth century, 39 generations after Christ, 26 percent of the world is evangelized, and 19.4 percent of the population is Christian. The church is 35 percent nonwhite, and Scriptures are available in 22 languages.

INFLUENTIAL CHRISTIANS OF THE CENTURY

Peter Abelard, Peter Valdes, Bernard of Clairvaux, Thomas of Becket

SIGNIFICANT EVENTS AND INFLUENCES

- The twelfth century witnessed two Crusades as the Christian West made desperate attempts to dislodge the Muslims from the Holy Land. The Second Crusade was preached by Bernard of Clairvaux in response to the Muslim conquest of Edessa, an ancient Christian city in Asia Minor and Crusader capital. It was led in 1147 by Louis VII of France and Emperor Conrad of Germany. It failed to relieve the besieged Christian garrisons, and in 1187 it was overcome by the army of Saladin, who captured Jerusalem and overran a great part of the Latin kingdom. The disaster provoked the Third Crusade of 1189–1192, led by Emperor Frederick Barbarossa, Richard I of England, and Philip II of France. They captured Cyprus, Acre, and Jaffa, but Jerusalem itself remained in the hands of Saladin.

- In 1174 the early precursors of the Reformation appeared in Europe. One of the most influential was a man called Peter Waldo, who inspired the Waldensian heresy. Waldo was a rich merchant of Lyons who underwent a personal conversion and gave all his wealth to the poor. His ministry was approved at first by Pope Alexander III on condition that he preach only at the invitation of the clergy. However, Waldo and his followers broke the church's ban on unofficial preaching and, in 1182 or 1183, they were excommunicated and expelled from Lyons. The Council of Verona in 1814 declared them schismatic and pertinacious and included them with the Cathars as heretics. The condemnation only seemed to have helped the movement, which was now spread by lay preachers, called the Poor Men of Lyons, all over Europe.

- In 1162 Henry II of England elevated his close friend and drinking companion, Thomas Becket, as archbishop of Canterbury and primate of England. Shortly thereafter, Becket opposed Henry's attempts to exert royal authority over the church and fell out of the king's favor. He paid a price for his independence when he was killed by the king's knights while celebrating

Mass. Miracles were soon recorded at Becket's tomb, and a widespread cultus developed. In 1173 he was canonized, and his shrine remained one of the principal centers of English pilgrimage until the Reformation.

• The Knights Templar, one of the powerful medieval military orders, was founded in 1119 by Hugh de Payens, a knight of Champagne, along with eight companions. The Knights' purpose was to protect Christians on pilgrimage to the Holy Land from Muslim bandits. In 1129 the order was approved by the Council of Troyes, and its rules were drawn up by Bernard of Clairvaux. The new order gained the support of the papacy, which granted it many privileges in a series of bulls. The Templars fought valiantly in the Second Crusade, but after the fall of Acre, they generally lost their influence. Their wealth led to their downfall as Philip the Fair, king of France, coveted their riches and sought to confiscate their possessions. The order was finally suppressed in 1312.

• The twelfth century was the golden age of the Cistercian Order. In 1112, a young French nobleman named Bernard knocked on the doors of the recently founded monastery of Citeaux and asked to be admitted to the cloisters. Three years later, he was asked by the abbot, Stephen Harding, to choose a place for a new monastery. Bernard established a house at Clairvaux, which soon became the focal point of the Cistercian order. Bernard's place in Western monasticism has never been rivaled in medieval or modern ages.

• The Seventh Ecumenical Council was the last universal council, but the Roman Catholic Church continued to hold councils of the Western Church, some of which were called Lateran Councils, after the Lateran Palace in Rome, where they were held. Three Lateran Councils were held in the twelfth century. The first of these ended the Investiture Controversy, and the third restricted the right to elect popes to the newly formed College of Cardinals.

• In 1121, Peter Abelard, a Scholastic theologian, published one of the most influential books of the Middle Ages, *Sic et Non* (*Yes and No*), a textbook for students of theology for more than four centuries. It was intended to help readers to reconcile apparent contradictions between statements from the Bible and the Church Fathers.

• The twelfth century saw the expansion of the Jacobite Church of Syria, an integral part of the Syriac Orthodox Church. At the close of the century, it had more than 20 metropolitan sees and 103 bishoprics in Syria, Iraq, and the Holy Land.

CHRONOLOGY

1100 The Armenian church is split by Paulicians, who believed the present, visible world was created by an evil spirit.

Baldwin I becomes king of Jerusalem and defender of the Holy Sepulchre.

The Christianization of Sweden and Poland is completed.

Christian converts first appear in Finland.

Hungary establishes Christianity as the national religion.

1106 Peter Abelard writes *Sic et Non* (*Yes and No*), reconciling some of the apparently contradictory statements of the Bible and the Church Fathers.

1108 Bernard of Cluny writes *De Contemptu Mundi* (*On Contempt of the World*), a 3000-line poem on life's transitoriness.

1110 Work begins on the Porto Cathedral in Portugal and the Worms Cathedral in Germany.

1113 The Knights of Saint John (the Hospitallers) are founded to care for pilgrims to Jerusalem.

The Abbey of Saint Victor in Paris is built. It is the house of the Victorines (a group of Canons Regular), who achieve great fame as theologians, poets, and mystics.

1115 Bernard of Clairvaux becomes abbot of the new monastery of Clairvaux. Under his leadership it becomes the most prominent house of the Cistercian Order.

1119 The Knights Templar, a military religious order, is founded with headquarters near the temple site in Jerusalem.

1120 The Order of Premonstratensian Canons, an austere Augustinian order, is founded. They are also known as the Norbertines or White Canons.

Thomas Becket (1120–1170), archbishop of Canterbury, is born.

1122 The Concordat of Worms settles the investiture controversy. The Concordat is between Pope Calixtus II and Holy Roman Emperor Henry V.

La Trappe Abbey is founded in Normandy, France. The Trappists, a branch of the Cistercians, would emerge from there in the seventeenth century.

1123 The First Lateran Council (the Ninth Ecumenical Council) abolishes lay princes' right to appoint bishops. It addresses recovery of the Holy Land and decides that a priest who is not married may not marry after ordination.

1125   The earliest mention of different colors being used for the different liturgical seasons is from the Augustinian canons in Jerusalem.

Hugh of Saint Victor begins his three mystical treatises on the Genesis account of Noah's ark.

The first bishop is appointed in Greenland.

1126   Bernard of Clairvaux writes *De Diligendo Dei* (*On Loving God*).

1127   The term "secular clergy" is first used to distinguish clergy attached to a diocese from those attached to monastic orders.

Hugh of Saint Victor writes *Treatise Concerning the Pursuit of Learning*.

1128   The Order of Knights Templar obtains recognition from the church.

William of Saint Thierry writes *Meditations on Prayer*.

1129-1135   Bernard of Clairvaux writes *On the Steps of Humility and Pride*.

1130   More than 90 monasteries are founded under the auspices of Bernard and the monastery at Clairvaux in the next 15 years.

Sculptor Gislebertus creates *Last Judgment* tympanum in Autun Cathedral.

The great church of Cluny, the largest church in Europe, is dedicated by the pope. It is destroyed in the French Revolution.

1132   Joachim of Fiore (1132–1202), an Italian apocalyptic theologian and scriptural commentator, is born.

1133   Durham Cathedral is consecrated. Work on Exter Cathedral begins.

Hugh of Saint Victor writes *Soliloquy on the Earnest Money of the Soul*.

1135   Peter Abelard writes *Historia Calamitatum* (*A History of My Calamities*).

1139   The Second Lateran Council (the Tenth Ecumenical Council) meets to condemn Arnold of Brescia, who maintained that confession should be made to other Christians, not a priest, and that a minister's sinfulness affects the efficacy of sacraments he administers. The council also makes clergy marriage illegal and invalid.

1140   The Crusaders begin renovating the Church of the Holy Sepulchre based on French Romanesque cathedral architecture.

Gratian, the father of the science of canon law, writes *Decretum Gratiani* (*Concordance of Discordant Canons*). It is based on the principles set down by Ivo of Chartres for interpreting and harmonizing texts.

Peter Waldo (1140–1217), founder of the Waldensians, is born.

The Council of Sens condemns Peter Abelard.

1146   Jews of Spain are forcibly converted to Christianity.

1147   The Second Crusade begins. The Crusaders are defeated and massacred.
Hildegard of Bingen begins building the convent at Bingen.

1150   The first stave church is built in Norway.
Stephen Langston (1150–1228), archbishop of Canterbury, is born.
The West Syrian (Jacobite) Church reaches its widest expansion with
two million adherents.
The College of Cardinals is established in Rome by the pope.
Aelred of Rievaulx writes *Spiritual Friendship*. Peter Lombard writes *Sententiarum Libri Quatuor* (*The Four Books of Sentences*).

1154   The Carmelite order, an extremely ascetic order, is formed by Berthold
of Calabria in Palestine.

1159   "Vicar of Christ" replaces "Vicar of Saint Peter" to describe the pope
during Hadrian IV's pontificate.

1160   Beads similar to rosary beads are placed in the tomb of Saint Rosalia.
They become the first archeological evidence of the rosary.
Christianity is introduced into Finland by English missionaries.
Richard of Saint Victor writes *Benjamin Minor* and *Benjamin Major*.

1162   Thomas Becket is named archbishop of Canterbury.

1163   Construction begins on the Cathedral of Notre Dame in Paris. It is consecrated in 1182.

1166   Peter Waldo and the Waldensian movement anticipate the Reformation.

1170   King Henry II sends four knights to assassinate Thomas Becket, archbishop of Canterbury, in Canterbury Cathedral.
Robert Grosseteste (1170–1253), an English bishop and scholar, is born.
Pope Alexander III establishes rules for the canonization of saints.

1171   Dominic (1171–1221), Spanish founder of the Dominican order, is born.

1175   Hugh of Lincoln builds the first English Carthusian monastery.
Intinctio panis (intinction), the dipping of the communion bread into
the consecrated wine, is forbidden by the Council of Westminster.

The use of candles on the altar is first noted. Before this time, they are probably put on the floor behind the altar.

1177 The Beguines and Beghards are organized as communal lay orders without religious vows.

1179 The Third Lateran Council (the Eleventh Ecumenical Council) addresses moral abuses of the church, condemns the Albigensians and Waldensians, proscribes ordination for money, and regulates the election of popes.

1181 Worms Cathedral is completed.

Eastern Catholic churches (churches that were previously Eastern Orthodox) begin to emerge in Syria.

Francis of Assisi (1181–1126), Italian saint and founder of the Franciscans, is born.

1184 The Inquisition is established.

1187 Saladin's army tears the cross from the Dome of the Rock and plunders churches and convents. Christians are allowed to use the Church of the Holy Sepulchre only if they pay a heavy tribute.

1189 The Third Crusade is prompted by the capture of Jerusalem by Saladin. The Crusade recovers Acre but not Jerusalem. A truce between Richard and Saladin makes pilgrimage possible. Key figures include Holy Roman Emperor Frederick I, King Philip II of France, and King Richard I of England.

1190 Teutonic Knights are founded in Acre. The Knights Hospitaller begin caring for the sick of Jerusalem, especially poor pilgrims.

1191 French Poet Robert de Boron writes *Joseph d'Arimathie* (*Joseph of Arimathea*), which first gives the Holy Grail myth an explicitly Christian dimension.

1193 Albertus Magnus (1193–1280), German friar, bishop, and theologian, is born.

Chartres Cathedral is begun, marking the beginning of the high Gothic period of architecture. A clerestory that is almost as high as the ground-story arcade adds additional height. This cathedral establishes the major divisions of the interior that become standard in all later Gothic churches.

1195 Anthony of Padua (1195–1231), a Portugese Franciscan priest, doctor of
the church, and miracle worker, is born.

1198 The Knights Hospitaller becomes the Teutonic order, a military order
under the Templar rule.

John of Matha founds the Trinitarians, who buy slaves in order to set
them free.

1200 Beatrice of Nazareth (1200–1268), a Belgian mystic and prioress, is born.

Jehan Bodel's *Jeau de Saint Nicolas* is the first French miracle play.

The Age of Scholasticism

THE STATUS OF THE CHRISTIAN CHURCH

At the end of the thirteenth century, 42 generations after Christ, 27 percent of the world is evangelized, and 22 of the population is Christian. The church is 36 percent nonwhite, and Scriptures are available in 25 languages.

INFLUENTIAL CHRISTIANS OF THE CENTURY

Francis of Assisi, Thomas Aquinas, Henry of Uppsala, Dominic

SIGNIFICANT EVENTS AND INFLUENCES

* In the thirteenth century, a new class of academic theologians had become influential in defining Christian beliefs and practices. In the West these writers were known as Scholastics. One of the foremost architects of Scholasticism was Thomas Aquinas, also called the Angelic Doctor, a Dominican monk who taught at Paris and was considered one of the most brilliant minds of the age. His *Summa Theologica*, published in 1255, is one of the seminal works of philosophy. It was the first to define theology as a science or as an ordered body of knowledge with its own laws. In Thomas's teaching, theology embraced the whole life of the church, including worship, morals, and spiritual practice.

* The thirteenth century witnessed the zenith of papal power. Pope Innocent III claimed the right of the pope to choose rulers and oversee their moral conduct. In 1231 the Papal Inquisition was established when Gregory IX appointed full-time papal inquisitors from the Dominican and Franciscan orders.

* Three Crusades were launched in the thirteenth century. The Fourth Crusade was launched in 1202 by Innocent III in Egypt, but under the influence of Boniface of Montferrat and the Venetians, it was deflected from its original purpose and ended in Constantinople, which it sacked for three days. A Latin Empire was established here in 1204, but its net result was a weakening of the Eastern Empire against Muslim expansion and a lingering residue of bitterness that poisoned the relations between Eastern and Western churches for centuries. In 1212 the Children's Crusade ended in disaster as all its juvenile combatants either died at sea or were sold into slavery.

* The Fifth Crusade, the largest ever, was launched in 1217. Jerusalem was recovered through negotiation by Frederick II and was once again in Latin hands from 1229 to 1244.

- The next one under Louis IX, also against Egypt, failed after a promising beginning. The Latin state was slowly overrun, and in 1291 the last remaining Christian possessions were overrun. The concept of crusades was sometimes extended to cover the extirpation of heretics, such as the Albigensians and the Cathars.

- In 1266 the church failed one of the greatest evangelistic opportunities by ignoring a call from the Mongol leader Kublai Khan. The Khan wrote to the pope, "Send me 100 teachers skilled in your religion…and so I shall be baptized, and then all my barons and great men, and then their subjects. And so there will be more Christians here than there are in your parts." Only two Dominicans were sent, but they turned back. In 1278 another team of five Franciscans were sent, but then it was too late, for the Great Khan was dead.

- The thirteenth century saw the founding of two of the most influential Roman Catholic orders—the Franciscans and the Dominicans. Francis of Assisi is the quintessential Catholic saint. Son of a rich cloth merchant of Assisi and on a pilgrimage to Rome, he was so moved by the plight of beggars outside Saint Peter's that he became one himself, and then overcame his fear of leprosy by embracing a leper. One day while attending Mass in the Porziuncola church near Assisi, Francis heard the Lord calling him to a life of self-denial and service. He discarded his staff and shoes, put on a long garment girded with a cord, and gathered a few followers, who eventually became the order of Franciscans. Francis's generosity, his simple and unaffected faith, and his passionate devotion to God, man, and nature have made him one of the most beloved saints of modern times.

- Dominic, a contemporary of Francis, also gave away all his goods to the poor and founded a monastic order for the preaching of the gospel. The Dominican Order was distinguished by the fact that the order adopted not only personal but corporate poverty, and each community was supported not by income or properties but by alms. The Dominicans were also active in education and scholarship.

- Christianity continued to expand in some of the smaller countries. In 1219 the independent Serbian Orthodox Church was founded. Finland was converted through Birger Jarl, a Swedish statesman, and the English bishop Henry of Uppsala. The Prussians were baptized, and pagan worship was eradicated.

- Two councils were held in this century. Lyon I (the Thirteenth Ecumenical Council) was convoked in 1245 by Pope Innocent IV to deal with what he called the Five Wounds of the Church: the bad lives of the clergy, the danger of the Muslims, the Greek schism, the invasion of Hungary, and the deposition of Emperor Frederick II. Lyon II (the Fourteenth Ecumenical Council) was convoked in 1274 by Gregory X to bring about union with the Greek Church, the reform of morals, and the liberation of the Holy Land.

CHRONOLOGY

1200 The Cluniacs Order becomes recognized as a distinct form of Cistercian monasticism. It stresses the spiritual life, especially the choir office. It incorporates less manual labor than the Benedictine or Cistercian Orders do.

Matthew Paris (1200–1259), a medieval historian, is born.

The papacy reaches its apex under Innocent III, pope from 1198 to 1216.

Europe is entirely Christianized except for Wends, Prussians, Lithuanians, and other Baltic races.

Albert the Great (1200–1280), a Dominican bishop and doctor of the church, is born.

Thomas Gallus (1200–1246), a French theologian, is born.

1201 *Intinctio panis* (intinction), the dipping of the communion bread into the consecrated wine, disappears in the West.

1202 The rosary is devised. It is traditionally thought to be invented by Spanish theologain Dominic.

Pope Innocent II launches the Fourth Crusade to capture more territory in and around the Holy Land, but it is diverted to Constantinople. The city is captured from the Greeks in 1204, and the Latin Empire of Constantinople is instituted. The key figure is Boniface of Montferrat.

Joachim of Fiore writes *Treatise of the Four Gospels*.

1204 The Crusader Baldwin is crowned Latin emperor in Constantinople. The animosity between Eastern and Western Christianity becomes irreparable.

1206 Dominic founds the first Dominican convent for women.

1207 Mechthild of Magdeburg (1207–1282), a German nun, mystic, and writer, is born.

1208 Pope Innocent III orders 20,000 Albigensians (Cathars, many of whom lived in the city of Albi, France) to be massacred as heretics.

The Carmelite Order (Brothers of Our Lady of Mount Carmel) is founded.

Francis of Assisi denounces wealth.

1209 Cambridge University is founded.

Francis of Assisi tries to convert the sultan of Egypt. He founds the Franciscan Order.

1210 Construction on the Cathedral of Reims is begun, marking the culmination of the high Gothic period of cathedral architecture.

Albert of Vercelli, Latin patriarch of Jerusalem, writes the Carmelite Rule. It is one of the most difficult monastic rules of the time, mandating poverty, vegetarianism, and solitude.

Francis of Assisi writes *Regula Primitiva* (*Simple Rule*), a monastic rule built mainly on the words of Jesus. It is the founding document for the Franciscans.

The feast of Corpus Christi is inaugurated.

1211 Genghis Khan, Supreme Khan of the Mongols, attacks China with an army of only 129,000 and massacres 35 million in a decade. (His mother was a Nestorian.)

1212 More than 20,000 children participate in the Children's Crusade, a disastrous venture in which most of the children die or become enslaved in Egypt. Fewer than 300 return home.

1214 Roger Bacon (1214–1292), an English philosopher, Franciscan friar, and scientist, is born.

Bonaventure (1214–1274), an Italian theologian and doctor of the church, is born.

1215 Francis of Assisi receives Clare, a young, wellborn nun of Assisi, into the Franciscan fellowship. She later founds the Order of the Poor Ladies (the Poor Clares) and the Second Order of Franciscans.

The Fourth Lateran Council (the Twelfth Ecumenical Council) is typically considered to be most important council of the Middle Ages.

- It uses the term "transubstantiation" for the first time and declares the doctrine *de fide* ("of the faith," or an essential part of it).
- It decrees each of the faithful must receive the Eucharist at least once each year at Easter.
- It establishes the modern system of private penance—confession, absolution, and light penance.
- It makes the seal of confession canonically binding.
- It regulates monastic observance. In general the regulation is based on the Cistercian system.
- It declares the doctrine of creation *ex nihilo* to be dogmatic.
- It condemns the Albigensians.
- It condemns the Trinitarian errors of Abbot Joachim.

- It declares that procession of the Holy Spirit from the Son is dogma.

Dominic founds the Order of Preachers (or Dominicans) in southern France.

New mendicant orders, including the Poor Clares, Franciscans, and Dominicans, send out thousands of preachers all over the world.

1216 Bonaventure (1216–1274), a Franciscan theologian titled Doctor Seraphicus, is born.

1217 The Fifth Crusade, the last Crusade launched by papal authority, is aimed against Egypt, the Muslim headquarters. The Crusaders have to be evacuated when Cairo floods.

1219 A Crusade led by King Valdemar II of Denmark and Archbishop Luna founds Talinn in Estonia as a diocese.

A monk named Sava founds the autonomous Serbian Church.

1220 Hugh of Lincoln is canonized, the first Carthusian to be declared a saint.

Scriptures are translated into German.

Alexander of Neva (1220–1263), a Russian ruler and saint, is born.

The Chartres cathedral is completed.

1223 Francis's *Regula Primitiva* receives papal approval.

1224 Francis of Assisi manifests stigmata (wounds that resemble those of the crucified Jesus). His is the first known case.

1225 Thomas Aquinas (1225–1274), prince of theologians, is born.

1227 The Christianization of Estonia is complete.

1228 In the Sixth Crusade, Holy Roman Emperor Frederick II claims jurisdiction over Jerusalem.

Lay people are forbidden to read Scripture.

Vernacular Scriptures are prohibited by Synod of Toulouse.

1229 The Treaty of Paris ends the Albigensian Crusade.

1231 Pope Gregory IX writes *Excommunicamus*. It marks the beginning of the Inquisition and places inquisitors, mostly Franciscans and Dominicans, under the special jurisdiction of the pope. It also lessens the bishops' responsibility for maintaining orthodoxy and establishes severe penalties for heresy.

1233 The Decretals of Pope Gregory IX lists 45 public feasts and holy days.

The Order of Servites is founded by wealthy Florentines who abandon their wealth to serve the Virgin Mary. They follow a modified Augustinan Rule.

Canon law dictates that the chalice and paten used during the Eucharist must be gold or silver. It allows the poorest parishes to use one made of pewter but forbids brass, copper, wood, and glass.

1235 Matthew Paris begins his *Chronica Majora*, one of his illuminated redactions of his work on English history.

1236 Jacopone da Todi (1236–1306), a Franciscan Italian poet, is born.

1237 Osmund, bishop of Salisbury, establishes the Sarum Rite, the variant of the Roman Rite in use at the Salisbury cathedral. The extant texts lend considerable insight into medieval church practices.

Extreme unction begins to be distinguished from rites for the healing of the sick.

1240 Cimabue (1240–1302), a Florentine painter, is born.

The Franciscan Breviary is designed to enable friars to continue to say the Office while on the road. It is the Liturgy of the Hours stripped to bare essentials. It becomes the basis for the modern Daily Office.

Albert the Great writes *Summa de Creaturis*.

1244 Jerusalem is finally recaptured by Muslims.

1245 Alexander of Hales begins the *Summa Universae Theologiae* (*Complete Theological Commentary*).

Innocent IV convenes the First Council of Lyon (the Thirteenth Ecumenical Council) to deal with what he called "the five wounds of the church": the degeneration of the church, the failure to recapture the Holy Land, the invasion of Hungary by the Tatars, the schism with the Eastern Church, and the conflict between the church and the emperor. The council excommunicated the emperor and ordered the preaching of a new Crusade, but this came to nothing.

Giovanni Pisano (1245–1314), an Italian sculptor, is born.

1248 The Seventh Crusade is launched against Egypt, the Muslim headquarters. Louis IX is eventually captured at Mansura.

1249 Finland is conquered and converted by Birger Jarl of Sweden. It is Christianized through English bishop Henry of Uppsala.

1250   The Catholic Church reaches the apex of its political power.

Prussians are forcibly baptized, and pagan worship is eradicated.

Portions of the Bible are available in Italian (Tuscan, Lombardic), Polish, and Spanish or Catalan.

Bonaventure writes his *Threefold Way to God* and *Reduction of the Arts to Theology*.

1252   The Church of Saint Francis is completed at Assisi.

1254   Thomas Aquinas writes *On Being and Essence*.

1256   Gertrude of Helfta (1256–1302), German Cistercian nun, writer, and saint, is born.

Thomas Aquinas writes *Disputed Questions on Truth*.

1257   The Sorbonne is founded at the University of Paris.

1258   Baghdad (and in 1260, Damascus) is sacked by Mongols in an attempt to destroy the Muslim world.

Thomas Aquinas writes *Summa Contra Gentiles*.

1259   A flagellant sect arises in Perugia, in central Italy.

Pietro Cavallini (1259–1330), an Italian painter, is born.

Bonaventure writes *Journey of the Mind to God*.

1260   Meister Eckhart (1260–1328), a German theologian, philosopher, and mystic, is born.

1263   Bonaventure writes *Life of Francis*, the official Franciscan biography of Francis of Assisi.

1265   Thomas Aquinas begins *Summa Theologica*. It is the greatest summation of medieval theology ever written. It has three parts: theology, ethics, and Christology.

Thomas Aquinas devises the classic doctrine of purgatory. He teaches that both punishment (*poena*) and guilt (*culpa*) are purged in purgatory.

Duns Scotus (1265–1308), a philosopher and theologian, is born.

Thomas Aquinas writes *Disputed Questions on the Power of God*.

Mechthild of Magdeburg writes *Flowing Light of the Godhead*.

Dante Alighieri (1265–1321), an Italian poet, is born. His *Divine Comedy* is widely considered the greatest literary work composed in the Italian language.

1266 Thomas Aquinas writes *Disputed Questions on Spiritual Creatures.*
Mongol leader Kublai Khan asks the pope, "Send me 100 men skilled in
your religion…and so I shall be baptized and then all my barons and
great men, and then their subjects. And so there will be more Christians here than in your parts." By the time two Dominicans and five
Franciscans are sent in response to this request, the Great Khan was
dead.

1267 Giotto di Bondone (1267–1337), a Florentine painter, is born.

1268 Thomas Aquinas writes *On Free Choice.* Roger Bacon writes *Opus Majus.*

1269 Thomas Aquinas writes *On the Virtues in General* and *On the Soul.*

1270 Mechthild of Magdeburg writes *The Flowing Light of the Divinity.* It is
an account of the visions of a German beguine in two volumes.
Louis IX dies in the Eighth Crusade. The Crusades end with the Muslim forces gradually overrunning Latin territory until 1291.

1271 *Rijmbijbel* (Scriptures in poetical Dutch) is written.

1274 Gregory X convenes the Second Council of Lyon (the Fourteenth Ecumenical Council) to win back the Holy Land, bring about reunion
with the Eastern Church, and reform the church. Many famous theologians attend, but Thomas Aquinas dies on the way there. In fact,
the Eastern Church is required to capitulate over its differences with
the Western Church, including the acceptance of the insertion of the
Latin word *filioque* into the creed—"The Holy Spirit proceeds from
the Father 'and the Son.'"

1275 Marsiglio of Padua (1275–1342), an Italian scholar and the author of
Defensor Pacis, is born.
A Nestorian archbishopric is established in Cambaluc (or Khanbaliq,
the capital of the dynasty founded by Kublai Khan in Mongolia), and
the hierarchy is restored throughout central Asia.

1277 Saint George's cross is emblazoned on the national flag of England.

1280 William of Ockham (1280–1348), an English Franciscan friar, theologian, and philosopher, is born.

1284 Simone Martini (1284–1344), an Italian painter, is born.

1290 Thomas Bradwardine (1290–1349), a forerunner of the Reformation, is
born.

Jews are expelled from England.

1291 The last Crusaders leave the Holy Land with the fall of Acre, the final Latin-held city to be captured by the Muslims.

1293 Jan van Ruysbroeck (1293–1381), a Flemish mystic and writer, is born.

1294 John of Montecorvino, a Franciscan priest, translates the New Testament and Psalms into Chinese and begins a journey to China.

1295 Henry Suso (1295–1366), a German Dominican friar, mystic, and writer, is born.

1296 Gregory Palamas (1296–1359), a Greek archbishop and saint and a preeminent Hesychastic theologian, is born.

Work begins on the Florence cathedral.

1298 The original four doctors of the church are named. They are the Western theologians Ambrose, Augustine, Jerome, and Gregory the Great.

1300 Richard Rolle (1300–1394), English Bible translator, mystic, and writer, is born.

John Tauler (1300–1364), a German preacher, theologian, and mystic, is born.

Guillaume de Machaut (1300–1377), a French poet and composer who wrote the earliest known complete setting of the Ordinary of the Mass, is born.

The Age of Babylonian Captivity

THE STATUS OF THE CHRISTIAN CHURCH

At the end of the fourteenth century, 47 generations after Christ, 24 percent of the world is evangelized, and 21 percent of the population is Christian. The church is 11 percent nonwhite, and Scriptures are available in 26 languages.

INFLUENTIAL CHRISTIANS OF THE CENTURY

John Wycliffe, Ramon Lull, Catherine of Siena

SIGNIFICANT EVENTS AND INFLUENCES

- It was called the Babylonian Captivity—a strange name that recalled the bondage of the Jews to Nebuchadnezzar—and it threatened to divide the Western Church. The name was first used by Francesco Petrarch and other writers to describe the exile of the popes in the French city of Avignon from 1309 to 1377. Clement V was the first pope to make his residence in Avignon. A puppet of King Philip IV of France, he favored the French and convened the Council of Vienne (the Fifteenth Ecumenical Council), which abolished the Order of the Knights Templar and gave their valuable property to the French king. Six other popes followed Clement, all of them Frenchmen. Meanwhile, antipopes were installed in Rome, prompting the later Avignon popes, including Urban V, to seek a return to Rome. Matters came to a head in 1378 when Catherine of Siena issued a personal appeal to Pope Gregory XI to resume residence in Rome. He did, but in the face of continuing hostilities in the Papal States, he returned to Avignon, where he died. His death led to a period of major disturbances in the papacy known as the Great Papal Schism, when there were two or three popes at a time. The College of Cardinals elected an Italian pope, Urban VI, the first in nearly 70 years, but later denied the validity of the election and chose the Frenchman Clement VII instead. Urban remained in Rome, but Clement went back to Avignon. The schism continued until 1417.

- In 1321 Dante Alighieri wrote the epic allegorical poem *The Divine Comedy*, one of the top-ten masterpieces in literary history. *The Divine Comedy* is an allegory divided into three parts. In "Inferno," the poet Virgil guides Dante through nine concentric circles of hell. In "Purgatory," Virgil guides him up a nine-tiered mountain, upon which saved souls work off their sins before entering paradise. In the final part, "Paradise," Beatrice (the woman Dante idolized all his life) and Bernard of Clairvaux lead him through the nine concentric circles of heaven, where he meets the saints of God. Dante's vision captured in lapidary language the beauty and the poetry of medieval theology.

- John Wycliffe appeared toward the end of the century, but he was a man far ahead of his times. Called the "Morning Star of the Reformation," Wycliffe left his stamp on his age. Although considered a Reformer, he remained a Catholic all his life and opposed the prevailing scepticism of his contemporaries. As a theologian he sought inspiration in the Bible and the Fathers rather than in the dry speculation of the Scholastics. In his *De Veritate Sacre Scripturae* (*On the Truth of Sacred Scripture*) and other books he maintained that the Bible was the sole criterion of doctrine to which no ecclesiastical authority might lawfully add. "For as much as the Bible contains Christ," he wrote, "that is all that is necessary for salvation, it is necessary for all men, not for priests alone." Despite the church's disapproval, he worked together with other scholars to translate the first complete English Bible, using a handwritten copy of the Vulgate. The second edition of this translation, published after Wycliffe's death, became known as the Wycliffe Bible.

- Between 1348 and 1351 the bubonic plague, also known as Black Death, killed 33 percent of all Europeans, or about 60 million people. People blamed the plague on the Avignon Papacy, or the Jews, or the immoral life of the princes.

- The fourteenth century saw the apogee of the Nestorian Church in Asia and its extermination. As the century opened, a large portion of Persia was still Christian. Geographically, the Nestorian Church flourished over a wider area than the Roman Catholic Church with a membership of more than 15 million. But beginning in 1358, Tamarlane (or Timur the Lame), the Muslim Mongol emperor, known to Christians as the Scourge of God, began his campaign of murder and pillage that wiped out Christian civilization from the entire region. In Isfahan alone he piled 70,000 skulls, and in Baghdad another 90,000.

- Meanwhile, Christianity was being extirpated from other countries in Asia and Africa. The Mamluk Dynasty of Egypt ordered the closure and destruction of all Christian churches between 1301 and 1321. The Ming Dynasty of China banned Nestorian Christianity from Mongolia and replaced it with Buddhism. Bulgaria fell to the Turks in 1396, signaling the rise of Ottoman power in the Balkans and another five centuries of Muslim supremacy.

- As a result of Muslim persecution, the non-European percentage of Christians rapidly shrank. White Europeans now constituted more than two-thirds of all Christians, and that percentage would continue to rise for the next three centuries. With the baptism of Jagiello, Grand Duke of Lithuania, all of Europe had become Christian.

CHRONOLOGY

1300   Many churches in England have installed wooden pews. The custom of standing or kneeling exclusively during worship gives way to occasional sitting.

The Ave Maria becomes a penitential exercise in part due to the custom of genuflecting or bowing deeply when it is said.

The Mongol world (Russia, Persia, Turkestan) is gradually being converted to Islam.

Franciscans work in 17 stations throughout the Mongol Empire with a monastery in Cambaluc.

Meister Eckhart writes *Sermons and Treatises*.

John Duns Scotus writes *De Primo Principio*.

The Mamluk Dynasty orders that all Egyptian churches be closed or destroyed.

1302   John Duns Scotus begins *Ordinatio: Oxford Commentary on the Sentences of Peter Lombard*, also called *Opus Oxoniense*.

Pope Boniface VIII declares that the "one holy and apostolic Church" is headed by the pope and that apart from the church there is "neither salvation nor remission of sins." In this the papacy claims unprecedented power for itself.

1303   Bridget of Sweden (1303–1373), a mystic and saint and the founder of the Bridgettine Order, is born.

1304   Pope Benedict XI officially sanctions the Order of Servites. Their principal service and devotion is to the Virgin Mary.

Francesco Petrarch (1304–1374), an Italian scholar and poet and the father of humanism, is born.

1306   Jews are expelled from France.

John of Montecorvino, a Franciscan priest, builds two churches in Cambaluc with 6000 converts and translates the New Testament into Ongut.

1309   Christians capture Gibraltar.

Pope Clement V moves the curia (the papal court) from Rome to Avignon, beginning the "Babylonian captivity of the church," which lasted until 1377.

1310   Margaret Porette, a French mystic and the author of *Mirror of Simple Souls*, is burned at the stake.

1311 Clement V, the first of the Avignon popes, convenes the Council of Vienne (the Fifteenth Ecumenical Council) to deal with the Templars, who were accused of heresy and immorality, and to promote a new Crusade. The Templars were suppressed, and King Philip IV of France promised to go on a Crusade within six years. The council also issued decrees against the Beguines and Beghards (lay religious orders), who were (wrongly) accused of immorality. More positively, it made provision for the teaching of Oriental languages in five universities to further missionary work.

1313 Dante Alighieri writes *De Monarchia*.

1314 Sergius of Radonezh (1314–1392), a spiritual leader and monastic reformer of Russia, is born.

1315 Ramon Lull, a Franciscan who is credited with writing the first major work of Catalan literature, is stoned to death at Bugia (modern Bejaia in Algeria) by Muslims.

1317 Pope John XXII decides against the Franciscan Spirituals and allows the Franciscans corporate ownership. The Spirituals split from the order and formally adopt the name *Fraticelli* (Little Brethren).

1318 Pope John XXII commends the practice of Angelus and recitation of Hail Mary three times. He creates an archdiocese in the Mongol capital of Cambaluc (now the Archdiocese of Beijing).

1320 King Kazimierz (Casimir III the Great) builds Saint Mary's Basilica in Kraków, Poland.

1321 Dante Alighieri writes *The Divine Comedy*, a poetic journey through purgatory and hell with a glimpse of heaven.

1322 The anonymous *Little Flowers of Saint Francis* is written.

1324 William of Ockham writes *De Corpore Christi*.

1325 The anonymous *Tournai Mass* is written. It is the first complete setting of the Ordinary of the Mass (that part of the mass that does not change with the seasons—Kyrie, Gloria, Credo, Sanctus, and Agnus Dei).

1327 Meister Eckhart writes *Treatises and Sermons*.

1330 John Wycliffe, an English philosopher, theologian, lay preacher, teacher, reformer, and Bible translator, is born.

Bonaventure writes *Meditations on the Life of Christ.*

Henry Suso writes *Little Book of Eternal Wisdom.*

John Tauler preaches sermons that are among the noblest in the German language. About 80 are compiled in the sixteenth century.

Jordanus (a Dominican) is sent by the Roman pope as a bishop to Quilon, south India, to convert Malabar Nestorians.

1331   Ottoman Turks capture Nicaea in Asia Minor.

1333   The pope sends 27 Franciscan missionaries to China.

1340   Geert Groote (1340–1384) is born. He eventually founds the Brethren of the Common Life in the Netherlands to foster personal spirituality and free, high-quality religious education.

Walter Hilton (1340–1396), an English Augustinian canon and mystic, is born. He is the author of *The Scale of Perfection.*

1342   The Stations of the Cross are popularized by the Franciscans.

Julian of Norwich (1342–1415), an English writer and one of the most important mystics, is born.

1343   Richard Rolle writes *The Fire of Love.*

Geoffrey Chaucer (1343–1400), the greatest English poet of the Middle Ages and the father of English literature, is born.

1346   Jan van Ruysbroeck writes *The Adornment of the Spiritual Marriage.*

1347   In the Black Death, one of the most devastating pandemics in history, the bubonic plague spreads through Europe, killing 33 percent of the population.

Catherine of Siena (1347–1380), a Dominican Scholastic philosopher and theologian, a doctor of the church, and a patron saint of Italy, is born.

1349   Bridget of Sweden (1303–1373), a mystic and saint, founds the Order of Bridgettine Sisters, based on a vision in which Christ commanded her to found a new strict religious order dedicated to reforming monastic life.

The Nestorian expansion across Asia reaches its apogee with more than 15 million members.

1350   The *Gottesfreunde* (Friends of God), a group of mystics in the Rhineland and Switzerland, downplay ecclesiastical life in favor of personal mystical experience with God. The short-lived movement was heavily influenced by Meister Eckhart, John Tauler, and Henry Suso.

Jan van Ruysbroeck writes *The Sparkling Stone*.

The anonymous *Theologia Germanica* is written.

1357 The Maronite Church, which had separated from Greek Orthodoxy in the seventh century, unites with Rome.

John of Thoresby, archbishop of York, writes *The Lay Folks' Catechism*.

1358 Mongol emperor Tamerlane begins to destroy Christian civilization from China and north India to the Mediterranean.

1360 The Dresden Bible, the first translation of the whole Bible into Czech, is published.

1363 Jean Charlier de Gerson (1363–1429), a French theologian, reformer, and poet, and educator known as Doctor Christianissimus, is born.

1364 Guillaume de Machaut composes the first known polyphonic setting of the Mass Ordinary.

1365 The anonymous *The Cloud of Unknowing* is written. It is a mystical guidebook, written for those given to a life of contemplation.

Mongol emperor Tamerlane ends Christian influence in Afghanistan.

1366 Mesrob Mashtots (1366–1439), theologian, hymnologist, and inventor of the Armenian alphabet, is born.

1367 Pope Urban V and the curia temporarily move back to Rome. Most of the papal bureaucracy remains in Avignon.

Francesco Petrarch writes *On His Own Ignorance and That of Many Others*.

1368 The Ming Dynasty ousts the Mongol Dynasty in China, and Christianity disappears.

1370 Pope Urban V returns the papacy to Avignon.

Jerome of Prague (1370–1416), a reformer, is born in Bohemia (in the modern-day Czech Republic).

Mongolia is converted from Nestorian influence to Buddhism.

John of Trevisa completes his translation of the whole Bible into Anglo-Norman, which contributed to Middle English.

Catherine of Siena writes *Dialogue*.

1371   Turks capture most of Macedonia.

Jan Hus (1371–1415), a Czech priest, philosopher, educator, and reformer who was burned at the stake, is born.

1373   Margery Kempe (1373–1438), an English mystic who dictated the first autobiography in the English language, is born.

1376   Catherine of Siena goes to Avignon to persuade Pope Gregory XI to return to Rome. He begins the papal curia's final move from Avignon to Rome.

John Wycliffe and his followers begin translating the Bible into English. The New Testament is completed in 1378, and the entire Bible is completed in 1382.

1377   Filippo Brunelleschi (1377–1446), one of the foremost architects and engineers of the Italian renaissance, is born.

1378   In the Western Schism, Western Christianity is divided between two or three popes or antipopes. The schism ends with the Council of Constance (the Sixteenth Ecumenical Council) (1414–1418).

Lorenzo Ghiberti (1378–1455), a Florentine sculptor, is born.

1380   John Wycliffe begins to send out the Poor Preachers, who preach his religious views across the country.

The term "Holy Father" is first used in English to refer to the pope.

Thomas à Kempis (1380–1471), a German canon regular and the mystical author of *The Imitation of Christ* (one of the best-known devotional works of all time), is born.

1382   John Wycliffe writes *Trialogus*.

1386   Work begins on the Milan cathedral.

Geoffrey Chaucer writes his magnum opus, *The Canterbury Tales*, describing pilgrims' visits to the tomb of Thomas Becket.

Jagiello, Grand Duke of Lithuania, is baptized. European paganism is no longer an organized religion. He marries Queen Jadwiga of Poland and becomes King of Poland.

Donatello (1386–1466), an early Renaissance Italian sculptor, is born.

1387   Followers of Wycliffe launch the Lollard movement.

1388   Juan de Torquemada (1388–1468), a Spanish theologian, is born.

1390   Jan van Eyck (1390–1441), a Flemish painter, is born.

1391 Anti-Semitic massacres begin in Spain and Portugal. In Seville, 4000 Jews are killed.

1393 Juliana of Norwich writes *Showings*, a first-person account of 16 ecstatic visions.

1395 Fra Angelico (1395–1455), an early Italian Renaissance painter, is born. In 1982 Pope John Paul II proclaimed his beatification.

1396 Johannes Gutenberg (1396–1468), inventor of printing with movable type, is born.
Bulgaria falls to Ottoman Turk invaders.

1397 Guillaume Dufay (1397–1474), a Netherlandish composer of the early Renaissance and the most famous and influential composer in Europe in the midfifteenth century, is born.

1399 Rogier van der Weyden (1399–1464), a Belgian painter, is born.

The Fall of Constantinople

THE STATUS OF CHRISTIANITY

At the end of the fifteenth century, 49 generations after Christ, 21 percent of the world is evangelized, and 19 percent of the population is Christian. The church is 8 percent nonwhite, and Scriptures are available in 12 languages.

INFLUENTIAL CHRISTIANS OF THE CENTURY

Joan of Arc, Christopher Columbus, Girolamo Savonarola, Thomas à Kempis

SIGNIFICANT EVENTS AND INFLUENCES

- The Crusades had failed. The Arab tide had weakened and subsided by the fifteenth century, but the Muslim jihad against Christians continued with the Turks invading Byzantium (Constantinople, or modern-day Istanbul), the citadel of Eastern Christianity. Since the tenth century, the newly converted Muslim Turks had continued to move from their Central Asian homelands into Armenia, Cilicia, Anatolia, Thrace, and Bulgaria. Brutal and inhuman warriors trained to pillage and kill, the nomadic Turks had only one goal—to extend the Ottoman power to the farthest corners of the world, dispossess the original inhabitants of the lands they conquered, convert them to Islam, and spread terror throughout the known world. Every square inch of the Ottoman Empire was stolen from other peoples. The zenith of their power was the siege and conquest of Constantinople, the jewel of the Eastern Empire, in 1453, considered the darkest year in the Byzantine calendar. The first act of the conquering Turks was to convert the magnificent *Hagia Sophia* into a mosque. Over the next five hundred years, the Turks would kill more than 10 million Christians, convert more than 20,000 churches into mosques, and forcibly convert more than 25 million Christians to Islam.

- The year 1450 is generally regarded as the beginning of the Renaissance. The term itself is significantly vague because it is not clear exactly what the Renaissance ushered in. There was a renaissance of learning as printing became a means of communicating knowledge faster. There was a renaissance of arts and culture as the fine arts and literature gained a notable momentum in this century. This was also the beginning of the great age of geographical discoveries.

- In 1492, one of the most momentous events in human history took place when Christopher Columbus, a Genoan by birth, accepted a commission from their Most Catholic Majesties, Ferdinand II of Aragon and Isabella I of Castile, to sail across the Atlantic. The expedition discovered the New World and added two continents to human civilization. This single act expanded the Christian world by more than half and compensated for the loss of the Middle East, North Africa, and Asia Minor to the Muslims. Christopher Columbus was a devout Catholic who considered himself as an apostle of the gospel and his expeditions as divinely ordained.

- Before the end of the century, Vasco da Gama sailed around the Cape of Good Hope to reach Kozhikode (also known as Calicut) on India's Malabar Coast. In 1493 Pope Alexander VI issued a bull dividing the New World between Portugal and Spain and assigning Africa and Asia to Portugal. The Treaty of Tordesillas of 1494 between Spain and Portugal confirmed the provisions of the bull. Immediately afterward, the great Roman Catholic orders—the Jesuits, Franciscans, and Dominicans—took the challenge and carried the cross to the unknown lands that beckoned them. As a result of their efforts, the first Christians are reported in Senegal, Guinea-Bissau, Mauritania, Haiti, Dominican Republic, Kenya, and Equatorial Africa.

- By a strange coincidence, 1492 also marked the final reconquest of Spain from the Moors, as Granada, the last Muslim stronghold, fell to the Christians.

- In 1418 Thomas à Kempis wrote one of the enduring classics of Christian literature, *The Imitation of Christ*. Thomas was a member of the Brethren of the Common Life, a celebrated medieval order.

- In 1431 Joan of Arc, a French peasant girl during the Hundred Years' War, began to see visions and hear voices asking her to save France from the Burgundians and their English allies. She led a successful military expedition that saved Orléans, and she was present at the coronation of Charles VII at Reims. Later, she was taken prisoner, tried for heresy, and burned. In 1456 the verdict was reversed, and she was canonized as a saint. Over the centuries she became an icon for Gallic pride and one of the patron saints of France.

- In 1453–1455 Johannes Gutenberg made history when he printed, with the help of a loan from banker Johann Fust, the 42-line Mazarin Bible, known to later generations as the Gutenberg Bible. It was the first printed book in the history of Europe, and it set in motion a revolution in communications and the transmission of knowledge that continues to this day. In 1457, Johann Fust and Peter Schöffer produced the first dated book, a beautiful psalter. More people could now afford to buy and read Bibles, a fact that encouraged more translations into European vernaculars. The first High German printed Bible appeared in 1466, the first Italian and Dutch printed Bibles in 1477, and the first Spanish and French printed Bibles in 1478 and 1487 respectively. The widespread printing of Bibles was one of the contributing causes of the Reformation.

- In 1497–1498 the Dominican friar Girolamo Savonarola began to preach reform, encouraging the people of Florence to burn their luxury items and return to a humbler life. He sold church property and gave the proceeds to the poor. For a while, he was the ruler of a theocratic republic. Soon he was embroiled in a conflict with Pope Alexander VI and was excommunicated, hanged, and burned.

- The Council of Constance (the Sixteenth Ecumenical Council), convened in 1414, rejected Wycliffe's teachings and burned Jan Hus at the stake as a heretic. The Council of Florence (the Seventeenth Ecumenical Council) in 1438 affirmed the primacy of the pope over general councils. It declared union between Western and Eastern churches, but its decree was not accepted by the Eastern Orthodox Church.

- The Great Papal Schism ended as Martin V was elected pope. This would be the last such schism in the Catholic Church.

- Although the Inquisition as an institution had atrophied by the fifteenth century, it was revived in 1477 by Ferdinand and Isabella of Spain, who were initially concerned about the problem of Marranos, or nominally converted Jews. In 1478 they obtained permission from Sixtus IV to set up a new Inquisition, backed by royal authority. Initially limited to Castile, it was gradually extended by 1484, in spite of papal objections, to Aragon and later all lands subject to the Spanish monarchy. It soon became a highly centralized organization, especially after the appointment of Tomás de Torquemada as the inquisitor general in 1483. (Incidentally, de Torquemada appears in Dostoevsky's *Brothers Karamazov* as the grand inquisitor.) Although the Inquisition has acquired a certain notoriety, it was considered by contemporaries as more benign than secular courts of the period.

- In 1480 Russia expelled Mongol Muslim rulers and became a Christian state. Earlier, in 1448, the Russian Orthodox Church became an autocephalous patriarchate.

CHRONOLOGY

1400 Alvarez of Córdoba symbolically represents Jerusalem's Way of the Cross in a series of small chapels at the Dominican friary of Cordoba. Scenes of the Passion are painted in each chapel.

Western Europe becomes the main center of Christianity worldwide.

The Scriptures are translated into Icelandic.

1401 Masaccio (1401–1428), an Italian Renaissance painter, is born.

Nicholas of Cusa (1401–1464), a German philosopher, theologian, astronomer, and mystical writer, is born.

1404 Leon Battista Alberti (1404–1472), a Florentine architect and sculptor, is born.

1406 Fra Filippo Lippi (1406–1469), a Florentine artist, is born.

1409 The Council of Pisa meets. Neither Antipope Benedict XIII nor Pope
Gregory XII attend. The council deposes both of them and elects
Alexander V antipope.

Jean Gerson (1363–1429) writes *On Ecclesiastical Unity*.

1410 Johannes Ockeghem (1410–1497), a Franco Flemish composer, is born.

Jan Hus is excommunicated. Riots break out in Prague in his support.

The Bible is translated into Hungarian.

Piero della Francesca (1410–1492), an Italian painter, is born.

The Limbourg brothers (Herman, Paul, and Johan) write *Très Riches
Heures du Duc de Berry*, a book of hours, for John, Duke of Berry. It
is possibly the best surviving example of French Gothic manuscript
illumination.

1412 Joan of Arc (1412–1431), the French "Maid of Orléans" who saved the
French from the English late in the Hundred Years' War, is born.

1413 Jan Hus writes *Treatise on the Church*.

1414 John XXIII convenes the Council of Constance (the Sixteenth Ecumenical Council, 1414–1418). He is one of three popes in office at the
same time (the others were Gregory XII and Benedict XIII). The purpose is to end what is known as the Great Papal Schism, when Avignon and Rome competed as rival centers of authority for Western
Christianity. It famously issued the decree *Haec Sancta* ("The Holy
Synod"), the culmination of Conciliarism. The decree states that
the council is above the pope, and on this basis the council resolved
the schism by deposing John XXIII and Benedict XIII (Gregory XII
resigned). (Because John XXIII was never officially recognized as
pope, the most famous twentieth-century pope felt free to use his
name.) The council called for general councils to be held regularly (at
intervals of at most ten years), but this never came about. It also acted
against John Wycliffe, ordering his body to be removed from its burial
place and burned. The council also condemned Jan Hus to be burned
at the stake.

1415 John Hus, a Bohemian religious reformer, is burned at the stake on July
6, his birthday. One of the earliest church reformers, he predated
the Protestant Reformation. The Hussite Wars begin in Bohemia in
response to his execution.

1416   Jerome of Prague, a follower of Wycliffe's teachings and associate of John Hus, is burned for heresy.

1417   Work begins on the Sistine Chapel. It is completed in 1484.

1418   Thomas à Kempis writes *The Imitation of Christ*, a manual of devotion in four parts: the spiritual life, inward things, internal consolation, and the communion. It was published anonymously.

1420   Francisco Jiménez (1420–1517), a Franciscan Counter-Reformation leader who founded the University of Alcala, is born.

Tomás de Torquemada (1420–1498) is born. He became the first inquisitor general of Spain, driving out the Moors and Jews.

1425   Pope Martin V founds the Catholic University of Louvain, the oldest Catholic university.

1430   Giovanni Bellini (1430–1516), a Venetian painter, is born.

1431   Pope Martin V convenes the Council of Florence (the Seventeenth Ecumenical Council), which began in Basel. Pope Eugene IV moved it to Ferrara (1438) and then to Florence (1439). It was convened to pacify Bohemia and reform the church. It formally affirms the list of seven sacraments: Eucharist, baptism, confirmation, penance, extreme unction, holy orders, and matrimony.

Joan of Arc is executed after having turned the tide of the Hundred Years' War in favor of France.

1433   Margery Kempe (1373–1438) dictates *The Book of Margery Kempe*, perhaps the first English autobiography.

1439   The papal bull *Laetentur Coeli* ("Let the Heavens Rejoice") unites the Eastern Orthodox and Roman Catholic Churches, but it was not widely accepted in the Eastern Church.

Joseph of Volotsky (or Volokolamsk) (1439–1515), the father of medieval Russian monasticism, is born.

1440   Nicholas of Cusa writes *On Learned Ignorance*.

Hugo van der Goes (1440–1482), a Dutch painter, is born.

Nil Sorsky (1443–1508), monk and reformer of Russian monasticism, is born.

1444   Donato Bramante (1444–1514), an Italian architect and painter, is born.

Christian Portuguese explorers reach Senegal and Equatorial Guinea.

1445 Sandro Botticelli (1445–1510), a Florentine painter, is born.

1447 Catherine of Genoa (1447–1510), an Italian mystic admired for her
work among the sick and the poor, is born.

1448 Christian traders (Portuguese, French, Dutch and English) reach
Mauritania.

The Russian Orthodox Church becomes an autocephalous patriarchate.

Pietro Perugino (1448–1523), an Italian painter and Raphael's teacher, is
born.

1449 Some portions of the Scriptures are available in 33 languages just prior
to the invention of printing.

1450 Pope Nicholas V founds the Vatican library. He also decrees a holy year,
to be celebrated every 50 years.

The Renaissance, humanism, the renewal of paganism, and an obsession
with wealth challenge Christianity in Europe.

Hieronymus Bosch (1450–1516) is born. He becomes an early Dutch
painter known for using fantastic imagery to illustrate moral and religious concepts.

Marcus Marulić (1450–1524), a Croatioan poet and Christian humanist, is born.

Josquin Des Prez (1450–1521), a Netherlandish composer, is born.

1451 Christopher Columbus (1451–1506), Italian discoverer of the Americas,
is born.

1452 Girolamo Savonarola (1452–1498), an Italian reformer and Dominican
friar, is born. In 1498 he was hanged and burned as a heretic. Relics
and medals containing his image begin to be circulated throughout
Europe.

Leonardo da Vinci (1452–1519) is born.

1453 Constantinople falls to the Ottoman Muslims. Sultan Mehmet converts
the *Hagia Sophia* into a mosque.

Saint Peter's Basilica in Rome is planned as world's largest church to
replace the *Hagia Sophia*.

Nicholas of Cusa writes *The Vision of God*.

1455 Johannes Gutenberg prints the Gutenberg Bible, an edition of the Latin
Vulgate, using movable type. More than 100 editions of the Bible are
produced by 1500.

Johann Reuchlin (1455–1522) is born in Germany. He becomes a renowned scholar of Greek and Hebrew.

1456 Pope Callistus calls for the recapture of Constantinople.
John Hunyadi and the Hungarians defeat Turks at Belgrade.

1457 *Unitas Fratrum* (Unity of Brethren, and later, the Moravian Church) establishs a Christian village in Moravia.

1458 The term "Stations" is first used to apply to the Way of the Cross in Jerusalem.
Turks conquer Athens and all Grecce.

1461 An Armenian patriarchate is established in Constantinople.

1463 Ottoman Turks conquer Bosnia, and many nobles convert to Islam.
Frederick III (1463–1525), Elector of Saxony, is born.

1465 Johann von Staupitz (1465–1524), German vicar-general of the Augustinians and a friend of Martin Luther, is born.

1466 A Bible is printed in High German—the first in any modern language.
Desiderius Erasmus (1466–1536), a Dutch priest, theologian, humanist, and Reformer, is born.

1471 Niccolò Malermi translates the Bible into Italian.
Christianity is introduced into Ghana.
Albrecht Dürer (1471–1528), a German Renaissance painter, is born.

1472 Lucas Cranach the Elder (1472–1533), a German Renaissance painter and printer, is born.
Thomas Wolsey (1472–1530), an English cardinal and statesman, is born.
Fra Bartolomeo (1472–1517), an Italian painter, is born.

1473 Nicolaus Copernicus (1473–1543), a German-Polish mathematician and astronomer, is born.

1475 An English morality play called *Everyman*, an allegory of death and the fate of the soul, is written anonymously. It is one of the first known morality plays.
Michelangelo (1475–1564), an Italian artist, is born. His influence on Western art is unparalled.

1476 Francisco Jiménez de Cisneros (1476–1517), a Spanish cardinal and
grand inquisitor, is born.

Pope Sixtus IV decrees that the entire Roman Catholic Church adopt
the Feast of the Immaculate Conception.

1477 The University of Württemberg is founded at Tübingen.

The Old Testament is printed in Dutch, and the New Testament is
printed in French.

1478 The Bible is printed in Spanish.

The Spanish Inquisition is established to ferret out hidden Jews and
Muslims, and 120,000 Spanish intellectuals are executed from 1481 to
1498.

Thomas More (1478–1535), an English statesman, humanist, and martyr, is born.

1479 The Dormition Cathedral is built in the Moscow Kremlin.

1480 Matthias Grünewald (1480–1528), an Austrian painter, is born.

Andreas Karlstadt (1480–1541), a German theologian, is born. He
becomes a friend of Luther but later joined the Anabaptists.

Russia expels Mongol Muslim rulers and becomes a Christian state.

Ferdinand Magellan (1480–1521), a Spanish explorer, is born.

1481 The Spanish inquisitor general Tomás de Torquemada conducts the first
"act of faith" in Seville—a public execution of persons condemned by
the Inquisition.

1482 Johannes Oecolampadius (1482–1531), an associate of Ulrich Zwingli, is
born.

Christians (Portuguese explorers) reach the Congo.

1483 Francisco de Vitoria (1483–1546), a Spanish theologian and philosopher, is born. He contributed to the theory of a just war and to international law.

Martin Luther (1483–1546), the German Reformer, is born.

Raphael (1483–1520), an Italian painter, is born.

The Sistine Chapel is consecrated.

1484 Bartolomé de las Casas (1484–1566), a Spanish missionary to the New
World, is born. He becomes the first priest to be ordained in the West-
ern Hemisphere and the first officially appointed "protector of the
Indians."

Ulrich Zwingli (1484–1531), a leader of the Swiss Reformation, is born.

1485 Hugh Latimer (1485–1555), Anglican bishop of Worcester and English Reformer, is born.

Andrea del Sarto (1485–1531), a Florentine painter, is born.

Titian (1485–1576), a Venetian painter, is born.

1486 Johann Eck (1486–1543), a German Scholastic theologian, is born.

1487 Miles Coverdale (1487–1569) is born. He produced the first complete printed English translation of the Bible.

Bernardino Ochino (1487–1564), an Italian Reformer, is born.

Portuguese Catholics reach Nigeria.

1489 Guillaume Farel (1489–1565), a French evangelist and Reformer, is born.

Thomas Cranmer (1489–1556), archbishop of Canterbury, is born.

Caspar Schwenckfeld (1489–1561), a German Anabaptist Reformer, is born.

1490 Thomas Müntzer (1490–1525), a German Reformer who led the Peasant's Revolt, is born.

Friedrich Muconius (1490–1546), a Luthern reformer of Thuringia (a German state), is born.

Adrian Willaert (1490–1562), a Flemish composer, is born.

1491 Ignatius of Loyola (1491–1556), Spanish founder of the Society of Jesus (Jesuits), is born.

Henry VIII (1491–1547), British monarch and founder of the Anglican Church of England, is born.

Martin Bucer (1491–1551), a German Reformer, is born.

1492 Granada, the last Muslim stronghold in Spain, is captured.

By this time in the Inquisition, 180,000 Jews have been driven from Spain, 300,000 others have been forcibly converted to Christianity, and 20,000 have been burned as heretics.

Ferdinand and Isabella, king and queen of Spain, conquer the Moors in their country. They order Spanish Jews and Muslims to convert, leave the country, or die.

Christopher Columbus discovers the New World, adding two new continents for evangelization. Within the next 50 years, millions of American Indians would be baptized.

1494 The Treaty of Tordesillas gives Portugal authority over Africa, much of

Asia, and later, Brazil. Spain receives authority over the rest of world west of a north-south line 345 miles west of the Azores.

William Tyndale (1494–1536), Reformer and Bible translator, is born.

1495 John of God (1495–1550) is born. He is the Portuguese founder of the Hospitaller Brothers, an order that serves the sick.

Melchior Hoffman (1495–1543) is born. He becomes an Anabaptist preacher and the father of Dutch Anabaptism.

1496 Menno Simons (1496–1561), Anabaptist priest and theologian, is born. His followers are called Mennonites.

1497 Philipp Melanchthon (1497–1560), a German Reformer, is born.

Hans Holbein (1497–1543), German painter and designer, is born.

1498 Leonardo da Vinci paints *The Last Supper*.

Vasco da Gama, a Portugese explorer, discovers a route to India around the Cape of Good Hope. He reaches Kenya, and 600 Kenyans are converted by 1597.

1499 Peter Martyr (1499–1502), an Italian reformer, is born.

Christianity is steadily shrinking as a world religion. It is extinguished in China, Central Asia, and across the Muslim world. Caucasians, Mongolians, and Africans have almost no contact with each other.

Peter Martyr Vermigli (1499–1562), a Catholic who converted and became a Reformation scholar, is born.

Michelangelo completes the *Pieta*.

The Reformation

THE STATUS OF THE CHRISTIAN CHURCH

At the end of the sixteenth century, 52 generations after Christ, 24 percent of the world is evangelized, and 20.7 percent of the population is Christian. The church is 14 percent nonwhite, and Scriptures are available in 36 languages.

INFLUENTIAL CHRISTIANS OF THE CENTURY

William Tyndale, Desiderius Erasmus, Martin Luther, John Calvin, Ulrich Zwingli, Philipp Melanchthon, Martin Bucer, Ignatius Loyola, Francis Xavier, Claudio Acquaviva, Matteo Ricci, Menno Simons

SIGNIFICANT EVENTS AND INFLUENCES

- The central event of the sixteenth century was the breakup of the monolithic Western Church through the Reformation. The Reformation was neither a single act nor led by a single person. But before the century ended, Germany, Scandinavia, Iceland, the Netherlands, and England had broken away from Rome and established national churches that did not subscribe to the Roman Catholic traditions or acknowledge the pope as their head.

- A series of Bibles published within a few years of each other heralded the Reformation. Erasmus, a scholar and humanist, published a Greek translation of the New Testament in 1516. Later editions of his Greek text became the *textus receptus* of translations by Martin Luther, William Tyndale, and the King James translators. Erasmus paved the way for the Reformation with his merciless satires on the doctrines and institutions of the Roman Church, but he himself had no desire to break away from Catholicism.

- In 1525 William Tyndale made an English translation of the New Testament from Greek without permission and smuggled copies into England. For that he was burned at the stake. In 1537 Matthew's Bible (produced by Thomas Matthew, an alias for John Rogers) became the first English language Bible published with royal permission.

- In 1517, a German Augustinian monk named Martin Luther ignited an ecclesiastical revolution by posting his manifesto, the 95 Theses, on the door of the Castle Church in Wittenberg. Luther primarily criticized the practice of selling indulgences. He had no plans to start a Reformation, but only a more modest and worthy goal of ridding the church of its corruption. The posting of the 95 Theses is generally considered the birth of the Reformation.

Ironically, Luther harked back to Augustine, one of the most revered of the Church Fathers, in defense of his theses.

- In 1518 Luther defended his position in the Heidelberg Disputation and won over several of his fellow monks, including the Dominican Martin Bucer. In the same year he was tried in his absence in Rome on charges of heresy and summoned before Cardinal Thomas Cajetan at Augsburg. Refusing to recant, Luther fled, but he met his opponents again in 1519 at the Leipzig Disputation, at which Luther denied both the primacy of the pope and the infallibility of the general councils.

- In 1520 Luther published three seminal works outlining his theology. In the first, *To the Christian Nobility of the German Nation*, he opposed the celibacy of the clergy, masses for the dead, and many other Catholic practices. This was followed by *Prelude on the Babylonian Captivity of the Church*, in which he attacked all sacraments other than baptism and the Eucharist, the doctrine of transubstantiation, and the division between clergy and laity. In the final work of the trilogy, *On the Freedom of a Christian*, Luther called for the liberation of a Christian from the bondage of works and affirmed the sufficiency and authority of the Scriptures and salvation by faith alone.

- In 1520 the pope condemned Luther in his bull *Exsurge Domine* ("Arise, O Lord"). Luther replied by burning the bull, and he was excommunicated in 1521.

- Two other streams flowed into the Reformation to make it a surging flood. In Switzerland John Calvin and Ulrich Zwingli advocated an even more radical version of Christianity. In 1536 Calvin published his *Institutes of the Christian Religion*, which became the foundation of Calvinism. Calvinism is distinguished from Lutheranism primarily by its more radical use of Scripture as a criterion of ecclesiastical doctrine and practice, its stress upon predestination and divine omnipotence, and on the importance of the certitude of salvation to the elect.

- Zwingli was the most radical of the three Reformation leaders. He denied transubstantiation, reduced the Eucharist to mere symbolism, and opposed the invocation of the saints, monasticism, purgatory, fasting, and icons. Calvin and Zwingli also promoted a more theocratic view of the gospel, encouraging civil authorities to more actively intervene in religious affairs.

- By 1529 the word "Protestant" had become accepted as a label for churches that broke away from Rome during the Reformation. All Protestant churches believed in the Bible as the only source of revealed truth, justification by faith alone, and the priesthood of all believers.

- In 1534 Henry VIII, England's dissolute monarch, seeking divorce from his Catholic queen, was led through a series of events that placed him as the head of a national church by the Act of Supremacy. (These events had nothing to do with theology.) The new Church of England, now known as the

Anglican Church, accepted many of the Protestant tenets but retained much of the Catholic ritual and ceremony. For its doctrinal basis, it adopted the 39 Articles of Religion in 1563. The 39 Articles did not comprise a creedal statement of Christian doctrine but rather were short and vague summaries of dogmatic tenets. They combined both high church (Catholic) teachings and low church (radical) teachings, and both strands continue to coexist in the Anglican Church today.

- In 1549 the Church of England issued *The Book of Common Prayer* as its official service book. It contains the Daily Offices of morning and evening prayer, the forms for administration of the sacraments, and other public and private rites.

- In 1555 Queen Mary Tudor reversed the Reformation and reestablished Catholicism in England, but Protestantism returned permanently with the accession of Queen Elizabeth in 1558. In 1570 the pope excommunicated Elizabeth, and relations between Rome and Canterbury were strained until the nineteenth century.

- In 1560 John Knox began the Reformation in Scotland. In the British Isles only Ireland remained faithful to the Catholic Church.

- In 1525 the Radical Reformation was born. The early forerunners of this movement were the Anabaptists, predecessors to the Brethren and the Mennonite churches, which teach believers' adult baptism, separation of church and state, and presbyterian or democratic church government. In 1534, Anabaptist extremists took over Münster to establish a communal sectarian government, but the rebellion was quelled in 1535. Later, under Menno Simons, the sect became an influential community, and many emigrated to North America.

- Throughout the sixteenth century, Protestants tried to codify their beliefs in a series of confessions or creeds. In 1530 the Augsburg Confession was adopted by the Lutherans. In 1562 the Heidelberg Catechism was issued, and it remained the most widely held doctrinal statement for centuries. The Formula of Concord of 1577 was the last of the classical Lutheran formulas of faith.

- Meanwhile, the Catholic Church, rather than becoming weakened by the rise of Protestantism, was entering a period of unusual growth, as evidenced by the celebrated Council of Trent, held between 1545 and 1563 (the Nineteenth Ecumenical Council). It began the Counter-Reformation— the most impressive renewal of the Catholic church under pressure. The decrees of the Council, known as the Tridentine Profession of Faith, or the Creed of Pius IV, affirmed the traditional beliefs of the Catholic Church but condemned the sale of indulgences, nepotism, and clerical immorality. It ordered the revision of the Vulgate. Based on the work of the council, Pius V issued the Roman Catechism in 1566, the Breviary in 1568, and the Missal in 1570. He also founded the Congregation of the Index in 1571.

- Closely following on the Council of Trent, Catholic scholars from Oxford led by Gregory Martin translated the Douay-Rheims Bible from the Vulgate Latin while in exile in France. It would remain the version of the Bible used by English-speaking Roman Catholics for three centuries.

- In 1540 the Society of Jesus, better known as Jesuits, founded by Ignatius Loyola and his nine companions, was approved by Pope Paul III. Among the more immediate goals of the society were the propagation of the faith and the promotion of Christian piety. Hardly had the society been approved when Francis Xavier established it in Japan and Manuel de Nóbrega in Brazil.

- The Jesuits have some distinguishing features. They vow to travel anywhere in the world that the pope may order, they vow not to accept any position in the hierarchy except under direct order of the pope, and they have no distinctive habit (uniform). The most characteristic institutions of the society, however, are the great humanist schools and universities they have established all over the world. By 1581, under Claudio Acquaviva, the fifth Jesuit superior general, the number of Jesuits had increased to 13,000.

- After many centuries of evangelistic inertia, the worldwide expansion of Christianity began again under Catholic auspices. Magellan took the gospel to the Philippines. Mass conversion of Mexican Indians began under Cortés on the orders of the Spanish monarch. Spanish missionaries reached Florida, California, and Texas. The first permanent Catholic community was founded in Saint Augustine, Florida, in 1565. Francis Xavier carried the gospel to South India, the East Indies, China, and Japan. Meanwhile, the first Protestant mission was founded in Tranquebar, India, in 1575.

- In 1503 Pope Julius II commissioned Michelangelo to paint the Sistine Chapel. The foundation stone of Saint Peter's Basilica was laid in 1506.

- In 1598, Henry IV of France issued the Edict of Nantes, granting freedom of worship to French Protestants, known as Huguenots, after 30 years of persecution. This edict would be revoked by Louis XIV in 1685.

CHRONOLOGY

1500 The Mozarabic Rite Missal is printed by Spanish cardinal Francisco Jiménez de Cisneros, who preserves the rite by founding the Corpus Christi Chapel in the Toledo Cathedral and endowing chaplains to use the rite in it.

Printing presses in Europe now number 40, with 8 million volumes printed, a large proportion being Christian works (including 98 distinct editions of the Vulgate). About 1000 books a year are published worldwide with the newly invented movable type.

Portuguese Christian explorers reach Brazil.

Portuguese missionaries baptize several African chiefs on the west coast and in Congo.

Portuguese missionaries discover 100,000 Christians of Saint Thomas (Syrian Orthodox) in Kerala in southern India.

The worldwide expansion of Christianity commences again, mainly through Spanish and Portuguese Catholics.

Charles V (1500–1558) is born. He rules the Spanish Empire (as Charles I) from 1516 and the Holy Roman Empire (as Charles V) from 1519 until his voluntary retirement in 1556.

Jacob Hutter (1500–1536), a German Anabaptist Reformer, is born.

1501 The Roman Catholic Church orders the burning of all books opposing the authority of the church.

1502 All Jews of Rhodes (Greece) are forcibly converted, expelled, or taken into slavery.

Queen Isabella of Castile gives the remaining Moors the choice between expulsion and baptism.

Cardinal Francisco Jiménes de Cisneros initiates the compilation of the six-column Complutensian polyglot Bible.

1503 Francesco Parmigianino (1503–1540), an Italian painter, is born.

Pope Julius II introduces the Swiss Guard.

Desiderius Erasmus writes *Enchiridion Militis Christiani* (*Handbook of a Christian Knight*).

Canterbury cathedral is completed.

1504 Heinrich Bullinger (1504–1575), a German Reformer who succeeded Zwingli at Zurich, is born.

Luis of Granada (1504–1588), a Spanish Dominican theologian, preacher, and writer, is born.

1505 Martin Luther joins the Augustinian Order after a near-death experience in a thunderstorm.

Thomas Tallis (1505–1585), one of England's greatest composers, is born.

1506 Johann Tetzel, former grand inquisitor, sells indulgences in Germany to raise money for the rebuilding of Saint Peter's Basilica in Rome, and construction begins.

Pierre Robert Olivétan (1506–1538) is born. He is the first to translate the Bible from Hebrew and Greek into French and is a cousin of fellow Reformer John Calvin.

Hundreds of new Christians (baptized Jews and Muslims) are killed in the Lisbon Massacre.

Francis Xavier (1506–1552), a Roman Catholic missionary to Asia, is born. He is cofounder of the Society of Jesus (Jesuits) and a study companion of Ignatius of Loyola.

1507 Thomas Cajetan writes a commentary on the *Summa Theologica* of Thomas Aquinas.

Martin Luther is ordained a priest.

1508 Andrea Palladio (1508–1580) is born. He is considered the most influential individual in the history of Western architecture.

1509 John Calvin (1509–1564), French Swiss Reformer and theologian, is born.

1511 The First Catholic diocese of the New World is established at Puerto Rico.

Desiderius Erasmus writes *In Praise of Folly*.

1512 Luis de Morales (1512–1586), a Spanish painter, is born.

Michelangelo begins work in the Sistine Chapel.

The Catholic University of Puerto Rico opens.

James Laynez (1512–1565) is born. He became the second superior general of the Jesuits and was sent by Pope Paul III to the Council of Trent as his theologian.

The Fifth Lateran Council (the Eighteenth Ecumenical Council) is held in Rome. Its decrees are mainly disciplinary.

Raphael paints the *Sistine Madonna*, commissioned by Pope Julius II as an altarpiece for the Church of San Sisto, Piacenza.

1513 The dissolution of monasteries in Norway begins.

1514 In the *Padroado* (Portugese for "Patronage"), Pope Leo X delegates the administration of local churches to the kings of Portugal.

John Knox (1513–1572), leader of the Scottish Reformation, is born.

1515 Teresa of Avila (1515–1582), a Spanish Carmelite nun and one of the most influential mystic writers, is born.

Philip Neri (1515–1595), known as the apostle of Rome, is born.

1516 Desiderius Erasmus writes *Novum Instrumentum* (*New Document*). The first critical edition of the Greek New Testament, it also contains a

parallel Latin text. It becomes the basis for Luther's German translation and, with some revisions, the King James Bible.

Thomas More writes *Utopia*.

Desiderius Erasmus writes *Paraclesis*.

1517 John Foxe (1517–1587), an English martyrologist, is born.

The Observants, Franciscans who want a return to strict observance of
the Rule, split from the Conventuals. Rome recognizes the Observants as the true Franciscans.

Luther nails his 95 Theses to the door of the Castle Church in
Wittenberg.

The Oratory of Divine Love, a Catholic brotherhood formed in 1497,
seeks moral reform in the Roman Church.

1518 Christianity is introduced into Ceylon (Sri Lanka).

Jacopo Tintoretto (1518–1594), a Venetian painter, is born.

1519 Theodore Beza (1519–1605), a French Reformer who succeeded Calvin
at Geneva, is born.

Ulrich Zwingli preaches expository sermons on the New Testament.
The Swiss Reformation begins.

Martin Luther and Johann Eck debate at Leipzig. Luther denies the
infallibility of the pope and the authority of the general councils.

1520 Thomas Müntzer opposes Luther and supports the Anabaptist movement in Germany.

Ulrich Zwingli adopts Luther's doctrines of *sola fide* (faith alone) and
sola scriptura (Scripture alone) to be the heart of his theology. He is
installed as the people's priest in Zurich and persuades the Zurich
town council to forbid all religious teaching without explicit foundation in Scripture. He also begins to denounce monasticism, purgatory, and relics and to preach predestination and the two (as opposed
to seven) sacraments.

Matthias Flacius Illyricas (1520–1575), a Reformer and professor at Wittenberg, is born.

The ebb of monasticism brings a decline in missionary endeavors.

The Ottoman Turk expansion into Christian Europe reaches its apex
with mass conversions of Christians to Islam.

Lutheran lay noblewoman Argula von Grumbach begins writing pamphlets, poems, and letters in support of Luther and Melanchthon.

Martin Luther writes *To the Christian Nobility of the German Nation*,
Prelude on the Babylonian Captivity of the Church, and *On the Freedom
of a Christian*.

Pope Leo X issues *Exsurge Dominus* ("Arise, O Lord"), a bull that centures 41 propositions and gives Luther 60 days to recant. Luther burns the bull in public.

1521 Emperor Charles V convenes the Diet of Worms.

Philipp Melanchthon writes *Loci Communes Rerum Theologicarum* (*Common Places in Theology* or *Fundamental Doctrinal Themes*), the first systematic Protestant theology.

Peter Canisius (1521–1597) is born. He becomes a German Jesuit who leads the Counter-Reformation in Germany and writes three catechisms.

King Henry VIII of England publishes *Assertio Septem Sacramentorum* (*Defense of the Seven Sacraments*). Directed at Reformation doctrine in general and at Martin Luther in particular, it asserts the Roman doctrine of the sacraments and wins him the title "Defender of the Faith" from Pope Leo X.

Martin Luther is called before the Diet of Worms. He refuses to recant, and Pope Leo X excommunicates him. Luther flees to the Wartburg castle.

Ignatius Loyola, a soldier at the time, is seriously wounded during the Battle of Pamplona in the Italian War. He spends a year at Manresa in recovery and meditation.

Andreas Karlstadt performs the first Reformed communion service. He wears secular clothing, does not mention sacrifice, does not require confession before communion, and lets the people take both the bread and the wine on their own.

1522 Martin Chemnitz (1522–1586), a Lutheran theologian, is born.

An expedition organized by Ferdinand Magellan circumnavigates the globe.

Luther translates the New Testament into German. He completes the entire Bible in 1534.

The University of Alcalá distributes the Complutensian Polyglot Bible in Latin, Greek, Hebrew, and Aramaic. It reflects a growing interest in biblical study.

1523 Ignatius Loyola writes *Spiritual Exercises*, including meditations, rules, and directions for use over four weeks to help the seeker to overcome self-will and to surrender to God.

Zwingli destroys the organ at Grossmünster Church in Zurich, knocks out the stained glass windows, whitewashes the walls, and installs plain benches. A wooden table replaces the altar, and a simple wooden cup replaces the chalice.

Augustinians Johann von Essen and Heinrich Voss from Antwerp are burned at the stake in Brussels. They are the first martyrs of the Reformation.

King Charles I of Spain orders Cortés to enforce mass conversion of Mexican Indians.

1524 The German Peasants' War breaks out. It is Europe's largest popular uprising prior to the French Revolution of 1789. The peasants' main demands are articulated in the 12 Articles, including the right to elect their pastors and to have fair living and working conditions. Luther approves of the 12 Articles but is against the use of force to implement them. The aristocracy slaughters up to a third of the 300,000 poorly armed peasants and farmers.

Thomas Cajetan and Giovanni Pietro Carafa (later Pope Paul IV) found the Theatines, a male religious order.

1525 William Tyndale prints the first portions of his English translation of the New Testament.

The Swiss Brethren, an Anabaptist group near Zurich, begins a fellowship distinguished by believer's baptism and a rejection of infant baptism.

Conrad Grebel rebaptizes George Blaurock, a former Roman Catholic priest, and several others, marking the beginnings of the Anabaptist movement.

The Anabaptists are expelled from Zurich.

At Zwingli's urging, the Zurich town council abolishes the Catholic Mass.

Anabaptists are being persecuted (and sometimes executed) by Catholics and Lutherans.

Martin Luther writes *On the Bondage of the Will*.

Pieter Bruegel the Elder (1525–1569), a Dutch painter, is born.

Giovanni Pierluigi da Palestrina (1525–1594) is born. He becomes *maestro di cappella* at Saint Peter's in Rome, and his work is considered the culmination of Renaissance polyphony.

1527 Martin Luther writes "A Mighty Fortress Is Our God."

The Schleitheim Confession is endorsed as the first Anabaptist doctrinal statement.

The University of Marburg is founded as the first Protestant university in Europe.

Sweden adopts the Lutheran Confession.

The first Baptist church is established in Zurich.

Francisco de Osuna writes *The Third Spiritual Alphabet*, a masterpiece of Franciscan mysticism.

1528 Paolo Veronese (1528–1588), a Venetian artist, is born.

Austrian authorities burn Balthasar Hubmaier (1480–1528), an Anabaptist leader, as a heretic.

In public "disputations," Johannes Oecolampadius, originally Johannes Hussgen, secures support of the Reformation in the canton of Bern, Switzerland.

Patrick Hamilton is burned at the stake in Scotland for advocating Lutheranism. His death fuels the Reformation in that country.

1529 Martin Luther publishes the Small and Large Catechisms.

Wars break out between the Swiss cantons.

In the Marburg Colloquy, a meeting at Marburg, Germany, Martin Luther and Ulrich Zwingli agree doctrinally on most things but differ on the Lord's Supper.

The term "Protestantism" is first used at the Diet of Speyer.

1530 Holy Roman Emperor Charles V summons German Lutheran leaders to the Diet of Augsburg to account for their Lutheran views. They present the emperor with Melanchthon's Augsburg Confession. Roman theologians issue a refutation, and Emperor Charles V declares that the Protestants have been defeated.

The Feast of the Holy Name is officially granted to the Franciscans.

Bartholomé de las Casas supports the rights of indigenous peoples of Central America and charges that Spanish conquistadores have killed 15 million Indians. He writes *On the Only Way of Conversion*.

Luther and Calvin teach that the Great Commission (Mark 16:15) was the work of the first-century apostles only and expired with them.

Jacques Lefèvre d'Étaples, a Catholic who anticipated some important Reformation ideas, produces the first French translation of the Bible.

Michael Wiesse, a Bohemian Brethren pastor, compiles the first Protestant hymnal, *Ein New Geseng Buchlen*.

Denmark adopts the Lutheran Creed.

1531 Zwingli dies in battle, attempting to force Zurich Protestantism on Catholic cantons.

Franciscans baptize one million Mexican Indians in the 12 years following the conquest.

The (Catholic) Swiss "forest" cantons win the Swiss Civil War. The progress of the Reformation is halted with the country split—half Catholic, half Protestant.

Michael Servetus writes *On the Errors of the Trinity*.

The Virgin Mary appears in Guadalupe, Mexico, to a young Aztec, Juan Diego, directing him to build her a shrine and imprinting a miraculous image on his shawl. The basilica now there is visited by 100,000 pilgrims each year on the anniversary of the appearance.

German Protestant princes form the Schmalkaldic League in religious and military opposition of Emperor Charles V.

The University of Granada opens.

1532 German Protestants are granted full religious freedom.

Orlando de Lassus (1532–1594) is born. A Franco-Flemish composer, he is one of the most famous and influential musicians in Europe at the end of the sixteenth century.

Ahmad Gran, a Muslim Imam who invaded Ethiopia and defeated several emperors there, bans monasteries and cathedrals in Ethiopia.

King Henry VIII makes himself head of the Church of England.

1533 King Henry VIII is excommunicated from the Roman Catholic Church.

Thomas Cranmer becomes archbishop of Canterbury.

Jacob Hutter organizes the Moravian community of Hutterites.

Goa (on the Indian coast) is made a Catholic bishopric by the Portuguese.

1534 Luther completes the first complete translation of the Bible in German.

Zacharias Ursinus (1534–1583) is born. A German Reformer, he co-writes the Heidelberg Catechism in 1563.

John Calvin leaves France for Basel.

In the Act of Supremacy, King Henry VIII is granted the title "the Only Supreme Head in Earth of the Church of England, Called Anglicana Ecclesia." The Church of England separates from Rome.

Ignatius Loyola founds the Society of Jesus (the Jesuits) at the University of Paris for "the defense and propagation of the faith through preaching." It is made into an order in 1539 and grows into a powerful worldwide missionary organization.

Thomas More writes *A Dialogue of Comfort Against Tribulation*.

Henry VIII requires subjects to sign the Oath of Succession, recognizing Henry's supremacy over the Catholic Church. John Fisher, bishop of Rochester; John Houghton, Carthusian prior; Thomas More, Lord Chancellor of England; and three other Carthusian monks are beheaded for refusing to sign the Oath of Succession.

1535 Miles Coverdale produces the first complete printed translation of the

Bible in English. It is based on the Vulgate, Tyndale's New Testament, and Lutheran texts.

Angela Merici founds the Ursulines, a Roman Catholic order of women dedicatied to the education of girls and the care of the sick and needy. It is named after Saint Ursula.

Luis de Molina (1535–1600), a Spanish Jesuit theologian, is born.

John Calvin publishes his *Institutes of the Christian Religion* at age 26.

1536   Kaspar Olevianus (1536–1587), a German Reformer, is born.

Thomas Cromwell spearheads the dissolution of English monasteries.

William Tyndale is kidnapped from the free city of Antwerp and taken into Brussels. There he is tried for heresy and burned at the stake.

Pope Paul III establishes a Commission of Cardinals to reform the papal court.

King Christian III introduces the Reformation to Denmark.

Menno Simons, a former Roman Catholic priest, renounces his connections to the Catholic Church and begins to lead the Anabaptists in Holland.

In the Wittenberg Concord, followers of Luther and Zwingli agree over the doctrine of the Eucharist, but the agreement soon collapses.

Heinrich Bullinger and others draft the First Helvetic Confession (also known as the Second Confession of Basle) as a confession of faith for German-speaking Protestant Switzerland.

Ulrich Zwingli writes *A Short and Clear Exposition of the Christian Faith*.

The Church of England issues the Ten Articles of Faith on the urging of Henry VIII.

King Joao III of Portugal establishes an Inquisition.

1537   John Rogers produces the Matthew Bible. Matthew is probably a pseudonym for Tyndale.

Luther writes the Schmalkald Articles, which are later incorporated into the Lutheran Confessions in *The Book of Concord*.

The English king is declared the head of the Church in Ireland.

1538   Charles Borromeo (1538–1584) is born. As cardinal, he leads the Reform party at the Council of Trent.

John Calvin is ordered to leave Geneva and moves to Strasbourg.

Miles Coverdale superintends the printing of the Great Bible.

1539   Mennos Simons writes *The Foundation of Christian Doctrine*.

Henry VIII imposes the Six Articles on the Church of England to stop the spread of Reformation doctrines and practices.

Lutheranism is adopted in Iceland.

1540 Denmark, Norway, and Sweden have adopted Lutheranism as the state religion by this time.

Ignatius of Loyola's Society of Jesus (the Jesuits) receives official confirmation from Pope Paul III. Throughout the next 15 years, they grow to be a dominant force in the Counter-Reformation.

The Brethren (Anabaptists) in Holland begin to be called Mennonites.

1541 John Calvin returns to Geneva and institutes a theocratic regime. The Reformed Church, backed by secular authority, closely regulates the behavior of Geneva's citizens.

Francis Xavier sails for India.

El Greco (Dominicos Theotokópoulos) (1541–1614), a Cretan-born painter, sculptor, and architect, is born.

Ignatius Loyola becomes the first superior general of the Jesuit order.

The first Catholic mission in Chile is established.

1542 Frances Xavier, a Jesuit, arrives in India and begins to carry the faith throughout the Far East until his death in 1552.

Largely in response to the Protestant threat, Pope Paul III establishes the Congregation of the Inquisition, also called the Holy Office, as the final appeal in cases of heresy. It is empowered to discover, try, and judge heretics.

John Calvin produces the Genevan Catechism, a series of questions and answers about basic Christian doctrine.

John of the Cross (1542–1591) is born. He becomes a Carmelite priest, a major figure of the Counter-Reformation, and one of the most influential mystic writers.

Robert Bellarmine (1542–1621), an Italian Jesuit theologian and cardinal, is born.

1543 Martin Luther's German translation of the Bible is translated into Swedish and named after Swedish king Gustav Vasa.

William Byrd (1543–1623), an English composer, is born.

Ahmad Gran is slain by the Ethiopians at the Battle of Woguera.

1544 Torquato Tasso (1544–1595), an Italian poet, is born.

John Calvin writes *The Necessity of Reforming the Church*.

1545 The Hungarian Lutheran Church adopts the Augsburg Confession.

Pope Paul III convenes the Council of Trent (the Nineteenth Ecumenical Council), which continues under two more popes until 1563. It addresses doctrines and practices in light of the Protestants' criticisms. It becomes immensely influential and shapes Roman Catholic life until the Second Vatican Council.

1546 The Schmalkaldic War breaks out in Germany. Emperor Charles V defeats Lutheran Schmalkaldic princes at the Battle of Mühlberg.

1547 Dionysius of Zakynthos (1547–1622), an Eastern Orthodox saint, is born.

1548 Michael Agricola translates the New Testament into Finnish.

Tomás Luis de Victoria (1548–1611) is born. He, Palestrina, and de Lassus are the three most famous composers in Europe at the close of the sixteenth century.

Francisco Suárez (1548–1617), a Spanish Jesuit theologian and priest, is born.

Catherine of Genoa writes *A Dialogue Between the Soul and the Body*.

1549 Francis Xavier establishes a Jesuit mission in Japan.

The Book of Common Prayer is produced.

Peter Martyr Vermigli, an influential figure in the early development of Reformed theology and in the English Reformation, writes *A Disputation of the Sacrament of the Eucharist*.

Johann Heinrich Bullinger writes *The Decades*.

1550 Iceland adopts Lutheranism as the state religion.

The Roman Inquisition has burned at least 30,000 alleged witches in the previous 150 years.

Thomas Cranmer writes *A Defense of the True and Catholic Doctrine of the Sacrament*.

1551 Tsar Ivan IV summons the Council of a Hundred Chapters to address Roman ritual practices that do not conform with those of the Greek Church.

Philipp Melanchthon writes the (Protestant) Saxon Confession for the (Catholic) Council of Trent.

Ignatius of Loyola founds the oldest of the Roman colleges for the education of future clergy. It is originally called *Collegio Romano* but later called the Pontifical Gregorian University.

1552 The Royal and Pontifical University of Mexico and Universidad National de San Marcos in Lima are founded.

The Second Prayer Book of Edward VI, a truly Protestant version of the *Book of Common Prayer*, is published.

Matteo Ricci (1552–1610), an Italian Jesuit priest and missionary to China, is born.

1553 John Knox flees Scotland as Mary Queen of Scots returns to take the throne. He goes to Geneva, where he meets and is influenced by John Calvin.

Michael Servetus, a Spanish radical reformer who has denounced predestination and infant baptism, passes through Geneva during his exile from Vienne. He confronts Calvin and is arrested, tried, and burned at the stake.

Thomas Cranmer directs the writing of the 42 Articles, an Anglican doctrinal collection.

Queen Mary restores Roman Catholicism in England. In the next three years, 300 Reformed leaders, including Thomas Cranmer, archbishop of Canterbury, are burned at the stake.

1554 Richard Hooker (1554–1600), an English Anglican priest and theologian, is born.

Lancelot Andrewes (1554–1626), an Anglican bishop and scholar, is born.

The first edition of *Actes and Monuments*, popularly known as *Foxe's Book of Martyrs*, is released. It is in Latin.

1555 Mary Tudor burns Nicholas Ridley and Hugh Latimer, English Protestants and social reformers, for heresy.

The Peace of Augsburg, a treaty between Charles V and the Schmalkaldic League, officially recognizes both Lutheranism and Catholicism (but not Calvinism) in the German Empire. It states that the doctrinal preference of the sovereign dictates that of the region.

Johann Arndt (1555–1621), a Lutheran theologian, is born.

In *Cum Quorundam* ("With Some"), Pope Paul IV affirms the perpetual virginity of Mary.

1556 In the world's worst earthquake disaster, 830,000 are killed in Shaanxi province, China.

At the death of Ingatius of Loyola, the Jesuits number 1000 and become the outstanding Catholic missionary society.

Giovanni Gabrieli (1556–1612), an Italian composer and organist, is born.

1557 *Index Librorum Prohibitorum* ("Index of Prohibited Books") lists the books Roman Catholics are forbidden to read or possess. It is first issued during the papacy of Pope Paul IV. The penalty for reading the books is excommunication.

Joseph Calasanz (1557–1648) is born. He is the founder of the Pious Schools, which provide free education to sons of the poor.

1558 Spanish Protestants are virtually wiped out (burned at the stake) by the Inquisition.

1559 The Reformed Church of France adopts the Gallican Confession, which is basically the work of John Calvin.

The Dutch revolt against Catholic domination.

The Act of Uniformity requires uniformity of worship in England. Dissenters are fined.

Under Queen Elizabeth I, the Act of Supremacy restores authority over the Church of England to the monarchy.

A separatist group, later known as Puritans, arises in England.

John Calvin founds the Genevan Academy to train theologians from all over Europe.

Matthias Flacius and other Lutheran scholars compile the *Magdeburg Centuries*, which becomes the basis of all modern church history.

1560 The members of the Protestant Reformed Church of France (Calvinists) are first called Huguenots.

The Reformed Church in Scotland is founded as a Presbyterian church.

Carlos Borromeo, archbishop of Milan, becomes a leading figure in the Counter-Reformation.

English Puritans prepare the Geneva Bible, an English translation, during their exile in Geneva under Mary Tudor. It is the most influential Calvinist Bible until the King James Version.

Anabaptists are the only Reformation group deliberately working to obey Jesus's Great Commission, especially through Hutterian Brethren itinerant evangelists.

The Reformed Church of Scotland adopts the Scots Confession, which is drawn up by John Knox and others.

Jacob Arminius (1560–1609), a Dutch theologian and the namesake of Arminianism, is born.

1561 French Catholic bishops and Protestant ministers attempt reconciliation at the Colloquy at Poissy in France.

Robert Southwell (1561–1595), an English poet, Jesuit priest, and martyr, is born.

The Belgic Confession is drawn up on the basis of the Gallican Confession. It establishes Calvinist principles in the Low Countries.

Francis Bacon (1561–1626), an Elizabethan scientist and Lord Chancellor, is born.

The Edict of Orléans suspends the persecution of Huguenots.

Saint Basil's Cathedral in Moscow is completed.

1562 Teresa of Avila writes *Life of Teresa of Jesus*. She founds the Convent of Saint Joseph at Avila, the first community of discalced Carmelite nuns.

The Edict of 1562 officially recognizes the French Protestants.

The War of Religion, a conflict between Roman Catholics and Huguenots, begins in France (1562–1594).

John Calvin publishes *The Genevan Psalter*.

Heinrich Bullinger writes the Second Helvetic Confession, which is adopted by Reformed Churches in Switzerland, Scotland, Hungary, France, and Poland by 1578. It remains in the *Book of Confessions* adopted by the Presbyterian Church (USA).

1563 The Heidelberg Catechism is written.

The 39 Articles, the final version of Anglican doctrine accepted during the reign of Elizabeth I, defines the doctrinal position of the Church of England and places the Anglican Church in contrast to both Roman Catholicism and Reformed churches.

Actes and Monuments, popularly known as *Foxe's Book of Martyrs*, is published in English by John Day.

Galileo Galilei (1563–1642), an Italian physicist, mathematician, astronomer, and philosopher, is born.

1564 Pope Pius IV promulgates a revised "Index of Prohibited Books."

Philip Neri founds the Congregation of the Oratory, a community of secular priests and clerics.

1565 The first American Roman Catholic parish is founded by secular priests in Saint Augustine, Florida.

The Roman Catechism (also called the Catechism of Pius V) is written. Based on the work of the Council of Trent, it is the first official catechism of the Roman Catholic Church.

1566 The first Unitarian churches are founded in Hungary, Romania, and Poland.

John Knox publishes *The History of the Reformation in Scotland* in five volumes.

1567 Claudio Monteverdi (1567–1643), an Italian composer, is born.

Francis de Sales (1567–1622) is born. He becomes an Italian mystic, saint, doctor of the church, and leader of the Counter-Reformation.

The Hungarian Reformed Church adopts the Second Helvetic Confession.

1568 Matthew Parker, archbishop of Canterbury, is the leading figure in translating the Bishops' Bible. It will be revised in 1572 and used as an important source for the King James Version of 1611.

John of the Cross founds the first Discalced Carmelite monastery.

Thomas Aquinas is made doctor of the church. The Eastern doctors of the church are named—Athanasius, Basil, John Chrysostom, and Gregory of Nazianzus.

The English College is founded at Douai by Cardinal William Allen.

1570 John Smyth (1570–1612), an English Baptist and champion of religious freedom, is born.

Pope Pius V excommunicates Elizabeth I of England.

Pope Pius V issues the Roman Missal.

The Inquisition is established in Lima, Peru.

The Bible is translated into Spanish.

1571 John Donne (1571–1631), an English metaphysical poet, is born.

The University of Oxford is founded.

Michelangelo Merisi da Caravaggio (1571–1610), an Italian painter, is born.

Johannes Kepler (1571–1630), a German mathematician and astronomer, is born.

The Synod of Emden marks the beginning of the Dutch Reformed Church.

An Inquisition is established in Mexico.

The Holy League of Venice and Spain defeats the Turks in the historic Battle of Lepanto. Pope Pius V attributes the victory to the Blessed Virgin Mary.

1572 The Saint Bartholomew's Day Massacre is the bloodiest episode in the French Wars of Religion. Catherine de Médicis, the French Queen Mother, persuades King Charles IX to kill Huguenot leaders.

Thomas Tomkins (1572–1656), an English composer, is born.

Cyril Lucaris (1572–1638), a patriarch of Constantinople, is born in Crete.

1573   William Laud (1573–1645), archbishop of Canterbury, is born.

1574   William the Silent founds the Calvinist University of Leiden.

1575   Jakob Boehme (1575–1624), a German Lutheran mystic, is born.
The Book of Bamberg, a Catholic hymnal, is published.

1577   The Formula of Concord, a Lutheran statement of faith, is written.
Martin Bucer writes *De Regno Christi* (*On the Kingdom of Christ*).
Sir Peter Paul Rubens (1577–1640), a Flemish baroque artist, is born.
Robert de Nobili (1577–1656), an Italian Jesuit missionary to India, is born.

1578   The Shroud of Turin first arrives in Turin.
The first Anglicans arrive in North America.
The English College at Douai moves to Reims.
The icon of Our Lady of Kazan is discovered.
Roman catacombs are discovered.

1579   John of the Cross writes *Noche Obscura del Alma* (*The Dark Night of the Soul*), a classic of mystical literature.
Martin de Porres (1579–1639), the Peruvian patron saint of people seeking interracial harmony, is born.

1580   Torquato Tasso wites the poem *Jerusalem Delivered*.
The Book of Concord, a Lutheran formula of faith, is published.
Vincent de Paul (1580–1660), Catholic priest and founder of the Congregation of the Misson (Lazarists) and the Sisters of Charity, is born.

1581   Edmund Campion (1540–1581) is executed for treason. One of the "Forty Martyrs of England," he is the best known of the English Jesuits who were martyred during the reign of Queen Elizabeth I.
Theodore Beza presents the Codex Bezae, a fifth-century copy of the Gospels, Acts, and a fragment of 3 John, to Cambridge University.
Claudio Acquaviva is elected the fifth general of the Society of Jesus. By his death in 1615, the Jesuits have increased from 5000 to 13,000.

1582   Gregory Martin and other Catholic scholars produce the Douay-Rheims translation of the New Testament. The Old Testament follows in 1609–1610.
Pope Gregory establishes the Gregorian calendar, which soon becomes universal.

Matteo Ricci, a Jesuit, begins his mission in Macao.

Robert Browne writes *A Treatise of Reformation Without Tarrying for Any*.

Teresa of Avila writes *The Way of Perfection*.

1583 Luis Ponce de León writes *Names of Christ*, a layman's guide to the essential principles of the church.

Girolamo Frescobaldi (1583–1643), an Italian composer, is born.

Orlando Gibbons (1583–1625), an English composer, is born.

Hugo Grotius (1583–1645), a Dutch jurist and a founder of international law, is born.

1584 The Third Council of Lima meets to organize the church in South America.

1585 Cornelius Otto Jansen (1585–1638), whose writings became the basis of Jansenism, is born.

Armand Jean du Plessis Richelieu (1585–1642), a French cardinal and secretay of state, is born.

Heinrich Schutz (1585–1672), a German baroque composer, is born.

The Bible appears in Icelandic and Slovenian.

1586 Pope Sixtus V fixes the number of cardinals at 70.

Rose of Lima (1586–1617), a Peruvian saint, is born.

Jesuit priest Alonso Sánchez drafts an evangelistic scheme for the invasion and military conquest of China.

1587 Shogun Toyotomi Hideyoshi expels missionaries from Japan.

Jesuits begin missionary work in Argentina, Brazil, and Paraguay.

Pope Sixtus V founds the Vatican Press.

Samuel Scheidt (1587–1654), a German composer, is born.

1588 John Winthrop (1588–1649), the founding governor of the Massachusetts Bay Colony, is born.

The Vatican library building, designed by Domenico Fontana, is completed.

Pope Sixtus V establishes the Sacred Congregation of Rites to deal with the process of beatification and canonization and to enforce the dictates of the Council of Trent.

Hadrian Saravia becomes one of the first non-Catholic advocates of foreign missions.

1589 The Russian Orthodox Church establishes its own patriarchate and becomes independent from Constantinople.

The Treatise of Erastus by Thomas Erastus (1524–1583) is published post-humously. It is reprinted in 1682 as *A Treatise of Excommunication*.

1590 The Bible is translated into Hungarian.

1591 Trinity College is founded in Dublin.

Alexander de Rhodes (1591–1660), a Jesuit missionary to Vietnam and Persia, is born.

1592 Francis Quarles (1592–1644), an English poet, is born.

John Amos Comenius (1592–1670) is born. He becomes a Moravian and one of the earliest champions of universal education.

Pope Clement VIII publishes a revised Vulgate.

William Byrd writes Masses for three, four, and five voices.

1593 King Henry IV of France converts to Roman Catholicism in an attempt to end religious wars.

George Herbert (1593–1633), a British priest and poet, is born.

Sweden adopts the Augsburg Confession and officially becomes Lutheran.

The Bible is translated into Czech, and Jesuit Jakub Wujek translates the Bible into Polish.

1594 Jesuits reach the court of Mogal emperor Akbar the Great. The construction of the first Christian church in Lahore (in modern Pakistan) is permitted with a few conversions.

Nicolas Poussin (1594–1665), a French baroque painter, is born.

1595 The Church of England issues the Lambeth Articles, nine doctrinal statements on the predestination to salvation of a definite number of people from eternity. They were not authorized.

The Hungarian Uniat Church is founded.

1596 At the Council of Brest, a majority of the Orthodox in Ukraine break relations with the partrarch of Constantinople and enter into communion with Rome.

1597 Christians are crucified in Nagasaki, Japan.

1598 King Henry IV of France issues the Edict of Nantes, which ends the French Wars of Religion and gives Huguenots (French Calvinist Protestants) freedom of religion.

Francisco de Zurbarán (1598–1664), a Spanish artist, is born.

Gian Lorenzo Bernini (1598–1680) is born in Italy. He becomes an architect and painter and the creator of the baroque style of sculpture.

Alessandro Algardi (1598–1654), an Italian sculptor, is born.

1599 The Synod of Diamper in India unites the Saint Thomas Christians of the Malabar Coast, India, with the Roman Catholic Church.

Jesuits introduce *Ratio Studiorum*, a celebrated system of teaching and learning.

Francesco Borromini (1599–1667), an Italian sculptor and architect, is born.

Oliver Cromwell (1599–1658), Lord Protector of the Commonwealth of England, Scotland, and Ireland, is born.

The Age of Christian Expansion

THE STATUS OF THE CHRISTIAN CHURCH

At the end of the seventeenth century, 56 generations after Christ, 25.2 percent of the world is evangelized, and 21.7 percent of the population is Christian. The church is 15 percent nonwhite, and printed Scriptures are available in 52 languages.

INFLUENTIAL CHRISTIANS OF THE CENTURY

Alexander de Rhodes, Philipp Spener, John Eliot, George Fox

SIGNIFICANT EVENTS AND INFLUENCES

- In 1601 the Jesuit missionary and scholar Matteo Ricci began evangelizing China by adopting the dress and customs of the land and incorporating Confucian traditions, such as ancestor worship. It sparked the prolonged and damaging Chinese Rites controversy that troubled missionary work in Asia and Africa until it was condemned by Clement XI in the eighteenth century. By 1692, when the Chinese emperor officially allowed Christianity to be practiced in his realm, the number of Christians numbered more than 300,000.

- In 1611 King James I of England commissioned 54 scholars to undertake a new Bible translation, which took six years to complete. The scholars used the Bishops' Bible and Tyndale's Bible as well as available Greek and Hebrew manuscripts. The result was the King James Version (the Authorized Version). Its majestic and evocative cadences made it the most popular Bible in the world for the next 300 years.

- In 1603 the Dutch Reformed theologian Jacob Arminius caused the first dissension within Calvinism by presenting, on the basis of the epistle to the Romans, doctrines that denied predestination and affirmed human ability to choose Christ and Christ's atoning death for all people (not merely for the elect). In 1618 the Dutch Reformed Synod of Dort denounced Arminianism with five points of Calvinism, known by their mnemonic initials, TULIP—total depravity, unconditional election, limited atonement, irresistibile grace, and the perseverance of the saints.

- Under James I, successor to Queen Elizabeth, the Puritan dissidents, known officially as Nonconformists, became more restless. Describing themselves as Separatists, they wanted to establish their own commonwealth, built on Calvinist ideas and untainted by the flaws of the Church of England, especially the episcopacy. They first went to Holland, where they found themselves to be strangers, or Pilgrims. They returned to England and then in 1620 set sail from Plymouth on a ship named *Mayflower* for the New World. Though they had intended to head for Virginia, a storm swept them off course, and they landed in Plymouth Rock, Massachusetts. One Pilgrim described the new land as "a hideous and desolate wilderness." But more than the wilderness, the Pilgrims feared the possible anarchy of an unregulated and ungodly community. To create an orderly government under God, 41 of the 101 Pilgrims, while huddled aboard the wind-tossed vessel, signed the Mayflower Compact. In it they agreed that the colony they were about to found would be for the glory of God and the advancement of Christianity.

- The first decades of the seventeenth century marked one of the bloodiest persecutions against Christians in modern times. The mission of Francis Xavier had converted hundreds of thousands of Japanese to Christianity, and Christians formed a sizable segment of the Japanese population. However, by 1587, under the suspicion that the missions were merely preparing the way for foreign conquest, Christianity was proscribed. The first wave of persecution claimed the lives of 26 Japanese Christians, who were crucified from 1596 to 1598. In 1613 it broke out again under Shogun Ieyesu, and by 1640 several thousands suffered martyrdom for their faith. Then all foreigners were banned from Japan under pain of death. The proscription against Christianity was not lifted until 1859, and complete freedom of religion was not allowed until 1890.

- From 1618 to 1648, Europe was ravaged by the last of the religious wars, known as the Thirty Years' War. Europe had by this time become a mosaic of Catholic, Lutheran, and Calvinist territories. Bohemia, a strongly Protestant territory, was under the Catholic Holy Roman Empire. In 1618 some Protestant rebels stormed the royal palace in Prague and threw the rulers out the window. This act, called the Defenestration of Prague, caused severe reprisals from Emperor Ferdinand II, who, with the help of Spanish forces, routed the rebels in the Battle of the White Mountain in 1620. Bohemia was declared officially Catholic, and Protestants were forced to leave. Among those who left was John Amos Comenius, the great educational innovator, who was a pastor of *Unitas Fratrum* (Unity of Brethren, and later, the Moravian Church). Comenius finally settled in Leszno, Poland, where he published his seminal books on education. Meanwhile, the war raged on until the Peace of Westphalia in 1648. It is estimated that Germany lost half her population in the war.

- Two of the greatest works of Christian literature appeared in this century. John Milton, the blind English poet, completed his epic *Paradise Lost* in 1667. In 1678, John Bunyan, while in prison as a Nonconformist, published his well-loved classic, *The Pilgrim's Progress*, an allegorical masterpiece that is as relevant today as when it was written.

- In 1608, a group of Nonconformists fled to Holland under the leadership of John Smyth. Smyth had been convinced by the Mennonites that only adult baptism was biblical, and he conducted the first adult baptism of believers. In 1610 Smyth tried to merge his group with the Mennonites but without success. Another splinter group led by Thomas Helwys took their beliefs about adult baptism back to London, where they founded the first Baptist church. Arminian Baptists became known as General Baptists, and Calvinist Baptists as were called Particular Baptists. In 1639 Roger Williams founded the first Baptist church in the New World at Providence, Rhode Island.

- In 1643 the British Parliament summoned an assembly at Westminister Abbey to draft a "confession of faith for the three kingdoms." After 27 months of deliberations, the assembly created the Westminster Confession (1646), the Shorter Westminster Catechism (1647), and the Larger Catechism (1648), all of them founded on Calvinism. The Confession expounded in 33 chapters all the leading articles of the Christian faith from the creation of the world to the last judgment. Although it reaffirmed predestination, it recognized freedom of the will. It recognized two covenants—the covenant of law and the covenant of grace. The observance of Sunday as the Lord's Day was made a cardinal tenet. The Confession remains to this day as the most authoritative definition of Presbyterianism.

- In 1647 an English radical preacher named George Fox heard an inner voice that told him, "There is only one, even Jesus Christ, who can speak to thy condition." Fox called it the Inner Light, and it became the central doctrine of a new group that he founded, Children of the Light, later known as the Society of Friends. Fox spent some time in jail because of his teachings, and when he was brought before Justice Bennett, he warned the judge to "tremble at the Word of God." "You are the tremblers, the quakers," the judge replied, and the name stuck. The Quaker movement reflected the religious ferment of the seventeenth century. Fox emphasized the immediacy of Christ's teachings and held that ordained ministers, sacraments (even baptism and Communion), and church buildings were unnecessary. Quakers had no church services, only meetings. They renounced oath taking, dressed simply, ate sparingly, and abhorred war.

- By the seventeenth century, the Lutheran Church had lost much of its early zeal for personal piety. The man who revived it was Philipp Jakob Spener, who led the great renewal of Protestantism known as Pietism. In 1675, he published the classic *Pia Desideria* (*Holy Desire*), which presented a six-point plan for kindling personal piety in Christians. First, he wanted Christians to have a deeper and more life-changing understanding of the Scriptures. He also wanted them to take their personal priesthood as believers seriously and waste less time in sterile controversies and polemics over minor theological doctrines. Spener instituted devotional circles for prayer and Bible study.

Pietism also gave a boost to hymnody, and hymnwriters like Paul Gerhardt, Joachim Neander, and Gerhard Tersteegen produced great hymns that would later be translated into English Methodist hymnbooks. The practical aspects of Pietism, especially the warmth, would have far-reaching effects, and they have been particularly influential in the development of American evangelical Christianity.

• From 1698 to 1701, the world's first two non-Catholic mission societies were formed under the aegis of the Church of England—the Society for the Promotion of Christian Knowledge and the Society for the Propagation of the Gospel in Foreign Parts. The Society of Foreign Mission was founded in Paris in 1660. In 1613 *De Procuranda Salute Omnium Gentium* (*On Procuring the Savation of All Peoples*) by Thomas á Jesu urged the conversion of the entire world to Christ. In 1622 the Vatican created the *Congregation de Propaganda Fide* (Congregation for the Propagation of the Faith) to direct Roman Catholic missionary efforts.

• In 1685, Louis XIV of France revoked the Edict of Nantes, forcing the large-scale exodus of Huguenots from France.

• In 1629 Cyril Lucar, the Orthodox patriarch of Constantinople, befriended Protestants and presented the earliest copy of the Bible in Greek, now known as Codex Alexandrinus, to Charles I of England.

CHRONOLOGY

1600 Jesuits establish "reductions" (cooperative Native American villages) in Bolivia among the Moxos and Chiquitos.

Christians in Japan number 750,000 (3.4 percent of the population), including most of the Nagasaki area, with 300,000 baptized as Roman Catholics.

Christianity experiences its final extinction in Nubia.

Jean-Joseph Surin (1600–1665), a French Jesuit mystic and exorcist, is born.

1601 Matteo Ricci enters Peking, where he lives until 1610.

1602 An Orthodox bishopric is erected at Astrakhan (Russia) near the mouth of the Volga River.

The Dutch government sends missionaries to convert the Malays in its East Indies domains.

Jules Mazarin (1602–1661) is born. He becomes a French cardinal and statesman and the owner of the Gutenberg Bible.

1603 Roman Catholics in England and Wales number 1.5 million, declining to 70,000 by 1780.

Roger Williams (1603–1683) is born in England. He becomes a Protestant theologian, founder of Rhode Island, and champion of religious liberty and the separation of church and state. He founded the first Baptist church in America, studied Native American languages, and may have been the first abolitionist in North America.

1604 Robert de Nobili arrives in India, where he begins converting Hindus by allowing them to continue some Hindu customs—later called Malabar rites—that are later condemned by the Pope.

John Eliot (1604–1690), a Puritan missionary known as the apostle to the American Indians, is born.

1605 The Armenian Catholic Church is created through Dominican activity in Iran. It is Uniate (adhering to an Eastern Rite but submitting to papal authority).

The Dutch replace Catholic missionaries in Indonesia with Dutch Reformed chaplains of the Dutch East India Company.

Giacomo Carissimi (1605–1674), an Italian composer, is born.

Christmas trees are first used (in Strasburg).

Christianity is introduced into Canada by French missionaries.

Nikon (1605–1681), a patriarch of the Russian Orthodox Church, is born.

Cardinal Federico Borromeo founds the Ambrosian Library in Milan, the second public library in Europe. (The Bodleian Library in Oxford was the first.)

1606 Rembrandt (1606–1669), the most important painter in Dutch history, is born.

Johann Arndt writes *True Christianity*.

1607 Jesuits establish a mission in Thailand.

Paul Gerhardt (1607–1676), a German hymnwriter, is born.

Anglicans begin evangelization with the foundation of the Virginia Colony at Jamestown.

1608 Jacob Arminius writes *Declaration of Sentiments*.

Benedict Canfield writes *Rule of Perfection*.

John Milton (1608–1674) is born in England.

António Vieira (1608–1697), a Portuguese theologian, is born.

Jean-Jacques Olier (1608–1657) is born in France. He becomes a priest and the founder of the Society and Seminary of Saint Sulpice.

Francis de Sales writes *Introduction to the Devout Life*. It becomes one of the most popular works of Christian spirituality at the time.

1609 Philip II of Spain expels all Moriscos (Spanish Muslims forcibly baptized), and 300,000 flee to Algeria, Morocco, and Tunisia.

Francis de Sales writes *On the Love of God*.

John Gerard writes *The Autobiography of a Hunted Priest*.

The Douay-Rheims Bible is completed. It is the English translation of the Bible most used by Roman Catholics during the next three centuries.

The first modern Baptist church is formed by English Separatist John Smythe, who is in exile in Amsterdam at the time.

1610 Catholics in Peking number 2000 at death of Jesuit superior Matteo Ricci.

1611 Cardinal Pierre de Bérulle founds the Congregation of the French Oratory, a society of priests.

The King James Version, or Authorized Version, is published. It is an English translation and revision of the Bible by 50 scholars at the behest of King James I of England.

The British East India Company begins trade in Surat, Bombay.

The Five Articles of Remonstrance, a statement of Arminian beliefs, is published.

Peter Paul Rubens paints *The Descent from the Cross*.

Brother Lawrence (1611–1691), French Catholic mystic and monk, is born.

1612 Anglican clergy first serve as chaplains with the East India Company.

The Philippine island of Luzon has 322,400 Christians.

Pope Paul V approves the Congregation of the Oratory. It is a congregation of secular priests living in community without vows, dedicated to evangelism through preaching and prayer.

England stops burning heretics.

Thomas Helwys founds the first Baptist church in England. These Baptists, who call themselves General Baptists, are Arminian.

1613 Thomas á Jesu, a Spanish discalced Carmelite monk, writes *De Procuranda Salute Omnium Gentium* (*On Procuring the Salvaton of All Peoples*), envisaging conversion of the entire world to Christ.

Francisco Suárez writes *Treatise on Law*.

Jeremy Taylor (1613–1667), an Anglican bishop and devotional writer, is born.

1614 A Japanese edict prohibits Christianity, which is then 3.5 percent of the population. Churches are destroyed, Jesuits and other missionaries are deported, and more than 40,000 Christians are killed.

Saint Peter's Basilica in Rome is completed.

1615 The Irish Episcopal Church adopts the Irish Articles. These 104 articles of faith are replaced in 1635 by the 39 Articles.

Richard Baxter (1615–1691), a Puritan clergyman and writer, is born.

Douai Abbey is built in France.

1616 Francis de Sales writes *Treatise on the Love of God*.

1617 Bartolomé Esteban Murillo (1617–1682), a Spanish painter, is born.

Vincent de Paul founds the first Confraternity of Charity, an organization of wealthy women ministering to the sick and poor in Châtillon-les-Dombes, near Lyon, France.

1618 The Synod of Dort, a Dutch Reformed assembly, convenes to deal with the Arminian controversy. It approves the five points of Calvinism.

The Jesuits are expelled from Bohemia, Moravia, and Silesia.

The Thirty Years' War begins. It becomes one of the longest and most destructive conflicts in European history.

1619 The Dutch colonize the Dutch East Indies (Indonesia).

In the 100 years since the conquest, Spaniards have reduced Mesoamericans from 20 million to 4 million through war, disease, starvation, and forced labor.

1620 At the Battle of White Mountain (near Prague), the German Catholic League and other armies defeat the (Protestant) Bohemian army.

The *Mayflower* lands at Plymouth Rock. Plymouth Colony is founded by the Pilgrims (Puritan Separatists).

Avvakum (1620–1682) is born. He will lead the Old Believers in Russia who refuse to accept the liturgical reforms of Patriarch Nikon.

The Diocese of Buenos Aires is established.

1621 Henry Vaughan (1621–1695), an English poet, is born.

1622 Pope Gregory XV establishes the *Congregation de Propaganda Fide* (the Congregation for the Propagation of the Faith).

Hugo Grotius writes *On the Truth of the Christian Religion*, the first Protestant textbook in Christian apologetics, in six books.

Emperor Susenyos I (Malak Sagad III) of Ethiopia converts to Roman Catholicism.

1623 Blaise Pascal (1623–1662), a French mathematician, physicist, and
Christian philosopher, is born.

Jakob Boehme writes *The Way to Christ*.

German Lutherans arrive in New York, organizing a congregation by
1649.

Paraguay has 23 Jesuit reductions (settlements) with a combined population of 100,000.

Benedictines found the University of Salzburg.

Francis Turretin (1623–1687), an Italian theologian, is born.

1624 Guarino Guarini (1624–1683), an Italian baroque architect, is born.

John Donne writes *Devotions upon Emergent Occasions*.

George Fox (1624–1691), the British founder of the Society of Friends
(the Quakers), is born.

Mateus Cardoso edits and publishes a Kongo translation of a popular
Portugese catechism by Marcos Jorge.

1625 Jean de Brébeuf arrives in Canada. A French Jesuit missionary to the
Huron in Quebec, he arrived with the French explorer Samuel de
Champlain.

Vincent de Paul founds the Congregation of the Mission, also called the
Lazarists. They are a congregation of priests who live from a common
fund and are dedicated to the education of the clergy and ministry in
rural dioceses.

The Sigan-Fu Stone is discovered. It has the earliest Christian inscription
in northwest China.

1626 Armand Jean le Bouthillier de Rancé (1626–1700), founder of the Trappist Cistercians, is born.

Nicholas Ferrar's extended family lives as an Anglican community at
Little Gidding in Huntingdonshire.

The Codex Alexandrinus (A), one of the earliest of the uncial manuscripts of the Greek New Testament, comes to England as a gift from
the patriarch of Constantinople.

Portugese Jesuit missionary António de Andrade is the first Christian to
enter Tibet, where he builds a church.

1627 Alexander de Rhodes baptizes 6700 in North Vietnam.

French Jesuit theologian and chronologist Denis Pétau adds BC to the
calendar before AD.

1628 Miguel de Molinos (1628–1697), the chief representative of the religious
revival known as Quietism, is born.

John Bunyan (1628–1688), Puritan author of *The Pilgrim's Progress*, is born.

The Dutch in New York organize the first Christian Reformed Church on Manhattan island.

Ireland experiences a revival under Rogert Blair and John Livingstone.

1629 Matthew's Gospel is printed in Malay. It is the first evangelistic pamphlet in a non-European language.

1630 The Massachusetts Bay Colony is established by English Puritans, who run it as a Calvinist theocracy.

1632 William Ames writes *Of Conscience, Its Power and Cases.*

Christopher Wren (1632–1723), an English architect, is born.

Peter Mogila becomes the Orthodox metropolitan of Kiev.

Antonio Bosio's *Roma Sotterranea* marks the beginning of Christian archaeology.

1633 George Herbert writes *The Temple.*

Particular Baptists are formed in London, led by Henry Jacob.

Cyril Lucaris, patriarch of Alexandria, publishes a controversial confession of faith based on justification.

1634 The Oberammergau Passion Play is first performed in Bavaria by amateurs in fulfillment of a vow. It is still produced today.

Lord Baltimore founds Maryland for Roman Catholic settlers in North America.

Pope Urban VIII institutes canonization requirements. The right of canonization and beatification is reserved to the papacy. Local bishops no longer have that authority.

Jesuits from the English missions arrive in Maryland to minister to the Catholics of that colony and to convert Native Americans.

Archbishop William Laud declares that altars in Anglican churches are to be returned to the east wall and altar rails are to be restored. He removes the pulpit from its central focus and in doing so incurs the hostility of the Puritans.

1635 Roger Williams founds Providence, Rhode Island.

Philipp Jakob Spener (1635–1705) is born in France. He will move to Germany and become known as the father of Pietism.

1636 Massachusetts Bay Colony Congregationalists found Harvard College in Cambridge.

1637 Dietrich Buxtehude (1637–1707), a Danish–German organist and composer, is born.

John of Saint Thomas writes *Cursus Theologici* in nine volumes. It is a commentary on the *Summa Theologica* of Thomas Aquinas.

Thomas Traherne (1637–1674) , an English clergyman and metaphysical poet, is born.

1638 Catholic peasants are defeated at the Shimabara Rebellion, marking the end of Christianity in Japan until the late nineteenth century.

1639 Roger Williams founds the first Baptist church in America.

1640 John Eliot produces the Mohican Bible, the first Native American translation.

The *Bay Psalm Book* is the first book printed in the American colonies.

1641 Jean-Pierre Camus writes *The Spirit of Saint Francis de Sales*.

Irish Catholics massacre thousands of Protestants in Ulster (Northern Ireland).

Jean-Jacques Olier founds the Society of Saint-Sulpice in France.

1642 The Orthodox Synod of Jussy opens. It endorses the confession of faith drafted by Peter Mogila, metropolitan of Kiev.

Thomas Browne writes *Religio Medici* (*The Religion of a Doctor*).

The Bible is translated into Finnish.

1643 Isaac Newton (1643–1727), one of the most influential scientists of all time, is born in England.

The first volume of *Acta Sanctorum* (*Acts of the Saints*) is published by the Bollandists (an association of Jesuit scholars), who continue to edit and publish it.

Catholic missionaries in China appeal to Rome over a rites controversy. In 1742, a final papal bull rejects Ricci's methods of incorporating Confucian traditions.

1644 Roger Williams writes *The Bloudy Tenet of Persecution for Cause of Conscience*, arguing for a wall of separation between church and state and for state toleration of various religious groups.

John Cotton writes *Keys of the Kingdom of Heaven*.

Samuel Rutherford writes *Lex, Rex*, defending the Scottish Presbyterian ideal in politics.

The heir to the Chinese throne is baptized by Jesuits with the name Constantine.

1645 Edward Herbert, First Lord of Cherbury, writes *De Religione Laici.*
Capuchin friars in the Congo and Angola baptize 600,000 Africans
(mainly infants) by 1700.

1646 The Westminster Assembly draws up the Westminster Confession of
Faith, the Presbyterian statement of doctrine.
Isaac Jogues and six other Jesuits (the North American Martyrs) are
killed by the Mohawk Native Americans while working as missionaries in Ontario, Quebec, and New York.

1647 The Puritan-led English parliament bans the celebration of Christmas,
causing riots in several cities.
George Fox founds the Religious Society of Friends.
Margaret Mary Alacoque (1647–1690), promoter of devotion to the
Sacred Heart of Jesus, is born.

1648 John Lilburne, first a Puritan and later a Quaker, writes *Foundations of
Freedom.*
Lancelot Andrewes, bishop of Winchester, writes *Preces Privatae.*
The Feast of the Immaculate Heart of Mary is first celebrated in France.
Jeanne-Marie Bouvier de la Motte-Guyon (Madame Guyon, 1648–
1717), a French mystic and one of the key advocates of Quietism, is
born.

1649 Christians are far more widely spread geographically than ever, but less
numerous proportionately than in AD 500.
Jean de Brebeuf (1593–1649), a French Jesuit, is martyred with seven
other missionaries when an Iroquois raid takes over a Huron (Canada) village.

1650 Jeremy Taylor writes *The Rule and Exercises of Holy Living.*
Richard Baxter writes *The Saints' Everlasting Rest.*
Anne Bradstreet writes *The Tenth Muse Lately Sprung Up in America*, the
first publication in British North America by a female writer.
The Manchu Conquest, a long period of war between the Qing and
Ming Dynasties, kills 25 million Chinese.
German pioneers of Pietistic evangelism include Gilbertus Voetius
(1589–1676), Jodocus van Lodenstein, Jean de Labadie, Theodore
Untereyck, Philipp Spener, and August Hermann Francke.

1651 Jeremy Taylor writes *The Rule and Exercises of Holy Dying.*
Juana Inés de la Cruz (1651–1695), a Mexican nun and scholar, is born.
John-Baptiste de la Salle (1651–1719) is born. He becomes a French

priest, the founder of the Brothers of Christian Schools, and the patron saint of teachers.

Francis Daniel Pastorius (1651–1720) is born. He founded Germantown, Pennsylvania, the first permanent German settlement in America. Raised as a Pietist Lutheran, he grew close to the Quakers and signed the first petition against slavery in the English colonies.

François Fénelon (1651–1715), a French archbishop and mystical writer, is born.

John Eliot baptizes the first Iroquois converts.

1652 Pope Innocent X condemns Jansenism.

Richard Crashaw writes *Carmen Deo Nostro*.

George Herbert writes *A Priest to the Temple*.

Nikon is appointed patriarch of Moscow. His reforms revive Greek traditions and are opposed by Old Believers.

1653 Johann Pachelbel (1653–1706), German baroque organist and composer, is born.

1654 James Ussher writes *Annals of the World*. Ussher establishes the date of creation as 4004 BCE. This date becomes widely accepted and is even included in the margins of many King James Version Bibles.

1656 Richard Baxter writes *The Reformed Pastor*.

Luo Wen Zao is the first priest ordained in China. He later becomes bishop.

Johann Bernhard Fischer von Erlach (1656–1723), a baroque Austrian architect, is born.

1657 John Amos Comenius writes *Didacta Magna*, in which he champions universal education.

1658 Thomas Bray (1658–1730), founder of the Society for the Promotion of Christian Knowledge, is born.

1659 The Ethiopian Church becomes independent.

Henry Purcell (1659–1695), an English baroque composer, is born.

1660 Alessandro Scarlatti (1660–1725), an Italian composer, is born.

Jeremy Taylor writes *Ductor Dubitantium* (*The Rule of Conscience*).

The Society of Foreign Missions in Paris is founded, promoting Roman Catholic missions to East and Southeast Asia.

Between and 1660 and 1685, Charles II of England imprisons 13,000 Quakers.

1661 John Eliot translates the Bible into Algonquin (a Native American language). His is the first American Bible translation.

1662 The 1662 Act of Uniformity requires all Church of England services to use the 1662 *Book of Common Prayer*. All ministers not ordained by a bishop are removed, and as a result 300,000 members choose to leave the church.

1663 Cotton Mather (1663–1728), an American Puritan and Congregational minister, is born.

August Hermann Francke (1663–1727), a German Lutheran clergyman, philanthropist, and scholar, is born.

1665 Richard Baxter writes *A Christian Directory*.

1666 The archbishop of Salzburg expels 15,000 Protestants from his principality.

Philipp Jakob Spener begins work at the parish in Frankfurt, where he becomes the leader of Pietism in German Lutheranism.

In London, Saint Paul's Cathedral is completely destroyed in the Great Fire.

The first Armenian Bible is printed.

John Bunyan writes *Grace Abounding to the Chief of Sinners*, a spiritual autobiography, while in prison for preaching without a license.

1667 John Milton writes *Paradise Lost*, the last epic poem in written English. Composed to "justify the ways of God to man," it details the story of Lucifer's rebellion and the fall of Adam and Eve.

Saint Peter's Basilica is completed in Vatican City.

The Cathedral of Mexico City is completed.

1670 Blaise Pascal writes *Pensées*.

1671 Rose of Lima is canonized by Pope Clement X. She is the first native-born South American saint.

Margaret Mary Alacoque enters the convent at Paray-le-Monial after attributing her recovery from paralysis to the Virgin Mary. While in the convent, she has numerous visions of the bleeding and compassionate heart of Christ.

1672 Patriarch Dositheos II of Jerusalem convenes the Synod of Jerusalem to counter the Calvinist confessions of Cyril Lucaris.

Jesuit Jacques Marquette founds a mission station in present-day Chicago.

1673 Louis de Montfort (1673–1716), a French monk and saint who led a Marian revival, is born.

1674 John Owen, an English Nonconformist, writes *Discourse Concerning the Holy Spirit*.

Nicholas Malebranche, a French priest and philosopher, writes *Treatise Concerning the Search After Truth*.

Isaac Watts (1674–1748), known as the father of English hymnody, is born. He is credited with writing approximately 750 hymn texts, including "Joy to the World."

1675 Sir Christopher Wren begins Saint Paul's Cathedral in London in the English baroque style. In this and other churches built after the Great Fire, Wren introduces the single square-tower belfry with tall steeple. Since his time, this steeple has become the hallmark of English and American church architecture.

Phillip Jakob Spener writes *Pia Desideria* (*Holy Desire*), a German Protestant book calling for a practical, biblical, laity-centered Christianity. It is the first programmatic statement of Pietism.

Jean-Pierre de Caussade (1675–1751), a French Jesuit priest and spiritual writer, is born.

1676 Henry Compton, bishop of London, conducts the first census of church affiliation (Anglicans, Nonconformists, and Roman Catholics).

1678 Robert Barclay, a Scottish Quaker, writes *An Apology for the True Christian Divinity*.

Ralph Cudworth, an English philosopher, writes *The True Intellectual System of the Universe*.

John Bunyan writes *The Pilgrim's Progress*. An allegory of the Christian life, it is one of the most widely read English books.

Jean-Baptiste de la Salle founds the Brothers of the Christian Schools to teach Christian doctrine to the poor and working class.

1681 Jacques-Bénigne Bossuet, a French bishop and theologian, writes *Discourse on Universal History*.

Georg Philipp Telemann (1681–1767), a German composer, is born.

Eusebio Francisco Kino, an Italian Jesuit priest, begins to establish missions to the Pima Indians in Mexico.

William Penn receives a charter for the colony of Pennsylvania.

1682 Stephen Charnock writes *Discourses upon the Existence and Attributes of God*.

James Gibbs (1682–1753), the British architect who built Saint Martin-in-the-Fields in London, is born.

The Declaration of the Clergy of France outlines the rights and privileges demanded by the clergy of France arising out of a dispute between King Louis XIV and Pope Innocent XI.

1683 Mennonites land in America to join William Penn's "holy experiment."

Francis Makemie, Scottish Presbyterian minister and the father of American Presbyterianism, comes to the American colonies.

1685 Louis XIV revokes the Edict of Nantes, and 400,000 Huguenots flee from France to England, South Africa, and elsewhere.

The Russian Orthodox Church sends its first missionaries to China.

Jeanne Guyon (known as Madame Guyon), a French mystic and one of the key advocates of Quietism, writes *A Short and Easy Method of Prayer*.

Johann Sebastian Bach (1685–1750), one of Germany's greatest composers, is born.

George Berkeley (1685–1753), an Irish philosopher and Anglican bishop, is born.

George Friderick Handel (1685–1759), composer of *Messiah*, is born in Germany. He settled in London in 1712.

1686 William Law (1686–1761), a priest in the Church of England and a writer on discipleship, is born.

1687 John Dryden, English poet laureate, writes *The Hind and the Panther*, celebrating his conversion to Roman Catholicism.

1688 The New Testament is translated into Malay. It is the first Bible translation in Southeast Asia. The Old Testament would be completed in 1734 (Roman script) and 1759 (Arabic script).

François Couperin (1688–1733), a French composer, is born.

Emanuel Swedenborg (1688–1772) is born in Sweden. He becomes a philosopher and the founder of Swedenborgian Church.

Bible is translated into Romanian.

1689 A student revival arises at Leipzig, Germany.

1690 The Scottish church is legally established as Presbyterian.
The Roman Catholic Diocese of Nanking in China is established.
Claude Fleury (1690–1723), a French ecclesiastical historian, is born.

1692 Chinese emperor Kangxi decrees freedom of worship to all Christians (a total of about 300,000 people).
Brother Lawrence (Nicholas Herman) writes *The Practice of the Presence of God*.
Joseph Butler (1692–1752), an Anglican theologian and bishop of Durham, is born.
Johann Michael Fischer (1692–1766), a German baroque architect, is born.

1693 A group led by Joseph Amman breaks away from the Mennonites. Later they emigrate to America and are known as the Amish.

1694 Paul of the Cross (1694–1775), founder of the Passionists, a Roman Catholic religious institute, is born.

1695 John Locke writes *The Reasonableness of Christianity*.

1696 John Toland writes *Christianity Not Mysterious*.
Giovanni Battista Tiepolo (1696–1770), a Venetian painter, is born.
Alphonsus Liguori (1696–1787), an Italian bishop and theologian, is born. He is founder of the Redemptorists, a religious order of men who spread the gospel to the poor and abandoned.

1697 John C. Gill (1697–1771), an English Baptist scholar and theologian, is born.
Gerhard Tersteegen (1697–1769), a German Protestant writer, is born.

1698 Thomas Bray founds the Society for the Promotion of Christian Knowledge in England. Essentially Anglican, it has a publishing house and a chain of bookshops and funds the provision of books in countries throughout the Commonwealth.

The Eighteenth Century (1700–1800)

The Age of Protestant Revivals

THE STATUS OF THE CHRISTIAN CHURCH

At the end of the eighteenth century, 59 generations after Christ, 27.2 percent of the world is evangelized, and 23.1 percent of the population is Christian. The church is 14 percent nonwhite, and printed Scriptures are available in 67 languages.

INFLUENTIAL CHRISTIANS OF THE CENTURY

John Wesley, Charles Wesley, George Whitefield, Isaac Watts, John Newton, Jonathan Edwards, Junipero Serra, William Carey, Robert Raikes, Nicholas von Zinzendorf

SIGNIFICANT EVENTS AND INFLUENCES

- In 1729 John Wesley and his brother Charles began a "Holy Club" at Oxford University, which their detractors named Methodists because of their methodical search for personal holiness. That search led the brothers on a missionary journey to Georgia in the American colonies in 1735. When they returned to London, they went to a Moravian meeting, where someone read from Luther's commentary on Romans. That night John Wesley wrote, "About a quaner before nine, while he was describing the change which God works in the heart through faith in Christ, I felt my heart strangely warmed. I felt I did trust in Christ, Christ alone for salvation; and an assurance was given me that He had taken away my sins, even mine, and saved me from the law of sin and death."

- Out of that conversion experience grew the worldwide Methodist Church. John Wesley began preaching in open fields because the Anglican churches were closed to him. For the remaining 63 years of his life, he traveled 250,000 miles on horseback, preached more than 40,000 sermons, and wrote hundreds of books and letters. Another member of the Holy Club, George Whitefield, was converted around the same time, and together they led England and America into a new age of revival. Methodism became successful because it primarily appealed to the lower classes, which were ostracized by the mainline churches.

- As the church grew, John Wesley assigned circuits, or districts, and each Methodist society was divided into fellowship classes and prayer bands. The brothers, especially Charles, had no intention of breaking away from the Church of England but rather wanted to reform the church from within. In 1771 John Wesley sent Francis Asbury to preach in America. The American Methodist Church became a separate entity in 1784.

- Although overshadowed by his brother, Charles too had great impact on Methodism. He wrote some of the sweetest hymn texts in the English language, some 5000 in all, including the unforgettable "Jesus, Lover of My Soul," "Hark the Herald Angels Sing," "O for a Thousand Tongues," and "And Can It Be That I Should Gain."

- The eighteenth century indeed was the age of great hymns. One of the first to write hymns that could be sung as part of a church service was Isaac Watts, who published his *Hymns and Spiritual Songs* in 1709. He based some of his songs on the Psalms, such as Psalm 98, which formed the basis of "Joy to the World." Watts wrote approximately 750 hymns, including "When I Survey the Wondrous Cross" and "O God Our Help in Ages Past," and became known as the father of English hymnody. In 1764, John Newton wrote "Amazing Grace." Newton was a former slave trader who was converted while his ship was battered by a storm in the North Sea. In 1779, Newton collaborated with William Cowper, the emotionally troubled English poet, to produce *The Olney Hymns*.

- Just as the spiritual fervor of the Puritan Commonwealth seemed to be dying out in America, Jonathan Edwards, a New England pastor, ignited a revival that swept New England and most of the 13 colonies. Drinking deeply from the wells of Calvinism, Edwards preached the necessity of a new birth, mixing fire-and-brimstone messages with pleas for changed lives and increased devotion. In the winter of 1734 and through the years that followed, a great change came over the church Edwards pastored at Northampton. "The Spirit of God began extraordinarily to set in," Edwards wrote. "The town seemed to be full of the presence of God. It never was so full of love and so full of joy." The revival was taken to New Jersey by Theodore Frelinghuysen, a pastor and leading politician who came from a distinguished Dutch family, and by Gilbert Tennent and his brothers. Towering above them all was George Whitefield, the most striking and eloquent orator of the Evangelical Revival. Tirelessly crisscrossing the colonies, he was the guiding spirit behind the Great Revival. It is estimated that 80 percent of the colonists heard Whitefield at one time or another. The Second Great Awakening took place almost half a century later in 1792. The movement was parallel to Continental Pietism and English Evangelicalism.

- In 1769 Father Junípero Serra, a Spanish Franciscan missionary, founded the first of the nine Californian missions in San Diego, thus bringing the gospel to the west coast of North America for the first time. He was instrumental in the settlement of what is California today.

- In 1741–1742 George Friderick Handel, a German-born composer living in London as a naturalized British subject, wrote *Messiah*, the most-performed oratorio in the world. Handel came from a German Pietist family, and he conveyed a deep evangelistic message in the oratorio, which was first performed before an audience that included the King of England.

- The year 1793 is a landmark in the history of Christian missions, for in that year William and Dorothy Carey set sail on a ship to India on the first Protestant missionary effort (apart from the Tranquebar mission). Even as a young man, Carey was obsessed with the Great Commission, in which Jesus Christ charged His followers to go into all the world and proclaim the gospel to every living creature. Three weeks after publishing his thesis, *An Enquiry into the Obligations of Christians to Use All Means for the Conversion of Heathens*, he issued the call for missionaries to "go into all the world" and cited the words that remained the motto of his life, "Expect great things from God, attempt great things for God." In 1800 the couple reached Calcutta, the capital of the English possessions in Bengal, and moved to Serampore, a Danish colony, where they gained their first convert. In the next 34 years, Carey, whose wife had by now succumbed to mental illness, translated the Bible into 44 languages and started several schools and mission stations that began the evangelization of northern India.

- In 1700 Peter the Great ordered the Christianization of Siberia, expanding the territorial extent of Christianity. In 1721 he abolished the patriarchate and appointed the Holy Synod, headed by an ober-procurator to lead the Russian Orthodox Church. The church would remain under state control until 1917.

- In 1780 one of the most beloved of Christian institutions had its genesis in the Gloucester kitchen of one Mrs. King, where a roomful of children were taught the Bible every Sunday from ten to twelve in the morning and from one to five in the afternoon. It was the pet project of Robert Raikes, the editor of *Gloucester Journal*, who publicized it in his journal. Soon a number of prominent Christians, including John Wesley and Queen Charlotte, applauded the idea. To extend the effort to all England, Raikes founded, with the help of William Fox, a London merchant, the Society for the Support and Encouragement of Sunday Schools in Different Counties of England. Within a century the movement had become worldwide and a part of Sunday services.

- In 1722 a group of Moravians and Bohemians who had been expelled from their homeland by Catholics appeared at the door of Count Nicolaus von Zinzendorf in Dresden seeking asylum. Zinzendorf was a wealthy and devout Lutheran who had been planning to open his vast estates to a community based on principles of Christian piety. Thus the noble and the refugees shared a common bond. Zinzendorf welcomed other Moravians into the new community, which he called Herrnhut ("the Lord's watch"). By 1726, Herrnhut grew to be 300 strong, and the next year, common worship services and a 24-hour-a-day prayer vigil were instituted. In 1732 the Moravians began sending out missionaries to all the new unreached colonial lands, including the West Indies, Greenland, Lapland, Suriname, South Africa, Guyana, Algeria, and Ceylon (modern Sri Lanka). Zinzendorf, meanwhile, revived the *Unitas Fratrum*, the original Moravian Church. After being expelled from Saxony by his political enemies, Zinzendorf began his missionary travels to the American colonies and England, establishing Moravian communities everywhere. By the time he died in 1760, more than 226 missionaries were serving in Moravian communities around the world.

- The French Revolution of 1789 was one of the catastrophic events that punctuate European history. The French revolutionaries, like most revolutionaries throughout modern history, were hostile to Christianity, and they attacked and pillaged the magnificent cathedrals and monasteries for which France was famous, killed thousands of priests and monks, converted Notre Dame into a temple, and instituted a cult of reason. The Jacobins, as the more radical of the revolutionaries were called, were eventually ruined by their own excesses and were, before the end of the century, suppressed by Napoleon, who then would dominate French history for the next two decades.

- In 1746 widespread and severe persecution of Christians began in China, lasting 38 years.

Chronology

1700 Armand Jean de Rancé restores the original practices of seclusion, silence, manual labor, and vegetarianism to his Cistercian monastery at La Trappe, France. Followers of his strict observance becomes known as the Order of Cistercians of the Strict Observance, or the Trappists.

Two thousand Quakers from England settle in Pennsylvania.

Ernst Christoph Hochmann von Hochenau, one of the chief proponents of radical Pietism, leaves his promising law career and begins conducting evangelistic campaigns in Germany.

The Wittgenstein revival movement begins in Germany and lasts 50 years.

Catholics are found in all provinces of China, numbering 250,000.

Nicolaus von Zinzendorf (1700–1760), a German nobleman who founded Herrnhut, is born.

1701 Thomas Bray forms the Society for the Propagation of the Gospel in Foreign Parts, an Anglican society. It fosters the spread of the Anglican Church into the British colonies.

Yale College is founded by conservative Congregationalists.

The Romanian Uniat Church is founded as 200,000 Romanian Orthodox submit to Rome.

1702 In the first attempt to found a church independent of Rome in black
Africa, 22-year-old prophetess Kimpa Vita (Dona Beatrice) founded
her Antonian sect in the Kingdom of Kongo. In 1706 she was burned
alive by King Pedro VI.

Cotton Mather publishes *Magnalia Christi Americana* (*The Glorious
Works of Christ in America*) in seven volumes.

1703 The Congregation of the Holy Spirit (Spiritans, or Holy Ghost Fathers),
are founded for the conversion of the heathen.

Jonathan Edwards (1703–1758) is born. He becomes an American congregational minister and a primary leader of the Great Awakening.

John Wesley (1703–1791), the English founder of Methodism, is born.

Saint Petersburg (Petrograd) is built as the imperial capital of Russia by
Peter the Great at the cost of 100,000 laborers' lives.

1704 Johann Sebastian Bach writes his first cantata to be a part of the
Lutheran liturgy.

Persecution begins throughout China.

François Fenelon writes *Christian Perfection*.

Pope Clement XI rules against the Jesuit practice of allowing Chinese
converts to continue the cult of ancestor worship.

1705 The first foreign mission society in Germany, the Lutheran Danish-
Halle Mission, sends Bartholomäos Ziegenbalg, Heinrich Plütschau,
and Christian Schwartz to Tranquebar, India, as pioneer missionaries.

1706 Seven Presbyterian ministers meet in Philadelphia and form the first
Presbytery in the New World. This is the origin of the Presbyterian
Church in the USA.

The Danish-Halle Mission begins in India.

1707 Isaac Watts publishes *Hymns and Spiritual Songs*. Though Watts is a
Nonconformist and his songs are not widely accepted in the Church
of England during his lifetime, some hymns in this hymnal eventually
become British and American favorites. Watts marks the trend away
from settings of literal Psalm translations and toward hymnody that
expresses the thoughts and feelings of the singer. The hymnal includes
"When I Survey the Wondrous Cross," "O God Our Help in Ages
Past," and "Joy to the World."

Selina Hastings, Countess of Huntingdon (1707–1791), is born. She
becomes a patron of Evangelical and Wesleyan revivals in England.

Charles Wesley (1707–1788), an English Methodist hymnwriter, is born.

1708 Pope Clement XI extends the Feast of the Immaculate Conception of the Blessed Virgin Mary to the universal church and makes it a Feast of Obligation.

1710 Christopher Wren finishes Saint Paul's Cathedral in London.

Karl von Canstein establishes the Canstein Bible Institute (the world's first modern Bible Society) in Halle, Germany, to print and distribute Bibles at low cost.

Thomas Reid (1710–1796), a Scottish Presbyterian philosopher, is born.

1711 Henry Melchior Muhlenberg (1711–1787), the father of the Lutheran Church in the United States, is born in Germany.

Bartholomäus Zigenbalg, a Lutheran pastor and the first Pietist missionary to India, translates the Bible into Tamil.

1712 Samuel Clarke writes *The Scripture Doctrine of the Trinity*.

1713 Junipero Serra (1713–1784), a Spanish missionary to the New World, is born.

1714 George Whitefield (1714–1770), an Angelican preacher and a key figure in the Great Awakening, is born.

1716 China bans Christian missionaries who do not permit converts to practice the cult of ancestor worship.

William Tennent evangelizes in the American colonies.

1719 The Jesuits are expelled from Russia.

1720 Pope Clement XI makes Anselm of Canterbury a doctor of the church.

Paul of the Cross writes the rules for the Passionists, or the Congregation of Discalced Clerks. In 1769, Pope Benedict XIV grants him permission to form the congregation.

1721 The Lutheran Church of Greenland is recognized as an integral part of the Evangelical Lutheran Church of Denmark.

Peter the Great abolishes the Russian Orthodox patriarchate and establishes a synod of bishops and a tsar-appointed ober-procurator, enabling tsars to rule the church through the synod until 1917.

Hans Egede, a Scandinavian Lutheran, begins a Protestant mission. He will become known as the apostle of Greenland.

1722 Nicolaus von Zinzendorf organizes groups of Brethren (who later evolve into the Moravian Church) in his home. He introduces a Pietistic tone to the organization.

Paisius Velichkovsky (1722–1794), a Ukrainian monk and writer, is born.

1724 Tikhon of Zadonsk (1724–1783), a Russian saint and mystic who inspired Dostoevsky, is born.

Friedrich Gottlieb Klopstock (1724–1803), German author of the epic poem *Der Messias* (*The Messiah*), is born.

1725 John Newton (1725–1807), author of "Amazing Grace" and hundreds of other hymns, is born.

The Great Awakening breaks out in the American colonies under Jonathan Edwards and T.J. Frelinghuysen.

Henry Venn (1725–1797) is born in England. He is founder of the Clapham Sect, which lobbied Parliament on social issues, especially the slave trade.

1726 Pope Benedict XIII canonizes Aloysius Gonzaga and John of the Cross.

The First Great Awakening begins among the Dutch Reformed Churches in New Jersey.

1727 The Ursuline convent is established in French New Orleans as the first regular religious community for women in America.

Jews are expelled from Russia and again in 1747.

1728 Johann Heinrich Callenberg, a Lutheran professor, founds the first Protestant mission to the Jews.

William Law writes *A Serious Call to a Devout and Holy Life*. It calls the Christian to a temperate and ascetical life. Based on the writings of Thomas à Kempis, Jan van Ruysbroeck, and other mystical writers, it exhorts the reader to glorify God in all aspects of life. It is one of the best-known post-Reformation spiritual classics.

1729 Johann Sebastian Bach writes the *Saint Matthew Passion*.

Methodism is founded in England by John Wesley.

1730 Matthew Tindal writes *Christianity as Old as the Creation*, the "Bible" of deism.

1731 William Cowper (1731–1800), an English poet, is born.

Pope Clement XIII fixes the Stations of the Cross at 14.

1732 Alphonsus Liguori, a Catholic bishop, founds the Redemptorists to spread Christianity among the poor.

The renewed Moravian Church begins missionary work, eventually going to the West Indies, Greenland, Tasmania, South Africa, and elsewhere.

Franz Joseph Haydn (1732–1809), an Austrian classical composer, is born.

1734 The translation of the entire Bible into Malay is completed.

1735 John and Charles Wesley travel to Georgia (America) as missionaries for the Society of the Preservation of the Gospel, but they meet hostility and return in 1737.

George Whitefield is converted.

John Carroll (1735–1815), the first American Catholic bishop of Baltimore, is born.

1736 Moravians send missionaries to Greenland.

Joseph Butler writes *Analogy of Religion, Natural and Revealed*.

Robert Raikes (1736–1811) is born. He is the British founder of the Sunday school movement.

The Bible is translated into Lithuanian.

1737 Alexander Cruden publishes the first Bible concordance.

Johann Michael Haydn (1737–1806), an Austrian composer and the younger brother of Franz Joseph Haydn, is born.

Moravian missionary George Schmidt begins work among the Khoikhoi in southwest Africa.

1738 John and Charles Wesley, founders of Methodism, are converted.

George Whitefield begins evangelistic campaigns in North America.

1739 John Wesley begins to form Methodist societies within the Anglican Church to provide guidance for the converts drawn to the church by his evangelistic efforts.

Charles Wesley publishes *Hymns and Sacred Poems*, his first collection of hymns.

George Whitefield (February 17) and John Wesley (April 2) preach the first evangelistic open-air sermons in England in centuries. John Wesley's evangelistic travels in Britain will average 8000 miles a year on horseback until his death in 1791.

1741 George Frideric Handel writes *Messiah*.

The Coptic Uniat and Armenain Uniat churches are founded.

Moravians under Nicolaus von Zinzendorf found the town of Bethlehem in Pennsylvania.

The oldest American-Indian independent church is formed—the Narragansett Indian Church in Charleston, Rhode Island.

1742 Henry Melchior Muhlenberg, a German Lutheran missionary, comes to America.

1743 William Paley (1743–1805), an English apologist, is born.

Charles Chauncy writes *Seasonable Thoughts on the State of Religion in New England.*

1745 Hannah More (1745–1833), a religious worker and philanthropist, is born.

Francis Asbury (1745–1816), one of the first two bishops of the Methodist Episcopal Church in the United States, is born.

1746 Princeton University is founded by New Light Presbyterians as the College of New Jersey.

Widespread and severe persecution of Christians begins in China and lasts 38 years.

Jonathan Edwards writes *A Treatise Concerning Religious Affections.*

1747 Johannes van der Kemp (1747–1811), a Dutch missionary physician to South Africa, is born.

The Shakers (the United Society of Believers in Christ's Second Appearing) are founded.

1748 Henry Melchior Muhlenberg founds the Pennsylvania Ministerium, the first Lutheran synod in North America.

Francis Xavier is declared the patron saint of the Orient.

Nicolaus von Zinzendorf writes *Nine Public Lectures on Important Subjects.*

1749 Richard Challoner publishes the Challoner Revision of the Douay-Rheims translation of the Bible.

The Diary of David Brainerd is published.

Nicodemus of the Holy Mountain (1749–1809), a Greek Orthodox theologian, is born.

1750 Christianity is now the prevailing religion of the West Indies.

About 95 percent of the people in the 13 colonies are professing Christians, but only 5 percent are affiliated as church members.

Alphonsus Maria de' Liguori writes *The Glories of Mary*.

Anne-Robert-Jacques Turgot, a French economist and statesman, writes *Two Discourses on Universal History*.

George Liele (1750–1828) is born. He is an African-American emancipated slave and the founding pastor of the First African-American Baptist Church in Savannah, Georgia. He became the first American missionary and the first Baptist missionary in Jamaica.

Antonio Salieri (1750–1825), a classical composer, is born in Italy but settles in Austria.

1752 Thomas Thompson, the first Anglican missionary, arrives in Ghana (then called the Cape Coast).

The Gregorian calendar is adopted in Great Britain and Ireland. Easter is celebrated on the same day throughout Western Christianity.

1754 Jonathan Edwards writes *The Freedom of the Will*.

Charles Maurice de Talleyrand-Périgord (1754–1838), a French statesman, is born.

Andrew Fuller (1754–1815), an English Baptist theologian, is born.

Columbia University is founded as King's College.

1756 Herman of Alaska (1756–1837), a Russian Orthodox missionary to Alaska, is born.

Wolfgang Amadeus Mozart (1756–1791), an Austrian composer, is born.

1757 William Blake (1757–1827), an English poet and artist, is born.

1758 Jonathan Edwards writes *The Great Christian Doctrine of Original Sin Defended*.

1759 The Jesuits are expelled from Brazil and Portugal.

Seraphim of Sarov (1759–1833) is born. He becomes one of the most renowned Russian monks and mystics in the Eastern Orthodox Church.

William Wilberforce (1759–1833) is born. As an English parliamentarian, he helped to end the slave trade.

1761 William Carey (1761–1834), an English missionary to India, is born.

1762 Thomas Campbell (1762–1854), the founder of the Disciples of Christ, is born.

Jean-Jacques Rousseau writes *The Profession of Faith of a Savoyard Priest.*

1764 The Feast of the Sacred Heart becomes a liturgical feast.
Robert Raikes begins Sunday schools in England.

1766 Catherine the Great grants religious freedom in Russia.
The first Methodist society in the New World formed in North America.
John Wesley writes *A Plain Account of Christian Perfection.*

1767 Jesuit missionaries are expelled from Mexico, Spain, and Spanish South
America.

1768 Friedrich Daniel Ernst Schleiermacher (1768–1834), a German theologian, is born.
Greek Orthodoxy comes to America when Greek pioneers found the
colony of New Smyrna south of Saint Augustine, Florida.

1769 Junipero Serra founds a series of missions in California.
John Wesley sends out Methodist missionaries to America.

1770 Bertel Thorvaldsen (1770–1844), a Danish sculptor, is born.
Georg Wilhelm Friedrich Hegel (1770–1831), a German philosopher, is
born.

1772 Barton Stone (1772–1844) is born. He becomes an American Presbyterian leader and associate of Alexander Campbell and helps organized
the Cane Ridge revival of 1801.
Francis Asbury begins reaching the American frontier through Methodist circuit riders.
Slavery is ruled illegal in Britain (but not in the colonies). Still, the
Atlantic slave trade delivers an average of 75,000 slaves a year from
1750 to 1800.

1773 The First independent American black Baptist congregation is formed
near Savannah, Georgia.
Pope Clement XIV dissolves the Society of Jesus (22,589 members
including 11,293 priests) and recalls 3000 Jesuit overseas missionaries.
The Syrian Catholic patriarchate is established.

1774 Mother Ann Lee leads a group of Shakers (the United Society of Believers in Christ's Second Appearing) from England to New York. For the
first time, this communal society begins to prosper.
The Journal of John Woolman is published.
Elizabeth Ann Seton (1774–1821) is born. She is the first native-born

citizen of the United States to be canonized by the Roman Catholic church. She also establishes the first American religious community for women.

1775 Friedrich Wilhelm Joseph von Schelling (1775–1854), a German philosopher, is born.

1776 Johann Joseph von Görres (1776–1848), a German Catholic author, is born.

1778 Universalists organize their first American church in 1778. Unitarians follow with their own church in 1796.

1779 David Hume writes *Dialogues Concerning Natural Religion*.
John Newton and William Cowper publish *Olney Hymns*.

1780 During the next ten years, Holy Roman Emperor Joseph II reforms both church and state to bring them in line with Enlightenment principles. He grants religious toleration to Protestants, simplifies the Catholic liturgy, closes many monasteries, and limits the power of the pope in Austria.
Túpac Amaru II leads a Quechua religious revolt against the Spanish in Peru. The revolt is crushed, and he is executed.
The Deutsche Christentumsgesellschaft (German Christendom Society) is founded in Germany.
Elizabeth Fry (1780–1845), an English Quaker prison reformer, is born.

1781 Henry Martyn (1781–1812), an Anglican priest and missionary to India and Persia, is born.

1782 Hugues-Filicité Robert de Lamennais (1782–1854), a French priest, philosopher, and political theorist, is born.
Robert Morrison (1782–1834), the first Protestant missionary to China, is born.
Jonathan Edwards promotes Concerts for Prayer, which started in Scotland.
William Miller (1782–1849) is born. An American Baptist preacher, he is credited with beginning Adventism.
Philokalia, a collection of mystical writings compiled by Nicodemus of the Holy Mountain and Macarius of Corinth, is published.

1783 The Eclectic Society and the Clapham Sect are formed in England.
Charles Simeon starts the Evangelical student movement in Cambridge, England.

Nikolaj Frederik Severin Grundtvig (1783–1872), a Danish Lutheran leader, is born.

Selina, Countess of Huntingdon, founds the Countess of Huntingdon's Connexion, a network of Calvinist churches.

1784 The first Catholic Church is established in Pyongyang, Korea.

The Christmas Conference of preachers is held in Baltimore. The Methodist Episcopal Church in the United States becomes a distinct body from the English Methodist structure. Francis Asbury and Thomas Coke are made bishops and become leaders of the new church.

Samuel Seabury is consecrated as bishop by nonjuring bishops of Scotland, becoming the first bishop of Connecticut and the first bishop of the Protestant Episcopal Church in the United States.

1785 Christianity is reintroduced into Korea, prospers for a while, and then is exterminated.

Evangelistic awakenings spread in Wales.

1786 The Methodist Missionary Society is founded.

Nathaniel William Taylor (1786–1858), an American theologian, is born.

1787 The Society of the United Brethren for Propagating the Gospel among the Heathen is founded in Pennsylvania.

The Episcopal Church in the United States obtains English parliamentary permission to have bishops consecrated. Bishops of the Church of England consecrate Samuel Provoost the first Episcopal bishop of New York, and William White the first bishop of Pennsylvania.

Christianity is introduced into Sierra Leone.

1788 The Edict of Versailles (the Edict of Tolerance) grants religious freedom to French Protestants.

Large colonies of German Mennonites and farmers (Stundists) settle in the Ukraine.

Alexander Campbell (1788–1866) is born in Scotland. He and his father, Thomas Campbell, join with Barton Stone to lead the restoration movement. Their congregations are known as Disciples of Christ or Christian Churches.

Adoniram Judson (1788–1850), the first American missionary in Burma, is born.

Christianity is founded in Australia.

1789 The French Revolution begins. It results in separation of church and state as well as religious liberty.

William Blake writes *Songs of Innocence. Songs of Experience* follows in 1794.

1790 The United States gets its first Roman Catholic bishop, John Carroll, who is appointed to the see in Baltimore.

The Society of Saint Sulpice arrives in America. Their mission is the training of future Catholic priests.

Georg Wilhelm Friedrich Hegel writes *Early Theological Writings* (published posthumously).

1791 Georgetown College is founded as the first Roman Catholic college in the United States.

1792 Charles Grandison Finney (1792–1875), an American evangelist, is born.

Macarius Glukharev (1792–1847), a Russian Orthodox missionary, is born.

John Keble (1792–1866), a leader of the Oxford movement, is born.

Lowell Mason (1792–1872), an American music educator and hymnwriter, is born.

Ferdinand Christian Baur (1792–1860), a German Protestant theologian and the founder of the Tübingen school of theology, is born.

The Second Great Awakening among Congregationalist and other New England churches begins. It will last 30 years.

Eight Russian Orthodox missionary monks arrive on Kodiak Island (Alaska).

William Carey publishes *An Enquiry into the Obligations of Christians, to Use All Means for the Conversion of the Heathens* and then sets sail for India under the auspices of the Particular Baptist Society for Propagating the Gospel Among the Heathen, thus beginning the modern era of Protestant world missions. He serves 41 years in Bengal and translates the Bible into 35 languages.

1793 Henry Francis Lyte (1793–1847), a hymnwriter, is born.

Immanuel Kant writes *Religion Within the Limits of Reason Alone*.

Samuel Hopkins writes *A System of Doctrines*.

1794 The first three Catholic American-Indian priests in Latin America are ordained.

1795 A group of Congregationalists, Presbyterians, Methodists, and Anglicans form the London Missionary Society. It becomes active in Asia and the South Pacific. David Livingstone was its most famous representative in Africa.

Leopold von Ranke (1795–1886), a German historian, is born.

Methodists in Britain separate from the Church of England after John Wesley's death in 1791.

Robert Moffat (1795–1883), a British missionary to Africa, is born.

1796 The New York Missionary Society is founded, marking the beginning of an interdenominational push to bring the spiritual and moral benefits of Christianity to the American frontier.

The first London Missionary Society missionaries are sent to the South Pacific (Tahiti).

The Edinburgh Tract Society and Edinburgh Missionary Society are formed in Scotland.

More than two million Uniate Eastern Europeans in Poland return to the Russian Orthodox Church.

The Scottish Missionary Society and Glasgow Missionary Society are formed.

Hans Nielsen Hauge leads the Norwegian Revival.

Rufus Anderson (1796–1880), an American congregational missionary, is born.

Johann Adam Möhler (1796–1838), a German theologian and member of the Catholic Tübingen school, is born.

Henry Venn (1796–1873), an English mission theorist, is born.

1797 Alexandre Vinet (1797–1847), a Swiss Reformer, is born.

The Netherlands Missionary Society is founded in Rotterdam.

William Wilberforce writes *Real Christianity*.

Charles Hodge (1797–1878), an American Presbyterian theologian, is born.

Franz Peter Schubert (1797–1828), an Austrian composer, is born.

Innocent of Alaska (Ivan Veniaminov) (1797–1878), a Russian Orthodox priest and missionary, is born.

The New Testament is translated into Tahitian.

1798 The Church Missionary Society is formed as the foreign missionary arm of the Church of England. It is the first Evangelical missionary society to send missionaries to Africa.

1799 Johann Joseph Ignaz von Döllinger (1799–1890) is born. He becomes a Catholic priest and historian who rejects the dogma of papal infallability.

Tholuck Friedrich August Gottreau (1799–1877), a German theologian, is born.

The London Missionary Society arrives in South Africa.

Johannes van der Kemp begins work among the Khoikhoi of southwestern Africa.

The Elberfeld-Barmen Missionary Society begins.

The New Religion of the Iroquois is founded by Handsome Lake, a Seneca Indian in the American Great Lakes region.

The Religious Tract Society is founded in Britain.

Friedrich Schleiermacher writes *On Religion: Speeches to Its Cultured Despisers.*

The Age of the Great Missionaries

THE STATUS OF THE CHRISTIAN CHURCH

At the end of the nineteenth century, 62 generations after Christ, 51.3 percent of the word is evangelized, and 34.4 percent of the population is Christian. The church is 18 percent nonwhite, and printed Scriptures are available in 537 languages.

INFLUENTIAL CHRISTIANS OF THE CENTURY

John Nelson Darby, David Livingstone, Adoniram Judson, Charles Finney, D.L. Moody, Charles Spurgeon, Hudson Taylor, Charles Martial Allemand Lavigerie, William Booth, John Henry Newman, Fyodor Dostoevsky, Søren Kierkegaard, John Keble, George Müller

SIGNIFICANT EVENTS AND INFLUENCES

- The nineteenth century represented the best and worst of times for the Christian church. Europe was still the bastion of the Christian church, but the church was being battered by a host of ideologies, including modernism, scientific rationalism, humanism, and deism. (Marxism was still nascent.)
- But 19 centuries after Jesus uttered the Great Commission, all the major denominations were taking it seriously, and marked progress was being made toward the conversion of whole continents. To accomplish this awesome task, God raised the most remarkable constellation of Christian leaders found in any century. They included John Nelson Darby, Adoniram Judson, David Livingstone, Charles Finney, D.L. Moody, Charles H. Spurgeon, and Hudson Taylor among Protestants and Charles Martial Allemand Lavigerie among Catholics. These were not great theologians or Church Fathers, but "doers"—men and women who braved all kinds of dangers to bring the gospel to all nations.
- The Congregation for the Propagation of the Faith, reestablished by Pope Pius VII, spurred Roman Catholic missionary efforts in Ethiopia, Mongolia, and North Africa. Under the auspices of the Congregation in 1868, Charles Martial Allemand Lavigerie founded the Society of Missionaries for Africa, popularly known as the White Fathers. As cardinal and primate of Africa, Lavigerie was instrumental in persuading the colonial powers to abolish slavery.
- Nineteenth-century revivalism was typified by three men—Americans D.L. Moody and Charles Finney, and Londoner Charles H. Spurgeon. Dwight Lyman Moody was a successful businessman who abandoned his business

correction

in 1860 to enter evangelistic work. In 1865 he met his lifelong associate Ira David Sankey, and for the next several decades the two toured America and the British Isles. In 1893 Moody organized a mission in connection with the World's Fair and Columbian Exposition, out of which grew the Bible Institute Colportage Association (now Moody Publishers) and the Moody Bible Institute. In 1865 Moody founded the nondenominational Northfield Conferences, which emphasized holiness, missions, evangelism, and the spirit-filled life.

- Charles Grandison Finney underwent a powerful conversion experience in 1821, and three years later began his spectacular rise to prominence as a revivalist preacher. Almost single-handedly, he introduced the concept of revivalist crusades in America. He popularized the so-called new measures, including protracted meetings (during which all secular activities ceased in the area for several days), the anxious bench for sinners, prayer meetings, public prayer for individuals by name, and a dramatic pulpit style. Later, with Asa Mahan, Finney became a proponent of Oberlin perfectionism.

- Charles Haddon Spurgeon, called the Prince of Preachers, was such a powerful preacher that a 20,000-seat Metropolitan Tabernacle in London had to be built to accommodate his ever-growing audience. His sermons and meditations are still read today. The 1870s were the heyday of British evangelists, including Henry Drummond (1851–1897), Wilson Carlisle (1847–1942), and Gipsy Smith (1860–1947).

- In 1840 a young Scot named David Livingstone decided to forsake a medical career and devote his life to the gospel in Africa, then known as the Dark Continent. By the time he died in 1873, the continent was dark no more because of him. He single-handedly evangelized half a continent, a feat that has never been equaled. Livingstone was also one of the century's great explorers, and his discovery of Lake Shirwa, Lake Malawi, Lake Bangweulu, and the Basin of the Upper Nile are part of the annals of geography. When he died, he was given a hero's burial in Westminster Abbey.

- In 1853 James Hudson Taylor heard the call to be a missionary and sailed for China. Despite many obstacles, he founded the China Inland Mission in 1865, which became the premier missionary organization there. A man of indomitable faith and great personal courage and devotion, he carried his missionary work into the very heart of China. By 1895 the China Inland Mission had a force of 641 missionaries working in every province.

- In 1865 one of the world's most unusual Christian groups was formed when William Booth, a freelance evangelist, began working among the destitutes of London. Gradually his work became known as the Christian Mission, and he was aided by his wife, Catherine, herself a gifted preacher. They combined evangelism with social work, including the supply of free meals to the hungry. Military terminology was then in vogue ("Onward Christian

Soldiers" was written about this time), and Booth's meetings were advertised as the Hallelujah Army Fighting for God, which was later shortened to the Salvation Army. Booth himself was titled general, and military titles and uniforms were used for all echelons in the Salvation Army. During the next 35 years, Booth traveled five million miles, preached 60,000 sermons, and enlisted 16,000 officers in his army. When he died in 1912, the world mourned—150,000 people filed past his coffin, and 40,000 attended his funeral. Vachel Lindsey, one of the best-known American poets at the time, wrote a special poem in honor of the occasion called "General William Booth Enters Heaven."

- One of the most important pontificates of the nineteenth century was that of Pius IX. Ironically, it was during his reign that the Vatican lost all its temporal possessions to the Risorgimento, and the pope became a virtual prisoner of the Vatican as a result of King Victor Emmanuel's Law of Guarantees. But the pontificate was one of the defining moments in the history of modern papacy.

- In 1854 the pope issued the controversial dogma of Immaculate Conception, which stated that "from the first moment of conception the Blessed Virgin Mary was, by the singular grace and privilege of Almighty God, and in view of the merits of Jesus Christ, Savior of mankind, kept free from all stain of original sin."

- In 1871 Pius IX convoked the First Vatican Council to deal with a variety of subjects, including faith and dogma. It was the Twentieth Ecumenical Council and the first in the nineteenth century. This council adopted the dogma of papal infallibility. The dogma stated that the pope is free from error when he speaks *ex cathedra*—that is, when he speaks as the supreme pastor and doctor of all Christians and when he defines a doctrine regarding faith and morals to be held by the universal church.

- In 1833 a group of scholars at Oxford began publishing a series of pamphlets with the somewhat undistinguished title, Tracts for the Times. The project was begun by John Henry Newman, and it soon gained many articulate supporters, including Edward Pusey, John Keble, R.H. Froude, and Robert Wilberforce. The purpose of the Tracts was to defend the Catholic and apostolic elements in the Church of England against liberal and humanist attack, and to decry what Pusey described as the "national apostasy." After the publication of the Tracts was suspended in 1841, a number of members of the movement, now called the Oxford movement, joined the Catholic Church, and Newman himself was later elevated as a cardinal. The Oxford movement left a permanent impress on the Church of England, especially by fostering monasticism, a higher order of worship, and patristic scholarship.

- In 1816, the Christianization of African-Americans took an important step forward when the first free black church was founded in Philadelphia by

Richard Allen. Called the African Methodist Episcopal Church, it was soon followed by other black churches, such as the African Methodist Episcopal Zion Church in 1821.

- In 1895, the struggle between Christian conservatives and liberals was joined when the conservative Evangelical Alliance published *The Fundamentals*, setting forth the five fundamentals of faith—the inspiration and inerrancy of Scripture, Jesus's virgin birth, the substitutionary atonement of the cross, Jesus's physical resurrection, and the historical reality of Jesus's miracles.

- In 1844 Christian Scholasticism was dealt its death blow by the *Philosophical Fragments*, written by a young Danish philosopher, Søren Aabye Kierkegaard, considered the father of modern existentialism. Although he wrote extensively, his major influence did not begin to be felt until the twentieth century. Kierkegaard is responsible for subjectifying modern theology. God is not an object, he maintained, but a living actual being, who, in the person of Jesus Christ, confronts us to save us. God is not reachable or knowable through reason, but only through a leap of faith. This leap requires full commitment, a rejection of the world's and the church's value systems. Kierkegaard also castigated the Lutheran Church for its emphasis on form as opposed to substance and spirit, and for its comfortable dalliance with the world system. Some of Kierkegaard's greatest books followed, especially *Either/Or*.

- The nineteenth century witnessed another phenomenon that has continued into the twentieth—the fragmentation of the Protestant church into sects and microdenominations, based sometimes on personality and sometimes on doctrine. African-Americans were among the first to form separate denominations.

- In 1830, John Nelson Darby, a relative of Admiral Nelson, became the leading spirit behind the Plymouth Brethren, a radical (for the times) group that tried to divest themselves of all unbiblical accoutrements. Communion was celebrated weekly, and there were no ordained ministers or fixed order of worship. The Brethren also believed in pacifism and the importance of prophecy and apocalypticism.

- Another member of the Plymouth Brethren was George Müller, who founded a faith orphanage— an orphanage that never sought funding, but trusted God to provide its needs. Müller's work was a testimony to the simple faith of the Brethren. Soon, rifts arose among the Brethren, and they split into Exclusive Brethren and Open Brethren and then into further smaller groups.

- The Campbells—Thomas and his son Alexander—were Irish Presbyterians who emigrated to the United States, which was a fertile ground for new sects. Affiliated at first with the Baptists, the Campbells worked for what they called a Restoration of the Ancient Order of Things. Eased out of the Baptist

Church for their radical ideas, Alexander Campbell joined with Barton Stone to found the Disciples of Christ, now a major denomination. The sect is important because they espoused one of the most elementary and simplest forms of the gospel.

- Meanwhile, even as Christianity expanded, the blood of the martyrs continued to flow to be transformed into the seeds of the church. In 1831, 1843, and 1846, Muslim Kurds engaged in large-scale massacres of Assyrians. Queen Ranavalona tried to eradicate Christianity in Madagascar by killing large numbers of Christians from 1835 to 1861. In 1843 millions were killed in China as the Great Peaceful Heavenly Kingdom (Tai Ping Tien Kueh), which began as a quasi-Christian sect with a Hakka founder strongly influenced by the New Testament, was suppressed. In Uganda some 250 Anglican and Catholic Christians were executed by King Mwanga at Namugongo. In 1885 a violent persecution against Christians broke out in Indochina, resulting in the martyrdom of 100,000 Catholics, including 115 priests. In 1895 the Turks, who over the centuries have killed more than 10 million Christians, massacred 850,000 Armenians, including 1200 who were burned alive in Urfa Cathedral. The massacre of Christians has become the longest and the bloodiest holocaust in history, lasting from the first century to the twentieth.

- Driving much of the global evangelism was the translation and publication of the Bible in hundreds of non-Western languages and the founding of the early Bible societies. The German Bible Society and the British and Foreign Bible Society were founded in 1804, the Russian Bible Society in 1810, and the American Bible Society in 1816. The American Tract Society was founded in 1825. In 1817 Robert Moffat completed his Tswana Bible. In 1817 Robert Morrison, the first Protestant missionary in China, translated the Bible into Chinese.

- Similarly, the nineteenth century was the birth period of some of the great parachurch organizations that came into full blossom in the twentieth century. In 1844 the Young Men's Christian Association was formed in London, followed by the World Evangelical Alliance in 1846, the Scripture Union in 1879, the Student Volunteer Movement for Foreign Missions in 1888, and the Young People's Society of Christian Endeavor in 1895. The Keswick Convention began in England in 1875 and would be associated with the Higher Life movement.

- In 1858 a young French peasant girl named Bernadette Soubirous received 18 apparitions of the Blessed Virgin Mary at Massabielle Rock, near Lourdes. The Virgin, who manifested herself as the Immaculate Conception, revealed her presence by supernatural occurrences (such as a miraculous spring of water) and commands (as the building of a church). Over the course of the next century, Lourdes would become a synonym for healing and miracles.

CHRONOLOGY

1800 Reginald Heber writes "Holy, Holy, Holy, Lord God Almighty."

John Nelson Darby (1800–1882), founder of Plymouth Brethren, is born.

Jacques Paul Migne (1800–1875) is born. A French priest, he published inexpensive theological works, encyclopedias, and texts of the Church Fathers.

Widespread evangelistic camp meetings begin in the United States. The Kentucky Revival sweeps over Kentucky, Tennessee, and the Carolinas with crowds of up to 25,000.

Protestant foreign missionaries number 100.

Local revivals begin in Scotland on Lewis and Harris Island and in Perthshire.

Edward Bouverie Pusey (1800–1882), an Anglican leader of the Oxford movement, is born.

1801 Korean king Sunjo executes Christians.

The Second Great Awakening begins at the revival in Cane Ridge, Kentucky.

The General Convention of the Episcopal Church in the United States approves a modified version of the 39 Articles of Religion.

The Concordat between Napoleon Bonaparte and Pope Pius VII solidifies the Roman Catholic Church as the majority church of France.

John Henry Newman (1801–1890) is born. He becomes an English cardinal, a Tractarian leader, and a member of the Oxford movement.

1802 François-Rene de Chateaubriand writes *The Genius of Christianity*, an apology for the Catholic faith.

The Massachusetts Baptist Mission Society is formed for the evangelization of frontier communities.

William Paley writes *Natural Theology*.

In the Organic Articles, an addition to the Concordat of 1801, Napoleon regulates public worship and defines the relations between church and state in France.

Marcus Whitman (1802–1847), an American Protestant missionary, is born.

The British and Foreign Bible Society is formed. It is the forerunner of hundreds of American and English Bible societies.

1803 Hector Berlioz (1803–1869), a French composer, is born.

1804 Absalom Jones is ordained in the Episcopal Church of the United States as its first black priest.

Alexei Khomyakov (1804–1860), a Russian Orthodox philosopher, theologian, and poet, is born.

William Blake writes *Jerusalem*.

1805 Frederick Denison Maurice (1805–1872), an Anglican theologian and Christian socialist, is born.

George Müller (1805–1898), an English philanthropist, is born.

Joseph Smith (1805–1844), American founder of the Church of Jesus Christ of Latter-day Saints, is born.

Johann Christoph Blumhardt founds a healing center at Bad Boll, Germany.

1806 The Haystack Prayer Meetings at Williams College in Williamstown, Massachusetts, inspire the foundation of the American Board of Commissioners of Foreign Missions in 1810. In 1961 it was renamed the United Church Board for World Ministries.

Nathan Södorblom (1806–1931) is born. He is a Lutheran archbishop of Uppsala and the founder of the Life and Work movement.

Napoleon abolishes the Holy Roman Empire.

In Britain, various groups secede from Methodism. The Independent Methodists are formed in 1806, the Camp Meeting Methodists in 1810, and the Primitive Methodists in 1812.

1807 The slave trade is prohibited by the British parliament.

Robert Morrison, of the London Missionary Society, becomes the first Protestant missionary in China. He arrives in Macao, translates Bible into Chinese by 1818, and compiles a dictionary by 1821. He dies in 1834 having seen only ten baptisms of Chinese.

Georg Wilhelm Friedrich Hegel writes *Phenomenology of Spirit*.

Phoebe Palmer (1807–1874), a Methodist preacher and one of the founders of the Holiness movement, is born.

Andover Theological Seminary is founded in Newton, Massachusetts. It merges with Newton Theological Institution in 1965.

1808 Fire partially destroys the Church of the Holy Sepulchre. The tomb is enclosed in the modern marble covering.

The last *auto-da-fé* (Portuguese for "act of faith") takes place. It is the public execution of persons condemned by the Inquisition. More than 340,000 persons suffered the *auto-da-fé*. Of these, 32,000 were burned.

John Wesley writes the 25 Articles, a Methodist adaptation of the Anglican 39 Articles.

Narcissa Prentiss Whitman (1808–1847), an America Protestant missionary, is born.

1809 The Restoration movement, also called Primitivism, includes the Churches of Christ, Disciples of Christ, the Christian Churches, and many Pentecostal churches.

Thomas and Alexander Campbell found the Christian Association of Washington, the first Disciples of Christ church, on the principle "Where the Bible speaks, we speak; where it is silent, we are silent." They are part of the Restoration movement.

Evangeliska Sällskapet (for Bibles and tracts) is founded in Sweden.

Isaak August Dorner (1809–1884), a German Lutheran priest and theologian, is born.

William Gladstone (1809–1898), four-time British prime minister and a committed Christian, is born.

Thomas Birch Freeman (1809–1890), a British Methodist missionary to Africa, is born.

Felix Mendelssohn (1809–1847), a German composer, pianist, organist, and conductor, is born.

1810 The Church of the Holy Sepulchre is rebuilt after being destroyed by fire.

The American Board of Commissioners for Foreign Missions, the first American society for foreign missions, is founded by New England Congregationalists. It becomes active in Hawaii.

Pope Leo XIII (1810–1903), the founder of Neo-Thomism, is born.

William Edwin Boardman (1810–1886), an American Presbyterian missionary, is born.

1811 Henry Martyn, an Anglican priest, is sent by the Church Missionary Society to Persia and begins translating the New Testament.

Hannah More writes *Practical Piety*.

Franz Liszt (1811–1886), a Hungarian composer, is born.

Sir George Gilbert Scott (1811–1878) , an English architect who promoted the Gothic revival, is born.

The Disciples of Christ is founded by Alexander Campbell

1812 Princeton Theological Seminary is founded.

1813 American Baptist missionary Adoniram Judson arrives in Burma.

Søren Aabye Kierkegaard (1813–1855), a Danish existentialist philosopher, is born.

David Livingstone (1813–1873), a British explorer and missionary to Africa, is born.

1814 Pope Pius VII restores the Jesuits after 41 years of official suppression in *Solicitudo Omnium Ecclesiarum* ("Care for All Churches").

The American Baptist Missionary Union is founded. It later becomes American Baptist International Ministries.

John William Colenso (1814–1883), an Anglican bishop of South Africa and missionary to the Zulus, is born.

1815 John Bosco (1815–1888), an Italian priest and the founder of the Salesian Order, is born.

Constantin von Tischendorf (1815–1874), the New Testament textual critic who discovered the Codex Sinaiticus, is born.

The Napoleonic Wars end, and the great century of worldwide Christian expansion begins.

The Basel Evangelical Missionary Society is founded in Switzerland.

Italian priest Caspar del Bufalo founds the Missioners of the Most Precious Blood for the evangelization of the world through charitable works.

1816 The American Bible Society is founded.

Several African Methodist Episcopal churches are organized into a denomination. Richard Allen becomes their first bishop.

The Society of Mary (Marists) is founded at Lyon by Jean-Claude Colin.

1817 In *The Conversion of the World*, Gordon Hall and Samuel Newell of the American Board of Commissioners for Foreign Missons propose a strategy to reach every person on earth through sending 30,000 Protestant missionaries from the United States and Europe in 21 years at a cost of four dollars from each Protestant and Anglican church member in Christendom.

Robert Moffat begins a 50-year ministry among the Tswana of Southern Africa. He completes the Tswana Bible in 1857.

1818 Franz Xavier Gruber composes "Silent Night" to a text written by Joseph Mohr two years earlier.

John Mason Neale (1818–1866), an Anglican hymnwriter, is born.

The Wesleyan Methodist Missionary Society begins in London. It later merges with other Methodist societies to form the Methodist Missionary Society.

Cecil Frances Alexander (1818–1895), an Irish hymnwriter and poet, is born.

1819 Charles Kingsley (1819–1875), an English writer, is born.

Isaac Thomas Hecker (1819–1888), founder of the Paulists, is born.

Philip Schaff (1819–1893), a German-American theologian and historian, is born.

The Missionary Society of the Methodist Episcopal Church is organized. It is reorganized in 1964 as the Board of Global Ministries of the United Methodist Church.

William Ellery Channing writes *Unitarian Christianity*.

1820 The Jesuits are expelled from Rome and from all of Russia.

The General Synod of the Evangelical Lutheran Church in the United States of America is founded. It brings together most of the Lutheran synods in the country (except the New York Ministerium).

Florence Nightingale (1820–1910), a British social reformer and the founder of modern nursing, is born.

London Jews' Society makes the first British missionary contact in Iraq.

The Georgian Orthodox Church is forcibly assimilated by the Russian Orthodox Church.

The Domestic and Foreign Missionary Society of the Episcopal Church is founded.

Frances Jane Crosby (1820–1915), an American poet and revivalist hymnwriter, is born.

Ivan Veniaminov (Innocent of Alaska) evangelizes Alaska.

1821 The Greek Orthodox Church revolts against the Ottomans and gains independence from the Muslims.

Frederick Temple (1821–1902), archbishop of Canterbury, is born.

John Malcolm Forbes Ludlow (1821–1911), an English lawyer and the founder of Christian socialism, is born.

The Danish Missionary Society is founded.

Friedrich Schleiermacher writes *Christian Faith*.

Fyodor Mikhailovich Dostoevsky (1821–1881), a Russian novelist, is born.

William Taylor (1821–1902) an American Methodist Episcopal bishop, author, and missionary, is born.

John Gibson Paton (1821–1902), a Scottish Protestant missionary to the New Hebrides Islands, is born.

1822 The Paris Evangelical Missionary Society is founded in France.

Providence Baptist Church in Monrovia (Liberia), the oldest Baptist congregation in Africa, is begun by the first American missionary to Africa, Lou Carey, a black slave from Virginia.

The Society for the Propagation of the Faith begins in Lyon (France).

Nicholas Ilminski (1822–1891), a Russian Orthodox missionary, is born.

Gregor Mendel (1822–1884), an Augustinian priest and geneticist, is born.

Albrecht Ritschl (1822–1889), a German theologian, is born.

1824 The America Sunday School Union is founded.

Richard Meux Benson (1824–1915) is born. He becomes a priest in the Church of England and the founder of the Society of Saint John the Evangelist.

The Berlin Missionary Society is formed.

Interdenominational citywide cooperative evangelism begins in the United States.

The first Anglican bishoprics in the Caribbean are established in Jamaica and Barbados.

Josef Anton Bruckner (1824–1896), an Austrian composer, is born.

George MacDonald (1824–1905), a Scottish writer, is born.

1825 The American Tract Society is formed as the first national tract-distribution society in America.

Charles Martial Allemand Lavigerie (1825–1892) is born. He becomes a French cardinal, a missionary in Africa, and the founder of the White Fathers and White Sisters, orders that crusaded against slavery.

The Bombay Missionary Union is formed in India for prayer and discussion among Anglican, Brethren, Congregionalist, and Presbyterian missionaries, eventually producing the principle of comity.

In Hawaii, a syncretistic cult announces the imminent end of world. Protestant missionaries burn its temple to ground.

The (Presbyterian) Church of Scotland Mission begins.

Samuel Taylor Coleridge writes *Aids to Reflection*.

Charles Grandison Finney begins holding revivals in the United States.

1826 Glasgow City Mission is founded as the first of 50 city missions in the United Kingdom.

1827 John Nelson Darby, an Anglican clergyman, begins the Plymouth Brethren movement in Dublin.

The Netherlands Missionary Society begins work in the Celebes Islands.

John Albert Broadus (1827–1895), an American Baptist pastor and theologian, is born.

Ellen G. White (1827–1915), the American founder of Seventh-day Adventist Church, is born.

1828 Joseph Barber Lightfoot (1828–1889), an English biblical scholar and bishop of Durham, is born.

Karl Gutzlaff, a German missionary, and Jacob Tomlin of the London Missionary Society arrive in Siam and begin translating the Bible into Siamese.

Dante Gabriel Rossetti (1828–1882), a pre-Raphaelite painter and poet, is born.

The Rhenish Missionary Society is formed in Germany and begins work among the Dayaks of Borneo.

England emancipates the Nonconformists, and the Roman Catholics a year later.

Karl Gützlaff, a Lutheran, begins work in the Far East, especially the Dutch East Indies, Siam, southern China, and Hong Kong.

Leo Nikolayevitch Tolstoy (1828–1910), a Russian novelist, is born.

1829 Christian Brethren send A.N. Groves and others as the first missionaries to Baghdad and later India. The organization is renamed as Christian Missions in Many Lands.

William Booth (1829–1912), founder of the Salvation Army, is born.

1830 Joseph Smith founds a Mormon settlement in Manchester, New York.

Christina Georgina Rossetti (1830–1894), an English poet, is born.

At Fayette, New York, Joseph Smith has visions that lead to the establishment of the Church of Jesus Christ of Latter-day Saints (Mormons).

In Paris, the Virgin Mary appears to a nun, Catherine Labouré, instructing her to have a medal struck and showing her the model for it. Millions of copies of the medal were struck and circulated all over the world. It becomes known as the miraculous medal.

The London Missionary Society sends John Williams to begin work in Samoa.

1831 Joseph Schereschewsky (1831–1906), Anglican bishop in Shanghai and Bible translator, is born.

1832 The American Baptist Home Missionary Society is formed.

The American Board of Comissioners for Foreign Missions establishes the first Protestant mission in Iran under the name Mission to the Nestorians.

Johann Adam Möhler writes *Symbolism.*

James Hudson Taylor (1832–1905), an English Methodist evangelist, author, and missionary to China, is born.

The Church of Christ (Disciples) is formed.

1833 William Miller, a Baptist preacher, and his followers spread the message that Christ will return in the year 1843.

John Keble preaches a sermon titled "National Apostasy." It is commonly regarded as the inception of the Oxford movement (Tractarianism), an Anglican movement that defended apostolic succession and elevated ritual and liturgy.

Frédéric Ozanam, a French scholar, founds the Society of Saint Vincent de Paul, a Roman Catholic lay organization. Their mission is to provide aid and advocacy for the poor.

The Greek Orthodox Church becomes independent from Constantinople.

Socially aware evangelicals found Oberlin College, the first coeducational college in the United States.

The Theological Institute of Connecticut (Hartford Seminary) is founded as a reaction against the revivalists of the Second Great Awakening.

Parliament abolishes slavery in the British Empire and compensates the owners of 70,000 freed slaves.

Thomas Chalmers writes *On the Adaptation of External Nature to the Moral and Intellectual Constitution of Man.*

Johannes Brahms (1833–1897), a German composer, is born.

1834 Gustav Warneck (1834–1910), a German missiologist, is born.

Charles Haddon Spurgeon (1834–1892), the English "Prince of Preachers," is born.

William Morris (1834–1896), an English artist and author, is born.

1835 Queen Ranavalona of Madagascar attempts to eradicate Christianity, and large numbers of Christians are killed from 1835 to 1861.

The Swedish Missionary Society is founded.

Charles Grandison Finney writes *Lectures on Revivals of Religion.*

David Friedrich Strauss scandalizes Christian Europe with *The Life of Jesus Critically Examined.*

Sunday schools are started throughout America. They become one of the largest sources of prospective church members.

Phillips Brooks (1835–1893), an American preacher and hymnwriter, is born. He wrote the text of "O Little Town of Bethlehem."

The first Protestant missionaries arrive in Korea.

1836   The Leipzig Evangelical Lutheran Mission is formed in Germany.

The Dresden Missionary Society is formed. It becomes the Leipzig Missionary Society in 1848.

Nikolai Kasatkin (Nicholas of Japan) (1836–1912), the founder of the Orthodox Church in Japan, is born.

Augustus H. Strong (1836–1921), an America Baptist theologian, is born.

The Ethiopian Uniat Church is founded.

Union Theological Seminary is founded in New York by New School Presbyterians.

1837   The Auburn Declaration is written to address conflict in American Presbyterianism.

The Board of Foreign Missions of the Presbyterian Church is established "to aid in the conversion of the world." In 1958 it became the Commission on Ecumenical Mission and Relations with the goal of "making the Lord Jesus Christ known to all men."

Abraham Kuyper (1837–1920), a Dutch evangelical statesman and theologian, is born.

Dwight Lyman Moody (1837–1899), an American evangelist, is born.

The Great Awakening reaches Hawaii and lasts until 1842 with 27,000 Protestant adult converts (20 percent of the population).

The electric telegraph is invented.

The Bible is translated into Japanese.

1838   Ralph Waldo Emerson delivers his Divinity School Address at Cambridge.

Frederick Denison Maurice writes *The Kingdom of Christ*.

Tenrikyo (Religion of Divine Wisdom), a Shinto-Christian amalgam, is founded in Japan as the first of the *shinko shukyo* (new religious movements).

Missionaries from the Dresden Missionary Society begin work among Australian aborigines.

1839   The cornerstone is laid for the Cathedral of Christ the Savior in Moscow.

In New Hebrides, missionary pioneer John Williams of the London Missionary Society is martyred on the Island of Erromango. Catholic missionaries also arrive, but systematic missions do not begin until 1887.

Alexander Campbell writes *The Christian System*.

Isaak August Dorner writes *A History of the Development of the Doctrine of the Person of Christ.*

Frances Elizabeth Willard (1839–1898), an America leader in the Women's Christian Temperance Union and the women's suffrage movement, is born.

1840 Christmas trees are introduced into France and England.

Father Damian (1840–1889), a Roman Catholic priest and missionary to lepers in Hawaii, is born.

Christianity is introduced into Nigeria.

1841 Church Missionary Society general secretary Henry Venn requires all missionaries to complete annual questionnaires recording church growth statistics. He propounds three self-goals of mission: to make churches become self-supporting, self-governing, and self-propagating.

Ludwig Feuerbach writes *The Essence of Christianity.*

Theodore Parker writes *The Transient and Permanent in Christianity.*

The Edinburgh Medical Missionary Society is founded in Scotland.

The Anglican bishopric in Jerusalem is established.

In the United Kingdom, 22,000 people are converted over seven years through the preaching of James Caughey of New York.

David Livingstone arrives in what is now Botswana.

1842 The Tübingen School begins to develop, led by Ferdinand Christian Baur. A group of largely German theologians apply Hegel's writings to the tensions between early Christian followers of Peter and Paul.

The University of Notre Dame is founded.

The Treaty of Nanking cedes Hong Kong to Britain and opens new territory to missions.

The Gossner Mission Society begins in Berlin.

Revival spreads through state church of Norway, and the Norwegian Mission Society begins.

Western missionaries are expelled from Ethiopia.

1843 Albert Benjamin Simpson (1843–1919), the American founder of Christian and Missionary Alliance, is born.

Cyrus Ingerson Scofield (1843–1921), editor of the Scofield Reference Bible, is born.

In the Disruption of 1843, Thomas Chalmers leads 473 clergy from the Church of Scotland to form the Free Church of Scotland.

Sierra Leonian former slave Samuel Ajayi Crowther is sent as a missionary to Nigeria. In 1864 he is consecrated as the first non-European Anglican bishop.

Søren Kierkegaard writes *Fear and Trembling*.

1844 Codex Vaticanus, one of the oldest extant manuscripts of the Greek Bible, is published. It had previously been secreted behind Vatican library doors.

George Williams forms the Young Men's Christian Association (YMCA) to give young men a Christian alternative to the temptations of urban life.

Bernadette Soubirous (1844–1879) is born. She receives visions of the Virgin at Lourdes beginning in 1858.

Gerard Manley Hopkins (1844–1889), an English Catholic poet, is born.

The South American Missionary Society is founded.

The Seventh-day Adventist movement begins in the United States.

J.L. Krapf is the first to begin modern missionary work in Kenya. His wife and child die of malaria in Mombasa.

Christadelphians are founded by John Thomas in Birmingham (England) and London.

Joseph Smith is murdered by an anti-Mormon mob.

1845 Andrew Kim is ordained as the first Korean priest. He is killed the next year.

Baptist missionaries enter Cambodia.

Baptist churches in the United States split into the Southern Baptist and the Northern (American) Baptists. The central issue is slaveholding by Southern missionaries. The Southern Baptist Convention founds the Board of Domestic Missions (later Home Mission Board) and Foreign Mission Board.

Phoebe Palmer writes *The Way of Holiness*. It popularizes the notion that Pentecostal Spirit baptism, which is available to all believers, is the route to holiness. It paves the way for the Pentecostal and Charismatic movements.

Marist missionaries reach the Solomon Islands. The bishop is killed on landing.

A potato blight from America devastates Ireland, with a million Irish killed by famine and typhus, resulting in another million migrating to Britain, America, and Australia, markedly influencing the development of Catholicism there.

As a result of the Oxford movement in England, 60 prominent Anglicans and 250 clergy enter the Church of Rome by 1862.

John Henry Newman writes *An Essay on the Development of Christian Doctrine*.

1846 The Melanesian Mission is founded.

Mormons under Brigham Young leave Nauvoo City for Great Salt Lake. Salt Lake City is founded the next year.

The Evangelical Alliance is formed in London by 800 Christians representing 52 confessions.

Søren Kierkegaard writes *Concluding Unscientific Postscript to the Philosophical Fragments*.

1847 Søren Kierkegaard writes *Purity of Heart Is to Will One Thing*.

Josiah Strong (1847–1916), an America preacher and advocate of the social gospel, is born.

The Lutheran Church–Missouri Synod is formed (originally as the German Evangelical Lutheran Synod of Missouri, Ohio, and other States). It is a German immigrant church based on *The Book of Concord*.

Pope Pius IX makes Joseph Valerga the Latin patriarch. The pope proclaims the title is no longer a mere formality and orders the new patriarch to take up his residence in Jerusalem, where he finds 4200 Catholics.

The New Testament is translated into Serbian.

1848 Wesleyan Methodists found Wheaton College, originally named Illinois Institute, as an independent, evangelical liberal arts college.

The Christadelphian Church is founded.

The Oneida Community is founded in Oneida, New York.

Karl Marx and Friedrich Engels publish *The Communist Manifesto* in Germany, calling for violent overthrow of the established order, including religion.

Søren Kierkegaard writes *Christian Discourses*.

1849 General C.G. Gordon proposes a site for Calvary and the Garden Tomb that is different from the traditional site. The new site becomes known as "Gordon's Calvary."

Charles G. Finney holds evangelistic campaigns in Britain in 1849–1851 and 1859–1861.

All foreign missionaries are ordered out of Thailand.

Robert Seymour Bridges (1849–1930), a British poet laureate, is born.

1850 British Quaker millionaire Robert Arthington donates millions to reach unreached peoples by supplying them with copies of the New Testament.

1851 Robert Laws (1851–1934), an English missionary to Malawi, is born.

A concordat between Queen Isabella II and the Vatican maintains the Cathlic faith as the only religion of the Spanish nation.

England and Wales conduct their only state Census of Religious Worship, revealing that 61 percent of the entire population attends church every Sunday.

The Edict of Tu Duc of Vietnam, following French intervention (1843), results in severe persecution of Christians. Approximately 70,000 Catholics (including 115 priests) are killed. In 1884, the French are granted the protectorate of the central and northern regions.

Adolf von Harnack (1851–1930), a German theologian, is born.

William M. Ramsay (1851–1939), archbishop of Canterbury, is born.

Benjamin B. Warfield (1851–1921), American conservative Presbyterian theologian, is born.

1852 Baron Friedrich von Hugel (1852–1925), a Roman Catholic theologian, is born.

Adolf Schlatter (1852–1938), a German Protestant theologian, is born.

In Canada, the Anglican Church separates from the state.

1853 Women are ordained in the Congregational Church in the United States. Initially their ordination is recognized only by their local churches.

Vladimir Soloviev (1853–1900), a Russian Orthodox theologian, is born.

1854 In the papal bull *Constitution Ineffabilis Deus* ("Ineffable God"), Pope Pius IX pronounces and defines the Immaculate Conception of the Blessed Virgin Mary.

The first Union Missionary Convention is held in New York under the leadership of Alexander Duff. Duff is later appointed first chair of evangelism and evangelical theology at New College, Edinburgh.

1855 The Young Women's Christian Association is founded in England by Emma Roberts and Lady Mary Jane Kinnaird, to "advance the physical, social, intellectual, moral, and spiritual interests of young women." It provides hostels and other facilities.

Marie-Joseph Lagrange (1855–1938), a French biblical scholar and Dominican priest, is born.

1856 The Amana Colonies, seven villages in Iowa, are founded by German Pietists.

Pope Pius IX extends the feast of the Devotion to the Sacred Heart of Jesus to the universal church.

Prayer meetings held during the midweek become common as a result of the "prayer meeting revival."

R.A. Torrey (1856–1928), a Congregational evangelist and leader of the Bible school movement, is born.

1857 The Anglican Universities' Mission to Central Africa is founded in response to an appeal in Cambridge by David Livingstone. In 1965 it unites with the Society for the Propagation of the Gospel to become the United Society for the Propagation of the Gospel.

In the Evangelical Awakening, led by Charles Grandison Finney and others, one million Americans are converted in two years. The Awakening spreads to Europe, India (1859), and China (1860).

A year of mass evangelism begins as American evangelist D.L. Moody begins crusades with singer and composer Ira Sankey. Moody preached to 750,000 people during his lifetime.

1858 Pandita Sarasvati Ramabai (1858–1922), an Indian Pentecostal pioneer, translator, and missionary, is born.

Isaac Hecker founds the Congregation of the Missionary Society of Saint Paul the Apostle (the Paulists) to provide a vehicle for evangelism. It is the first American Catholic order for men.

Charles Eugene de Foucauld (1858–1916), a French explorer, hermit, and missionary, is born.

The Hindu Church of the Lord Jesus (in Tinnevelly) is the first of more than 150 attempts to establish indigenous Hindu-Christian movements or churches in India.

David Livingstone begins exploration of the Zambesi and Shire Rivers, attracting others to begin missionary work in Nyasaland (now Malawi).

Queen Victoria proclaims religious freedom and impartiality in India. "Relying ourselves on the truth of Christianity...we have no desire to impose our convictions on any of our subjects." India's population includes more than one million Roman Catholics and 100,000 Protestants and Anglicans.

The Virgin Mary appears 18 times in a cave in Lourdes in southern France to Bernadette Soubirous, revealing herself as the Immaculate Conception. Lourdes eventually becomes a destination for many pilgrims who hope to be healed.

1859 The Higher Christian Life movement spreads throughout the United States and England in the late nineteenth and early twentieth centuries, emphasizing a "second blessing" after salvation that enables a believer to rise above the tendency to sin.

Francis Thompson (1859–1907), a Roman Catholic poet, is born.

More than 1.1 million people are converted in the second Evangelical Awakening in Britain.

The Society of Saint Francis de Sales (Silesians of Don Bosco) is founded for the Christian education of youth.

1860 The General Conference Mennonite Church is founded.

The Greek Uniat Church is founded.

Revival in South Africa erupts under Andrew Murray (Dutch Reformed), sweeping the Afrikaner churches.

Horace Bushnell publishes *Christian Nurture*.

William Jennings Bryan (1860–1925), an American Christian statesman and three-time Democratic presidential candidate, is born.

E.Y. Mullins (1860–1928), an American Baptist theologian, is born.

1861 Henry Alford publishes the *The New Testament in Greek* in eight volumes.

The Oxford movement produces *Hymns Ancient and Modern*, the first Anglican hymnal, to encourage congregational singing.

Russian Orthodox monk Nicolai (Ivan Kasatkin) arrives in Japan. In 1868 he baptizes three converts and eventually becomes bishop (1880) and then archbishop (1906) in Tokyo. By the time he dies in 1912, 30,000 people have been converted.

The Woman's Union Missionary Society of America for Heathen Lands is founded in New York.

The Russian Orthodox Church begins evangelism in Mongolia and Japan.

Jean-Pierre de Caussade publishes *Self-Abandonment to Divine Providence*.

Walter Rauschenbusch (1861–1918), an American Baptist and the father of the social gospel, is born.

1862 The Congregation of the Immaculate Heart of Mary is founded.

Billy Sunday (1862–1935), an American evangelist, is born.

1863 Ernest Renan writes *Life of Jesus*.

Archimandrite Innocent Figourovsky (1863–1931), a Russian Orthodox missionary, is born.

A.T. Robertson (1863–1934), a Southern Baptist scholar, is born.

Robert Parmelee Wilder (1863–1938), an American missionary and the founder of the Student Volunteer Movement for Foreign Missions, is born.

1864 The Seventh-day Adventist Church is formed in the United States.

A small group of New Orleans Greek merchants builds the first Greek Orthodox church in America.

Pope Pius IX produces *Syllabus Errorum* ("The Syllabus of Errors"), a compendium of "the principal errors of our time."

The British and Foreign Bible Society is founded.

John Henry Cardinal Newman writes *Apologia pro Vita Sua* in response to Charles Kingsley's attacks on Newman's religious opinions, the priesthood, and Catholic doctrine.

1865 James Hudson Taylor founds the China Inland Mission, later called the Overseas Missionary Fellowship and then OMF International. It begins the Faith Mission movement.

Richard Benson founds the Cowley Fathers (the Society of Saint John the Evangelist), the first official Anglican monastic order.

John Raleigh Mott (1865–1955), a Methodist leader and ecumenist, is born.

From 1820 to 1865, nearly two million Irish Roman Catholics emigrate to America.

The Christian Revival Association is founded in London by Methodist evangelist William Booth to work in the slums of London. In 1878 it is renamed as the Salvation Army. Its emphasis is "the supremacy of evangelism in fulfilling the Lord's Great Commission...To work to that end that every man and woman and child has the opportunity to heart the good news of the Gospel." Its twofold mission is the salvation of souls and the relief of human suffering.

Ernst Troeltsch (1865–1923), a German theologian, is born.

Robert Jermain Thomas is the first Protestant missionary in Korea. He is killed the next year.

Samuel Crowther is the first black Anglican bishop of Nigeria.

1866 Tikhon of Moscow (born as Vasily Ivanovich Belavin, 1866–1925), the first patriarch of the Russian Orthodox Church, is born.

Korea's 25,000 Catholics suffer severe persecution. Ten thousand are martyred, including two bishops and seven priests.

C.H. Mason (1866–1961), the African-American founder of the Church of God in Christ, is born.

1867 The Dutch Reformed Church in America drops the "Dutch" from its name to become the Reformed Church in America.

The Anglican Church ceases to be the state religion in Ireland.

George Washington Truett (1867–1944), a Southern Baptist pastor and leader, is born.

Samuel Zwemer (1867–1952), an American missionary of the Muslims, is born.

The first Lambeth Conference (the assembly of Anglican bishops) includes 76 bishops.

1868 Charles Allemand Martial Lavigerie founds the White Fathers (Missionaries of Our Lady of Africa) to evangelize Africa.

1869 The First Vatican Council (the Twentieth Ecumenical Council) is convened.

- It decrees the pope is infallible when speaking *ex cathedra*.
- It passes several canons relating to the faith.
- It limits the pope's temporal authority. No longer does the papacy rule a large part of central Italy.

Henri Leclercq (1869–1945), a Benedictine scholar, is born.

Rudolph Otto (1869–1937), a Protestant theologian, is born.

Charles Haddon Spurgeon writes *John Ploughman's Talk*.

1870 Joseph Hilaire Belloc (1870–1933), a Catholic writer, is born.

Albrecht Ritschl writes *The Christian Doctrine of Justification and Reconciliation*.

The Old Catholic Church is founded. It refuses to accept the Vatican I doctrines of infallibility and universal jurisdiction of the pope.

The Jehovah's Witnesses are formed as the Watch Tower Bible and Tract Society of Pennsylvania.

Protestant activists begin a campaign against birth control.

The Russian Orthodox Church establishes its first diocese in the United States.

The Nuremberg Declaration protests the decrees of Vatican I and the dogma of papal infallibility.

James Moffat (1870–1944), a New Testament scholar, is born.

This is the heyday of British evangelists William Booth (1829–1912), Charles Spurgeon (1834–1892), Henry Drummond (1851–1897), Wilson Carlile (1847–1942), and Gipsy Smith (1860–1947).

The Orthodox Missionary Society is organized in Russia by Innocent of Alaska (Ivan Veniaminov), metropolitan of Moscow.

1871 John Nelson Darby publishes his translation of the Bible.

Sergei Bulgakov (1871–1944), a Russian Orthodox theologian, is born. He taught sophiology (devotion to wisdom).

Fifty churches and missions destroyed in the Great Fire of Chicago.

Charles Hodge publishes his *Systematic Theology*.

Georges Rouault (1871–1958), a French painter, is born.

1872 Ralph Vaughan Williams (1872–1958), an English composer, is born.

Revivals occur in Japan and again in 1883.

1873 D.L. Moody conducts large and successful evangelistic meetings in the eastern United States and England, becoming the best-known evangelist of his time.

Thérèse of Lisieux (1873–1897), a Carmelite nun and saint known as the Little Flower, is born.

Robert Jaffray (1873–1945), a Canadian missionary to China, is born.

Charles Peguy (1873–1914), a French Catholic writer, is born.

Christianity is legalized in Japan.

1874 Verdi's *Requiem* is first performed in the Milan cathedral.

Jakob Hutter establishes the Hutterites, a communal utopian colony in the American Northwest. It is one of many such utopian experiments throughout the United States and Europe in the nineteenth century.

The Seventh-day Adventist Church sends out its first missionary.

The Women's Christian Temperance movement is founded.

Joseph Holdsworth Oldham (1874–1969), a leader of the ecumenical movement, is born.

Oswald Chambers (1874–1917), the English author of *My Utmost for His Highest*, is born.

Gilbert Keith Chesterton (1874–1936), an English apologist and writer, is born.

Nikolai Alexandrovich Berdyaev (1874–1948), a Russian theologian, is born.

1875 Hannah Whitall Smith writes *The Christian's Secret of a Happy Life*.

The Bible conference movement begins in America. The Believers' Meeting for Bible Study, later the Niagara Bible Conference, is dominated by premillennialists.

The Society of the Divine Word is inaugurated in Germany.

The Keswick Convention for higher spiritual life begins in England under the theme "All One in Christ Jesus."

The World Alliance of Reformed Churches is founded.

Mary Baker Eddy publishes *Science and Health with Key to the Scriptures*.

Albert Schweitzer (1875–1965), a German Protestant humanitarian, is born.

Paul Ivanovsky (1875–1920), a Russian Orthodox missionary and monk, is born.

The World Methodist Conference is founded.

The Mothers' Union is founded in England by Mary Elizabeth Sumner. It is an Anglican organization aimed at preserving the sanctity of marriage and helping mothers to bring up children responsibly.

1876 Evelyn Underhill (1876–1941), an English mystic, is born.

1877 John Franklyn Norris (1877–1952), an American preacher and conservative spokesman, is born.

The first General Foreign Missions Conference is held in Shanghai with 473 missionaries from 20 Protestant missionary societies.

Phillips Brooks publishes *Lectures on Preaching*.

1878 Evan Roberts (1878–1951), a Welsh evangelist, is born.

King Chulalongkorn of Thailand proclaims the Edict of Religious Toleration.

The first American Bible and Prophetic Conference is held at the Church of the Holy Trinity in New York City.

The second Lambeth Conference is held with 100 Anglican bishops present.

Vladimir Solovyev publishes *Lectures on Godmanhood*.

Franklin Nathan Daniel Buchman (1878–1961), founder of the Moral Re-Armament, is born.

Harry Emerson Fosdick (1878–1969), an American pastor and leader of the modernist movement, is born.

1879 Pope Leo XIII publishes the papal encyclical *Aeterni Patris* ("Eternal Father").

Mary Baker Eddy founds the First Church of Christ, Scientist as a worldwide movement centering on spiritual healing.

The Scripture Union is founded. By 1987, it has 300,000 members in the United Kingdom alone.

Saint Patrick's Cathedral in New York City is completed.

1880 Frances Xavier Cabrini founds the Order of the Missionary Sisters of the Sacred Heart.

The Thirty Years' Revival begins in Germany. Several hundred thousand people are converted in state churches.

A.T. Pearson publishes "A Plan to Evangelize the World" in *The Missionary Review*, calling for an ecumenical council to oversee global evangelization.

Fyodor Dostoevsky writes *The Brothers Karamazov*.

Garfield T. Haywood (1880–1931), an African-American evangelist, is born.

Abraham Kuyper founds the Free University of Amsterdam as the first Protestant university.

The new Cologne Cathedral is consecrated.

1881 The English Revised Version of the Bible is prepared by 65 English scholars.

The Church of God (Anderson, Indiana) is formed by a Holiness group believing in instantaneous and entire sanctification.

The first of 40 International Eucharistic Congresses is held in Lille (France) with 800 present. The forty-first is held in 1976 in Philadelphia with one million present.

The Young People's Society of Christian Endeavor is formed in the United States. In 1895 it becomes the World Christian Endeavor.

John Gresham Machen (1881–1937), an American Presbyterian theologian, is born.

Pierre Teilhard de Chardin (1881–1955), a French paleontologist and theologian, is born.

William Temple (1881–1944), archbishop of Canterbury, is born.

1882 Jacques Maritain (1882–1973), a French Catholic intellectual, is born.

The International Bible Reading Association is founded in Britain. It has 100,000 members by 1886.

A treaty between Korea and America ensures religious freedom in Korea. Presbyterian anti-Methodist missionaries enter Korea three years later.

Leo Tolstoy writes *What I Believe*.

Pavel Florensky (1882–1937), author of *Pillar and Ground of the Truth* (an exposition of Orthodox theology), is born.

1883 Robert Henry Lighfoot (1883–1953), a New Testament scholar, is born in England.

The General Conference of Protestant Missionaries of Japan reports several revivals and states, "Japan is now embracing Christianity with a rapidity unexampled since the days of Constantine...will be predominantly Christian within 20 years."

William Smith founds the Boys' Brigade in England. The organization combines games and sport with hymns and prayers, transforming traditional Sunday schools into volunteer bands with military order, obedience, and discipline. The boys wear a distinctive uniform of cap, belt, and haversack. It has branches in many Commonwealth countries.

Bob Jones Sr. (1883–1968), an American evangelist, is born.

1884 *The Christian Oracle* is first published in Des Moines, Iowa, as a Disciples of Christ denominational magazine. In 1900 it is renamed *Christian Century* and eventually moves to Chicago, Illinois.

Martin Dibelius (1884–1947), a German New Testament scholar, is born.

The German Evangelization Society is founded.

The anonymous *Way of a Pilgrim* is published.

Rudolph Bultmann (1884–1976), a German theologian, is born.

Charles Harold Dodd (1884–1973), a British New Testament scholar, is born.

Étienne Gilson (1884–1978), a French Thomist philosopher, is born.

Frank Charles Laubach (1884–1970), the American mystic and "apostle to the illiterates," is born.

Kenneth Scott Latourette (1884–1968), an American historian of the church and missions, is born.

1885 American Roman Catholic bishops of the Third Plenary Council of Baltimore, Maryland, produce "A Catechism of Christian Doctrine." For almost 60 years, it dominates American Catholic catechesis as the Baltimore Catechism.

The first African ordinations to Anglican ministry are held in Kenya.

In violent persecutions in Indochina, 100,000 Catholics and 115 local priests are killed.

In Uganda, approximately 250 Catholic and Anglican Christians are executed by King Mwanga at Namugongo.

Under Hugh Price Hughes of the West London Mission, the (Methodist) Wesleyan Forward Movement establishes central halls and stresses social evangelism.

François Charles Mauriac (1885–1970), a French Catholic novelist, is born. In 1952 he wins the Nobel Prize in Literature.

1886 The Church of God (Cleveland) begins as a study and fellowship group in Cleveland, Tennessee. In 1906 it becomes the first Pentecostal church in America.

Augustus Hopkins Strong begins publishing his *Systematic Theology*.

Karl Barth (1886–1968), a Swiss Reformed theologian, is born. He is often regarded as the greatest Protestant theologian of the twentieth century.

Charles Williams (1886–1945), an English poet and essayist, is born.

Paul Tillich (1886–1965), a German theologian, is born.

1887 The Moody Bible Institute is founded.

Padre Pio (1887–1968), a Capuchin priest, is born.

Scriptures (the Gospel of Luke) are translated in the Philippines for the first time.

Evangelists Hugh Thomas Crossley and John Edwin Hunter conduct evangelistic campaigns in Canadian cities.

Albert Benjamin Simpson organizes the Christian Alliance and the Evangelical Missionary Alliance. They merge in 1897 to form the Christian and Missionary Alliance, which eventually has one of the largest contingents of missionaries per capita.

Charles Edward Fuller (1887–1968), an American Baptist evangelist, is born.

1888 Toyohiko Kagawa (1888–1960), a Japanese Christian pacifist, reformer, and labor activist is born.

The Student Volunteer Movement for Foreign Missions forms in America with the watchword "The Evangelization of the World in This Generation."

The Conference on Protestant Missions of the World in London includes 1576 missionaries and representatives of 140 agencies. It is the first of the great international conferences.

The third Lambeth Conference includes 145 Anglican bishops.

1889 Simon Kimbangu (1889–1951), the Congolese founder of the Church of Jesus Christ on Earth, is born.

The Catholic University of America is founded as the only pontifical university in the United States.

Gipsy Smith holds evangelistic campaigns in America.

Emil Brunner (1889–1966), a Swiss theologian, is born.

Martin Heidegger (1889–1976), a German existentialist philosopher, is born.

Sadhu Sundar Singh (1889–1929), an Indian Christian ascetic, is born.

1890 William Booth publishes *In Darkest England and the Way Out*.

The Scandinavian Alliance Mission of North America is founded for worldwide evangelism and church planting. In 1949 it is renamed The Evangelical Alliance Mission (TEAM).

Aimee Semple McPherson (1890–1944), an American preacher and the founder of the International Church of the Foursquare Gospel, is born.

The Bible is translated into Swahili.

1891 Pope Leo XIII issues the papal encyclical *Rerum Novarum* ("Of New Things"), which addresses the condition of the working classes.

Abraham Kuyper helps organize the Christian Social Congress in the Netherlands.

Edith Stein (1891–1942), a Jewish-born Christian philosopher and martyr, is born.

1892 Reinhold Niebuhr (1892–1971), an American Protestant theologian and social ethicist, is born.

Martin Niemoller (1892–1984), a German pastor, is born.

John Ronald Reuel Tolkien (1892–1973), a South African scholar and author of the *The Hobbit* and the Lord of the Rings trilogy, is born.

1893 Dorothy L. Sayers (1893–1957), an English essayist and novelist, is born.

Construction begins on *Segrada Familia*, a basilica in Barcelona, Spain, designed by Antoni Gaudi.

Georges Florovsky (1893–1979), a Russian Orthodox theologian, patrologist, philosopher, and historian, is born.

The Sudan Interior Mission begins.

Francis Thompson publishes *Hound of Heaven and Other Poems*.

1894 Maximilian Kolbe (1894–1941), a Polish martyr, is born.

Helmut Richard Niebuhr (1894–1962), an American theologian, is born.

1895 Turks begin to massacre Armenian Christians.
    1895–1896—200,000 are killed.
    1905—20,000 killed in Cilicia.
    1909—30,000 killed in the district of Adana.
    1915—600,000 killed in Anatolia.
    1920—30,000 killed at Marash and Hadjin.

The Church of God in Christ is formed in America. It is a Pentecostal Holiness denomination with a predominately African-American membership.

The Young People's Society of Christian Endeavor movement numbers 38,000 societies worldwide with 2,225,000 members.

The World Student Christian Federation is founded in Sweden under the leadership of John R. Mott, then student secretary of the YMCA.

Donald Grey Barnhouse (1895–1960), an American Bible expositor, is born.

Cornelius Van Til (1895–1987), an American Calvinist theologian, is born.

Fulton Sheen (1895–1979), an American Roman Catholic bishop and speaker, is born.

The Los Angeles First Church of the Nazarene is founded in Los Angeles. It becomes the mother church of the western branch of the Church of the Nazarene.

1896 Billy Sunday conducts his first revival.

Pope Leo XIII issues *Satis Cognitum* ("On the Unity of the Church"), a papal encyclical declaring that unity among the various branches of the church is possible only when they all acknowledge the primacy of the papacy.

Henri de Lubac (1896–1991), a French Jesuit theologian, is born.

Charles Monroe Sheldon writes *In His Steps*.

Henri de Lubac (1896–1991), a French Jesuit theologian and writer, is born.

James Stuart Stewart (1896–1990), a Scottish preacher, is born.

William Cameron Townsend (1896–1982), founder of Wycliffe Bible Translators and Summer Institute of Linguistics, is born.

1897 The Christian Alliance and the Evangelical Missionary Alliance merge to form the Christian and Missionary Alliance.

The Oxyrhynchus Papyri are discovered in Egypt. The collection dates from the first to the sixth century and includes a Greek variant of the Gospel of Thomas, fragments of the Old and New Testaments, and the oldest known example of church music.

The fourth Lambeth Conference includes 194 Anglican bishops.

Dorothy Day (1897–1980), an American Catholic social activist and founder of *Catholic Worker*, is born.

The Association of Pentecostal Churches of America (one of the groups that would merge to form the Church of the Nazarene) begins foreign missions.

Donald Anderson McGavran (1897–1990), an American scholar and exponent of church growth, is born.

A.W. Tozer (1897–1963), a Christian and Missionary Alliance pastor and author, is born.

1898 The Society for Promoting Christian Knowledge is formed to spread charity schools, Bibles, and religious tracts throughout England and Wales.

The Russian Orthodox Church sends missionaries to Korea.

Church and state separate in Cuba when it gains independence from Spain.

C.S. Lewis (1898–1963), an English apologist, scholar, and writer, is born.

1899 The Christian Commercial Travelers Association of America is founded and eventually becomes the Gideons International. The organization evangelizes through the distribution of Scripture.

William Ralph Inge writes *Christian Mysticism*.

Thérèse of Lisieux writes *Story of a Soul*.

David Martyn Lloyd-Jones (1899–1981), a Welsh evangelist, is born.

The Twentieth Century (1900–2000)

The Age of Expectancy

THE STATUS OF THE CHRISTIAN CHURCH

At the end of the twentieth century and the close of the Christian bimillennium, 67 generations after Christ, 78.4 percent of the world is evangelized, and 33 percent of the population is Christian. The church is 51 percent nonwhite, and printed Scriptures are available in nearly 2000 languages.

INFLUENTIAL CHRISTIANS OF THE CENTURY

Dietrich Bonhoeffer, Billy Graham, Mother Teresa, Cameron Townsend, C.S. Lewis, Brother Roger Schutz

SIGNIFICANT EVENTS AND INFLUENCES

- After 2000 years, the church is still struggling to survive and to spread against a host of enemies from within and without. Striking a balance sheet at 2000, a momentous divide in human history, Christians form about a third of the world's population. Roman Catholics make up roughly half of this number, with members of the Orthodox Church and the 20,000 Protestant denominations accounting for the remaining.

- The hideous persecutions have not ceased. In fact, the Diocletian and Decian persecutions under the Roman Empire pale into insignificance compared to the bloody massacres of Christians in the twentieth century under Communism and Islam. More than 600,000 Armenian Christians and 200,000 Greek Christians were killed by Turks during World War I. More than five million Christians perished under Lenin and Stalin, and another three million when Communists took over China in midcentury. There were other scattered outbursts of violence against Christians, as during the Boxer Rebellion in China in 1900, when 50,000 Christians were killed. But the church strangely has managed to survive and to flourish. The gates of hell, to claim the biblical promise, have not prevailed against it.

- By the middle of the twentieth century, a great transition took place. From the birth of the church through the sixth century, non-Europeans were in the majority. From the tenth to the twentieth centuries, Europeans constituted the majority of Christians. The tide turned again around 1980 when, as a result of mass conversions in the Third World, especially Africa, non-Europeans again became the majority. This trend is likely to continue if Europe becomes more and more apostate and the Third World more open to the gospel.

- The Bible is available in nearly 2000 languages. More than three billion copies of the Bible are in print—more than any other book in the world. The Christian church is close to fulfilling the Lord's command to go to every country and to every tribe. Only four countries in the world are without a Christian presence (Saudi Arabia, Yemen, Afghanistan, and Maldives), all of them Muslim. There are rumblings of the end, but nothing visible, nothing certain. It is still the age of expectancy, a church still waiting for its Bridegroom.

- The central event of twentieth-century Christianity was the survival of the Russian Orthodox Church under the Bolsheviks for more than 75 years. The extirpation of Christianity was one of the principal goals of Lenin, Stalin, and Kruschchev. They used every means in their power to wipe out the Orthodox Church, converting tens of thousands of churches into museums, sending thousands of priests into Siberian gulags, shutting down seminaries and monasteries, and banning baptisms and other sacraments, bell ringing, and the celebration of Christmas. Kruschchev promised that by 1971 the last Christian priest in Russia would be put on display as a relic. Yet Kruschchev and the Communists did not last. Their empire dismantled, and their vaunted Marxist ideology was exposed and discredited. The Orthodox Church has emerged from this dark chapter of history as a phoenix and as the very embodiment of the soul of the great Russian people.

- In 1906 a one-eyed illiterate black preacher, William Seymour, went to Los Angeles to start a church. He rented a run-down warehouse in the seedy part of town on Azusa Street. He began holding services there without any fanfare, sometimes covering his face with a brown paper bag. His audience, which grew larger day by day, began to be boisterous, praying in strange tongues under the guidance of the Holy Spirit. This was the beginning of the modern phenomenon known as Pentecostalism. Within weeks, Azusa Street services were on the front pages of national newspapers as people experienced miracles and healings and spoke in tongues. The Azusa phenomenon was soon replicated not only in many other cities in the United States but also in far countries, such as England, Chile, and India. Within eight years, Pentecostal denominations began to appear, eventually including the Assemblies of God, the Church of God, and the International Church of the Foursquare Gospel. Pentecostalism would leave a permanent impress on the Christian faith, and Pentecostal churches would form the fastest-growing Christian movement in the world before the end of the century. In the 1960s and 1970s, the so-called Jesus movement provided a rich harvest of souls, and many of its members became Pentecostal church planters and evangelists. The Catholic Church would later welcome the second wave of the Charismatic movement. Led by Cardinal Suenens of Belgium, the Catholic

Charismatic movement spread to Europe and then to many countries in Asia and Africa.

- Longtime Pentecostal leader David du Plessis worked for many years as an unofficial ambassador, bringing together Pentecostals, Charismatics, and mainline churches. Charismatics and Pentecostals have become one of the most dynamic expressions of Christianity in the twentieth century, effectively reaching out to those not touched by more traditional churches.

- The twentieth century witnessed a remarkable recovery from the liberalism and agnosticism of the nineteenth century. The horrors of two world wars and seven decades of Marxist Leninism have convinced thinking men and women that the socialist and humanist utopias of endless progress and prosperity cannot be sustained by unregenerate human nature. The magisterial voice of the church was once again heard in the twentieth century as the custodian of the conscience of humanity. Atheism has been shrinking as an ideology and as an ideal, and even Christian liberalism has been shriveling despite the entirely materialistic cultural environment. Unitarian churches have dwindled and may soon entirely disappear. The great liberal theologians of the nineteenth century and the early twentieth century have lost much of their influence in the seminaries, and orthodoxy, as represented by Karl Barth and his school, became the dominant influence by the end of the twentieth century.

- Similarly, the twentieth century produced some of the great crusaders and preachers in history. The list is led by Billy Graham, who, since 1948, has preached to more people, both in person and on radio and television, than any evangelist in history. The other great itinerant evangelists include Billy Sunday (the "baseball preacher"), the Latin American Luis Palau, and the German Reinhard Bonnke. More and larger crusades were held than ever before. In 1980, the World Evangelization Crusade in South Korea was attended by 16.5 million people.

- In 1934, some 550 years after the death of John Wycliffe, Cameron Townsend founded the Wycliffe Translators for the translation of the Bible into all languages of the world. By 1914 the Bible had been translated into only 600 languages, but by 1999, the number of Bible translations had risen to nearly 2000.

- The twentieth century was also the century of ecumenism. Ecumenism is the fulfillment of Christ's directive that all His believers should form one, indivisible body. The first steps in this direction were taken at the Edinburgh Conference of 1910, with John R. Mott presiding. It was followed by the Oxford and Edinburgh conferences in 1938. These conferences led to the founding of two movements: Life and Work, and Faith and Order. These merged through the founding, in 1948, of the World Council of Churches. The Council is defined as a "fellowship of churches which confess the Lord Jesus as God and Savior according to the Scriptures and therefore seek to fulfill together their common calling to the glory of the one God, Father, Son and Holy Spirit." The Council comprises 322 member churches from every continent and country. The Roman Catholic Church, the only major nonmember, has the status of an observer and actively participates in many agencies of the World Council of Churches.

- The major event in twentieth century Catholic history was the convocation of the Second Vatican Council in 1962 by Pope John XXIII. The council's goal was *aggiornamento*, or "bringing the church up to date." More than one-fourth of the 2000-plus delegates were from Africa and Asia. Without making any sweeping changes in the structure or the mission of the church, the Council cut away some deadwood and set a new course for Catholicism. Latin is no longer the sole language of the liturgy, but the Mass may be said in native languages. Both the clergy and the laity are accepted as people of God, each with their share of ministerial functions. The Council document "On Divine Revelation" emphasized that Scripture—not tradition—is the primary basis of divine truth. In the Decree on Ecumenism, non-Catholic Christians are called "separated brethren" and not heretics.

- After the death of John XXIII and his next two successors, a new pope of Polish origin, John Paul II, would give meaning and substance to the decrees of the Council. One of the most traveled and popular of modern popes, John Paul II would preside over the church during the final decades of the twentieth century and bring extraordinary luster to his apostolic office.

- For 19 centuries, the only means of preaching the word was through sermons and open-air meetings. In the early part of the twentieth century, technology added broadcasting as another means, one never envisioned by the apostles. In 1921, a year after Westinghouse began radio broadcasting, the church service of Calvary Episcopal Church in Pittsburgh was broadcast over station KDKA. Others followed in the next two years, notably Paul Rader broadcasting for 14 hours every Sunday (when regular broadcasting was suspended) on WJBT in Chicago, R.R. Brown on WOW in Omaha, and the Moody Bible Institute on WGES in Chicago. In 1928 Donald Grey Barnhouse became the first radio preacher to buy time on CBS to air his service from Philadelphia's Tenth Presbyterian Church. In 1930 HCJB in Quito, Ecuador, became the world's first Christian-owned missionary radio station. Within the next 70 years, Christian media grew phenomenally, and now it blankets the world.

- In the 1960s and 1970s, Billy Graham, Rex Humbard, Oral Roberts, Pat Robertson, and Bishop Fulton Sheen blazed the trail into television. At least two Christian television networks, Christian Broadcasting Network and Trinity Broadcasting Network, have global affiliates. Without Christian radio and television, it is doubtful whether Evangelical and Pentecostal

Christianity would have spread as wide and as fast as they did in the second half of the twentieth century.

- The media also helped to bring into focus the lives and works of some of the modern heroes of the faith. C.S. Lewis, an icon among Protestants, is unusual in that he was an Oxford don who brought clarity to basic theological propositions. Mother Teresa, an Albanian nun, adopted India as her home and worked among the destitute and the dying. Dietrich Bonhoeffer, a Lutheran pastor, defied Hitler and paid for his stance with his life. It is a powerful testimony to the Christian faith that 20 centuries after Calvary, it can still produce men and women of the same caliber and devotion as the apostles.

- The first two millennia of Christian history end with the same hope as that of the aged apostle John, an exile on the rocky islet of Patmos, as he wrote his last words in the book of Revelation: "Come, Lord Jesus."

CHRONOLOGY

1900 The United Presbyterian Church and Free Church of Scotland merge to from the United Free Church of Scotland.

Khrisanf Shchetkovsky, a Russian Orthodox missionary, arrives in Korea and opens a school and mission.

Wang Mingdao (1900–1991), a Chinese church leader, is born.

Adolf von Harnack, a German Lutheran theologian and church historian, writes *What Is Christianity?*

John R. Mott publishes the influential classic, *The Evangelization of the World in This Generation* and names the twentieth century "the Christian Century."

In China, 47,000 Catholics die in the Boxer Rebellion.

The International Council of Unitarian and other Liberal Religious Thinkers and Workers is founded in America. In 1910 it is renamed the International Congress of Free Christians and Other Religious Liberals. In 1930 it is renamed the International Association for Liberal Christianity and Religious Freedom.

1901 The American Standard Version of the Bible is released. It is an Americanized version of the Revised Version.

Since 1808, the British and Foreign Bible Society has issued...
46,030,124 Bibles
71,178,373 New Testaments
52,763,047 copies of other portions of Scripture.

Charles F. Parham opens Bethel Bible School near Topeka, Kansas, teaching his students about the infilling of the Holy Spirit as evidenced by speaking in tongues. The gifts of the Holy Spirit are restored to the church and are reinforced by Latter Rain teaching.

R.P. Augustine Poulain writes *Graces of Interior Prayer*.

John Sung (1901–1944), a Chinese Methodist evangelist and revivalist, is born.

1902 Gladys Aylward (1902–1970), a missionary to China, is born.

Adolf von Harnack publishes *The Mission and Expansion of Christianity During the First Three Centuries*.

Between 1902 and 1908, 130,000 people are converted through the preaching of R.A. Torrey and C.M. Alexander.

The Young People's Missionary Education Movement is founded by 15 denominational boards in the United States to enlist missionaries.

Alfred Loisy writes *The Gospel and the Church*.

Hilaire Belloc writes *The Path to Rome*.

William James writes *The Varieties of Religious Experience*.

Oscar Cullmann (1902–1999), a German-speaking French biblical scholar, is born.

Peter Marshall (1902–1949), chaplain of the US Senate, is born.

1903 Richard F. Weymouth publishes The New Testament in Modern Speech.

Vladimir N. Lossky (1903–1958), a Russian Orthodox theologian, is born.

Malcolm Muggeridge (1903–1990), a British author, satirist, journalist, and Christian apologist, is born.

The Church of God of Prophecy (the All Nations Flag Church) is founded. In 1911, it begins overseas work in the Bahamas.

John Piper (1903–1992), an English artist whose works include stained glass windows and tapestries, is born.

Watchman Nee (1903–1972), the Chinese founder of Christian Assembly (the Little Flock), is born.

1904 Karl Rahner (1904–1984), a German Jesuit theologian and an advisor at the Second Vatican Council, is born.

Evan Roberts conducts revivals in Wales with 100,000 converts in six months.

Joseph Ayodele Babalola (1904–1959), Nigerian founder of the Christ Apostolic Church, is born.

Yves Congar (1904–1995), a French Catholic theologian, is born.

Graham Greene (1904–1991), an English Catholic novelist, is born.

Bernard Lonergan (1904–1984), a Canadian Catholic theologian, is born.

John Courtney Murray (1904–1967), an America Jesuit theologian, is born.

1905 Dag Hammarskjold (1905–1961), a Christian thinker and United Nations secretary general, is born.

Max Weber writes *The Protestant Ethic and the Spirit of Capitalism.*

The Baptist World Alliance is founded.

In France, the Catholic Church separates from the state.

Evangelistic Faith Missions (USA) is formed.

The Evangelistic Council of London sponsors a greater London crusade with R.A.Torrey and C.M. Alexander. It includes 202 meetings with 1.1 million attenders and 14,000 conversions.

Hans Urs von Balthasar (1905–1988), a Swiss Roman Catholic theologian, is born.

David Johannes du Plessis (1905–1987), a South African Pentecostal leader and faith healer, is born.

Maria Faustina (1905–1938), a Catholic nun known as Apostle of Divine Mercy, is born.

Marcel Lefebvre (1905–1991), a conservative French Catholic archbishop, is born.

The Protestant Federation of France is founded.

1906 Albert Schweitzer writes *The Quest of the Historical Jesus.*

William J. Seymour leads the Azusa Street Revival, one of the earliest instances of Pentecostal worship.

Bede Griffiths (1906–1993), an English mystic, is born.

The first General Conference of Missionaries to the World of Islam is held in Cairo under the leadership of Samuel Zwemer.

The Laymen's Missionary Movement is launched as a foreign missions auxiliary agency.

Dietrich Bonhoeffer (1906–1945), a German theologian and pastor who opposed Hitler, is born.

The Pentecostal Church of God is founded in Cleveland, Tennessee.

1907 Kathryn Johanna Kuhlman (1907–1976), an American faith healer and leader in the Charismatic movement, is born.

Walter Rauschenbusch writes *Christianity and the Social Crisis*, bringing the social gospel into the public arena.

In the encyclical *Pascendi dominici gregis* ("Feeding the Lord's Flock"), Pope Pius X condemns 65 modernist propositions and places several modernist works on the Index of Forbidden Books.

The United Church of Christ is founded.

Korea experiences a massive revival and the phenomenal growth of
churches.

1908 Olivier Messiaen (1908–1992), a French Catholic composer, is born.

Jonathan Goforth leads the Manchurian Revival at Changde.

J. Wilbur Chapman conducts a six-week evangelistic campaign in Philadelphia that includes 400 churches and 1.5 million attenders. Seven
thousand people inquire about the faith.

Thirty-one denominations form the Federal Council of Churches (later
the National Council of Churches).

Gilbert Keith Chesterton writes *Orthodoxy*.

Friedrich von Hügel writes *The Mystical Element of Religion*.

1909 The Scofield Reference Bible is published.

Pope Pius X issues the encyclical *Lamentabili Sane Exitu* ("With Truly
Lamentable Results") condemning the errors of the modernists.

W.A. Criswell (1909–2002), a Southern Baptist theologian, is born.

Torrey Maynard Johnson (1909–2002), the American founder of Youth
for Christ International, is born.

Lesslie Newbigin (1909–1998), an English theologian and missionary in
India, is born.

Simone Weil (1909–1943), a French Catholic philosopher, is born.

Hélder Câmara (1909–1999), a Brazilian Roman Catholic bishop and
champion of the poor, is born.

1910 Frederick Fyvie Bruce (1910–1990), a Scottish theologian, is born.

Mother Teresa (1910–1997), an Albanian-born Catholic nun who min-
istered to the destitutes in Calcutta, is born. She wins the Nobel Peace
Prize in 1979.

Graduale Romanum, the official Vatican collection of chant melodies,
is compiled from medieval manuscripts by scholars, most from the
Benedictine Solesmes Abbey in France.

The Fundamentals is published. It eventually includes 90 essays in 12
tracts.

The World Missionary Conference (Edinburgh) marks the beginning
of modern ecumenism. It has three facets: evangelism, service, and
doctrine.

The Faith and Order movement, an initiative of the Protestant Episcopal
Church in Cincinnati, begins.

The Million Souls movement (aiming at one million converts) begins in
Korea.

Between 1910 and 1930, one million people are converted through the preaching of Billy Sunday and Homer Rodeheaver.

1911 Evelyn Underhill writes *Mysticism*.

The Catholic Foreign Mission Society of America, better known as the Maryknoll Missioners, is formed as a group of American Catholic priests dedicated to foreign missions. It is headed by James Anthony Walsh and Thomas Frederick Price.

Mahalia Jackson (1911–1972), the queen of gospel music, is born.

1912 V.S. Azariah becomes the first Indian to be consecrated bishop.

J.H. Oldham becomes editor of *The International Review of Missions*.

Mordecai Ham conducts evangelistic campaigns in America from 1912 to 1945. William J. Ramsey is his musical director.

In the first attempt by a mission body to systematically reach every home in an entire nation, the Oriental Missionary Society reaches 10.3 million homes in Japan.

Jacques Ellul (1912–1994), a French theologian, is born.

Francis August Schaeffer (1912–1984), an American Christian intellectual, is born.

1913 James Moffatt publishes The Holy Bible Containing the Old and New Testaments, a New Translation.

George W. Hensley introduces the practice of snake handling to Pentecostals in Tennessee.

"Oneness" or "Jesus only" Pentecostals begin to baptize in the name of Jesus rather than using the traditional trinitarian formula. The innovation creates a permanent split among Pentecostals.

Liberian prophet William Wade Harris preaches in the Ivory Coast. By 1915, 120,000 people are converted.

C.T. Studd begins the Worldwide Evangelization Crusade in England.

Carl F.H. Henry (1913–2003), an American New Evangelical theologian and professor, is born.

Demos Shakarian (1913–1993), an Armenian philanthropist who founded the Full Gospel Businessmen's Fellowship International, is born.

1914 The Assemblies of God denomination is formed under William H. Durham.

Edward Schillebeeckx (1914–2009), a Belgian Domincan friar and theologian, is born.

Nomiya Luo Mission, the first of Kenya's independent indigenous churches, begins as a schism from the Anglican Church.

All Roman Catholic bishops worldwide are of European origin except for four Indians in Kerala.

Bruce Metzger (1914–2007), an American Bible scholar and translator, is born.

1915 Thomas Merton (1915–1968), a Trappist monk and mystical author, is born.

In the third major Turkish persecution, at least 600,000 Armenians are killed, and 600,000 flee or are deported from Turkey.

Pentecostal healer George Jeffreys begins the Elim Foursquare Gospel Alliance in Britain. He later also founds the World Revival Crusade.

Roger Louis Schütz-Marsauche (Brother Roger) (1915–2005), the Swiss founder and prior of the Taizé Community, is born.

1916 Bernard L. Ramm (1916–1992), an American theologian and apologist, is born.

Walker Percy (1916–1990), an American Catholic novelist, is born.

1917 Edward Joseph Flanagan sets up the Home for Homeless Boys, which is later renamed Boys Town.

The Balfour Declaration recognizes Palestine as the national homeland of the Jews.

When the Russian army withdraws from Turkey and Persia, Turks and Kurds kill 20,000 Nestorians.

The Bolshevik Revolution begins in Russia, followed by civil war. One and a half million people, mostly Christians, are killed. In 1918, church and state separate. Another 1.5 million flee the country.

The True Jesus Church begins in China. It is a Charismatic split from the Apostolic Faith Movement.

The Interdenominational Foreign Missions Association of North America is founded by a number of evangelical organizations.

Rudolf Otto writes *The Idea of the Holy*.

Walter Rauschenbusch writes *A Theology for the Social Gospel*.

Dennis Bennett (1917–1991), an Episcopal priest and the father of the modern Charismatic movement, is born.

Oscar Arnulfo Romero (1917–1980), the Catholic archbishop of El Salvador, is born.

Pope Benedict XV issues *Codex Juris Canonici* ("Code of Canon Law").

The Sacred Congregation of the Index, the Vatican censor, is abolished after 346 years.

1918   Aleksandr Solzhenitsyn (1918–2008), a Russian Christian novelist, historian, and critic of totalitarianism, is born.

The church and state separate in Germany, though the Lutheran Church still receives income from taxes.

William Franklin Graham, an American evangelist, is born.

In Nigeria, an influenza epidemic (part of a worldwide swine flu epidemic) brings about formation of prayer and healing groups, which later grow into large indigenous churches: Cherubim and Seraphim, the Church of the Lord, and Christ Apostolic Church.

The fundamentalism versus modernism controversy erupts in American Protestantism, splitting every major denomination. Premillennialism becomes a major part of all revivalist preaching.

Oral Roberts (1918–2009), an American radio preacher with a widespread healing ministry, is born.

Benjamin B. Warfield writes *The Plan of Salvation*.

1919   Karl Barth publishes his commentary *Epistle to the Romans*.

More than 6000 people attend the World Conference on Christian Fundamentals in Philadelphia.

The Cao Dai Missionary Church is founded by Lê Văn Trung in Vietnam. It is a syncretistic mixture of popular Buddhism, Confucian ethics, the ancestral cult, and Catholic-type organization, with a membership of about 2.8 million by 1975.

The International Missionary Council is launched with a preliminary conference in Crans-Montana, Switzerland.

The Mennonite Central Committee is formed in Akron, Pennsylvania.

The General Council of Co-operating Baptist Missions of North America is organized. It is renamed Baptist Mid-Missions in 1953.

John Macquarrie (1919–2007), an English Christian existentialist philosopher, is born.

1920   The Friends (Quakers) hold their first World Conference in London.

The Evangelization Society is chartered at the Pittsburgh Bible Institute.

1921   The Grail, a Catholic Women's organization, is founded in the Netherlands.

The first broadcast of a church worship service is on Sunday evening, January 2, from Calvary Episcopal Church in Pittsburgh.

The International Missionary Council is founded at Lake Mohonk, New York.

Simon Kimbangu's revival in the Lower Congo leads to mass

conversions, persecutions, and by 1960, a massive indigenous church, the Church of Jesus Christ on Earth.

The Oxford Group begins in Britain. It is later renamed Moral Re-Armament.

The Pentecostal World Conference is formed in Amsterdam.

Max Scheler writes *On the Eternal in Man*.

William Lee Bonner, an American leader of the Church of Our Lord Jesus Christ of the Apostolic Faith, is born.

Bill Bright (1921–2003), founder of Campus Crusade for Christ, is born.

Alexander Schmemann (1921–1983), an Estonian-born Orthodox theologian, is born.

John R.W. Stott (1921–2011), an English theologian, is born.

1922 The National Christian Council of China is founded.

Ten thousand Russian Orthodox bishops, priests, monks, and nuns are executed by Bolsheviks under Stalin.

The Bible Reading Fellowship is founded in Britain for Anglicans.

Hans Wilhelm Frei (1922–1988), a German-born American theologian, is born.

1923 George Lindbeck, an American Lutheran theologian, is born.

Edgar Johnson Goodspeed publishes The New Testament: An American Translation. In 1935, with John Merlin Powis Smith, he releases The Bible: An American Translation (the Goodspeed Bible). In 1939, he includes his translation of the Apocrypha in The Complete Bible: An American Translation.

Don Falkenberg founds the Bible Literature International to produce and distribute Bibles, tracts, and Bible study material worldwide.

George T.B. Davis begins the Million Testaments Campaign in Philadelphia.

John Gresham Machen writes *Christianity and Liberalism*.

One and a half million Greek Orthodox believers in Turkey are deported to Greece, and 400,000 Muslim Turks in Greece are deported to Turkey.

Not long after opening Angelus Temple in Los Angeles, Aimee Semple McPherson establishes the Echo Park Evangelistic and Missionary Training Institute. In 1926 its name is changed to L.I.F.E. (Lighthouse of International Foursquare Evangelism) Bible College. Today the school is known as Life Pacific College.

1924 Stanley Jaki, a Hungarian Catholic priest and philosopher, is born.

James William McClendon Jr. (1924–2000), an American Baptist theologian, is born.

The Near East Christian Council is founded at Mount of Olives, Jerusalem.

The first international Christian radio station, NCRV, begins broadcasting in the Netherlands.

1925 John Thomas Scopes, an American high school instructor, is accused of teaching evolution. In the ensuing trial, the prosecutor is William Jennings Bryan, and the defender is Clarence Darrow. Scopes is convicted and fined $100, but the verdict is overturned on a technicality. Five days after the trial, Bryan dies in his sleep.

The Mennonite World Conference is formed in Basel, Switzerland.

The Universal Christian Conference on Life and Work is held in Stockholm, Sweden.

Methodists, Presbyterians, and Congregationalists join to form the United Church of Canada.

Gilbert Keith Chesterton writes *Everlasting Man*.

Fulton J. Sheen writes *God and Intelligence in Modern Philosophy*.

Charles Caldwell Ryrie, an American theologian, is born.

Flannery O'Connor (1925–1964), an American novelist, is born.

Juan Luis Segundo (1925–1996), a Latin American Jesuit priest and theologian of liberation theology, is born.

When Patriarch Tikhon of the Russian Orthodox Church dies, no successor is appointed until 1943.

Lew Wallace's 1880 novel *Ben-Hur: A Tale of the Christ* is produced as a movie.

1926 James I. Packer, an English theologian, is born.

The Benedictines of Saint John's Abbey in Collegeville, Minnesota, begin to publish the periodical *Orate Fratres*, later titled *Worship*, marking the beginning of the liturgical movement in the United States.

Jürgen Moltmann, a German Reformed theologian, is born.

The German Association for Mass Evangelism begins.

The Unevangelized Tribes Mission of Borneo is formed in America.

Watchman Nee forms the Assembly Hall churches (the Little Flock) in China.

The largest schism in the Roman Catholic Church in Mexico leads to the formation of the Orthodox Catholic Apostolic Mexican Church. By 1970 it has ten bishops and 60,000 members.

Timothy Dudley-Smith, an English hymnwriter and bishop of the Church of England, is born.

John Meyendorff (1926–1992), an American Orthodox theologian, is born.

1927 The first World Conference on Faith and Order is held in Lausanne, Switzerland, as a part of the movement toward doctrinal ecumenism. It is the first in a series of meetings that lay the foundation for the World Council of Churches.

The Cistercian Order brings all its congregations under an Abbot General in Rome.

Stalin threatens to execute the entire Orthodox clergy of Russia (146,000 people, including monks and nuns). The acting patriarch capitulates.

Fifty American radio stations are now licensed to religious bodies.

As a result of an anti-Christian movement in China, 5000 of the 8000 Protestant missionaries leave the country.

Seven Protestant denominations join to form the Church of Christ in China.

The Association of Baptists for Evangelism in the Orient is formed.

Friedrich von Hügel publishes *Selected Letters*.

Thomas J.J. Altizer, the American "death of God" radical theologian, is born.

Heribert Mühlen (1927–2006), a German Catholic systematic theologian, is born.

Charles Ward "Chuck" Smith (1927–2013), the American founder of the Calvary Chapel churches, is born.

John Howard Yoder (1927–1997), an America Mennonite theologian, is born.

Aimee Semple McPherson founds the International Church of the Foursquare Gospel.

Cecil B. DeMille produces *The King of Kings*.

1928 Josemaría Escrivá de Balaguer forms *Opus Dei* in Spain to promote Christian ideals in secular life. It is a conservative, right-wing, Catholic organization.

Hans Küng, a Swiss Catholic priest, theologian, and author, is born.

The Unevangelized Africa Mission and the Unevangelized Tribes Mission of Africa are both founded in America.

The National Conference of Christians and Jews forms in New York City to combat religious and social prejudice. It is a member of the International Council of Christians and Jews.

Anglican evangelist Bryan Green begins 50 years of ministry as a diocesan missioner in Britain, America, Canada, South Africa, Australia, and elsewhere.

The World Fundamental Baptist Missionary Fellowship is founded in Texas. It is later renamed as the World Baptist Fellowship Mission.

In the encyclical *Mortalium Animos* ("Minds of Men or Mortal Souls"), Pius XI condemns the ecumenical movement, forbidding Roman Catholics to be involved.

Donald G. Bloesch, an American Evangelical theologian, is born.

Gustavo Gutiérrez Merino, a Peruvian Domincan priest and the founder of liberation theology, is born.

Wolfhart Pannenberg, a German theologian, is born.

The British InterVarsity sends its vice chairman, Howard Guinness, to Canada to start campus groups there. In 1938, Stacy Woods, the Canadian InterVarsity director, meets with students at the University of Michigan, and the first American chapter is formed.

1929 Martin Luther King Jr. (1929–1968), an African-American preacher and civil-rights leader, is born.

In the Lateran Treaty, the Kingdom of Italy and the Roman Catholic Church create Vatican City as an independent sovereign state known as the Holy See.

The first major international Protestant radio station, Voice of the Andes (HCJB), is founded at Quito, Ecuador. Its first broadcast is on Christmas Day 1931.

Congregationalist missionary Frank C. Laubach begins his Each One Teach One literacy program in the Philippines. In 1950 he describes his method in *Literacy as Evangelism.*

Jay Edward Adams, the American founder of nouthetic counseling, is born.

J. Gresham Machen founds the Westminster Theological Seminary.

Antonina Maria Izabela Wilucka-Kowalska is ordained as the first female bishop in the Netherlands.

1930 The Malabarese Uniat Church is founded in South India.

The Japanese Kingdom of God movement begins under evangelist Toyohiko Kagawa and reaches more than one million people in two years.

Christian Businessmen's Committee International is formed in Chicago.

The Missouri Synod (USA) begins *Lutheran Hour* broadcasts. In 1931, the program reaches five million listeners a week. In 1945, it reaches 20 million a week worldwide.

The World Conference for Life and Work is formed.

Thomas Cochrane, a Scottish medical missionary, begins the Mildmay Movement for World Evangelization in London.

Benjamin Davidson of Scotland begins the India Mission. The name is changed to International Missions in 1953.

Foundation Farthest Out begins as a belt of prayer around the world.

Anders Nygren writes *Eros and Agape*, and the next year, Gustaf Aulen writes *Christus Victor*. These are the two most significant works of the Lundensian school, named for Lund University in Sweden.

José Severino Croatto (1930–2004), an Argentinian Catholic scholar, is born.

Robert W. Jenson, an American systematic theologian, is born.

Pat Robertson, an America televangelist, is born.

Pope Pius XI condemns contraception in his encyclical *Casti Connubii* ("Chaste Wedlock").

Aladura, a movement started in Nigeria in 1918, becomes a mass movement in that country. The name means "praying people." It later morphs into Faith Tabernacle and finally to Christ Apostolic Church, but today, most churches in Western Nigeria can correctly be called Aladura.

1931 Desmond Tutu, a South African Episcopal archbishop and global social rights activist, is born.

The Unevangelized Fields Mission, named UFM International in 1985 and Crossworld in 2004, is founded in London.

Church and state separate in Spain. Thousands of priests and Catholics are murdered, and churches are burned in mob riots.

Pius XI inaugurates Radio Vatican in Rome and entrusts it to Jesuits.

The Worldwide Prayer and Missionary Union is founded in Chicago.

Abraham Kuyper publishes *Lectures on Calvinism*.

Albert Schweitzer writes *Out of My Life and Thought*.

Paul Landowski's huge sculpture of Christ the Redeemer in Rio de Janeiro is dedicated.

1932 In the Soviet Union, the League of Militant Atheists numbers 7 million adults and 1.5 million children.

The All-India Forward Movement in Evangelism is launched in Nagpur.

Thirty thousand Muslims are converted around Mojowarno, East Java, Indonesia.

Karl Barth writes *Church Dogmatics*.

Emil Brunner writes *Divine Imperative*.

Alvin Plantinga, an American philosopher, is born.

Henri Nouwen (1932–1996), a Dutch Catholic priest and writer, is born.

1933 Dorothy Day establishes the Catholic Worker movement, a lay organization advocating nonviolence, voluntary poverty, aid for the poor. She serves as editor of the *Catholic Worker* newspaper.

In a Soviet collectivization drive and famine, seven million kulaks and others are killed—mainly Christians in the Ukraine.

The Shanghai Christian Broadcasting Association is organized (XMHD), covering the entire Far East. In 1935, XLKA (Peking) is formed.

The Sacred Congregation of Propaganda (Rome) begins *Bibliografia Missionaria*, a periodical that covers contemporary mission literature.

Dawson Trotman forms the Navigators in Southern California. It is a one-on-one discipling agency that specializes in memorization of the Bible and multiplication of believers.

1934 W. Cameron Townsend begins Wycliffe Bible Translators for Scripture translation by professional linguists with overseas work under the name of Summer Institute of Linguistics. In 1959 it adopts the slogan, "Two Thousand Tongues to Go."

The Theological Declaration of Barmen, issued by Karl Barth and other leaders in the German Confessing Church, defines the belief of the church in the face of threats from Nazi Germany.

Richard Granville Swinburne, an English theological philosopher, is born.

The Student Volunteer Missionary Union updates its watchword: "Evangelize to a Finish to Bring Back the King."

1935 Alexander Men (1935–1990), a Russian Orthodox priest, theologian, writer, and martyr, is born.

The term "Judeo-Christian tradition" is first used as a unifying slogan to rally Christians and Jews together for the aid of European Jews.

Pentecostal leader George Jeffreys begins the World Revival Crusade.

World Intercessors, the Prayer Circle of the Oriental Missionary Society, is begun as a worldwide prayer movement for evangelization.

Charles Harold Dodd writes *The Parables of the Kingdom*.

Virgilio Elizond, a Catholic priest and professor and the father of Hispanic theology, is born.

1936 J. Gresham Machen organizes the Orthodox Presbyterian Church, which distances itself from the modernism of the Presbyterian Church (USA).

The International General Assembly of Spiritualists forms in America.

The Student Foreign Missions Fellowship begins in the United States. It holds triennial mass conventions.

D. Elton Trueblood writes *The Essence of Spiritual Religion*.

1937　Evelyn Underhill writes *Worship*.

Kenneth Scott Latourette's seven-volume *A History of the Expansion of Christianity* is published between 1937 and 1945.

Italian invaders remove missionaries from Ethiopia, but widespread revival erupts among Protestant (Sudan Interior Mission) churches in the south.

Japan's largest indigenous Christian church, the Spirit of Jesus Church, is formed as a split from the Assemblies of God.

The second World Conference on Faith and Order is held in Edinburgh, Scotland.

The second World Conference on Life and Work is held in Oxford, England, under the banner, "Church, Community, and State."

Child Evangelism Fellowship is founded in Warrenton, Missouri.

Dietrich Bonhoeffer writes *The Cost of Discipleship* and *Letters and Papers from Prison*.

Frank C. Laubach writes *Letters by a Modern Mystic*.

Pius XI issues the encyclical *Mit Brennender Sorge* ("With the Deepest Anxiety") on the church and the German Reich.

Justo Luis González, a Methodist pastor and theologian, is born.

Edwin Masao Yamauchi, an American theologian, is born.

1938　Hendrik Kraemer writes *The Christian Message in a Non-Christian World*, a powerful statement of traditional views of mission.

The World Council of Churches is "in the process of formation," in Utrecht, Netherlands.

The fourth World Missionary Conference and the Meeting of the International Missionary Council are held in Tambaram, Madras, India, including 471 delegates from 69 countries.

George MacLeod and the clergy and laymen of the Church of Scotland form the Iona Community.

The American Home Bible League is founded in Chicago. It is later called the World Home Bible League and then Bible League International.

Amy Wilson Carmichael writes *If*.

Leonardo Bol, a Brazilian liberation theologian, is born.

Jon Sobrino, a Spanish Jesuit priest and liberation theologian, is born.

1939　David Tracy, an American Catholic theologian, is born.

The Methodist Episcopal Church, the Methodist Protestant Church, and the Methodist Episcopal Church, South unite into the Methodist Church.

Reinhold Niebuhr writes *The Nature and Destiny of Man*.

The Protestant international radio station PRA7 begins in Sao Paulo, Brazil.

Radio Vatican begins broadcasting in ten languages.

The first World Conference of Christian Youth is held in Amsterdam, Netherlands.

Worldwide Signs Following Evangelism is begun under United Fundamentalist Church.

Jim Rayburn begins Young Life, an interdenominational outreach to youth.

T.S. Eliot writes *The Idea of a Christian Society*.

1940 Roger Louis Schütz-Marsauche (Brother Roger) establishes the Taizé Community.

The Japanese government forces 33 diverse Protestant groups to unite, forming the United Church of Christ in Japan.

John Frum cargo cults begin on Tanna Island, New Hebrides, growing in strength with the arrival of US military personnel and their extensive material possessions.

The Evangelical Mission Council begins in Algeria.

The Soviet army conquers Estonia, Latvia, and Lithuania, and 200,000 people are deported to labor camps in Siberia. Most bishops, church leaders, and clergy are shot or deported. Between 1944 and 1953, 500,000 more are deported.

Stanley Hauerwas, an American theologian and professor at Duke University, is born.

1941 Emmaus Bible School is founded in Toronto, Canada. It is the first international organization to provide Bible correspondence courses.

The siege of Leningrad by the Nazis lasts 880 days. Of the 1.4 million people who are killed, about half are Christans.

The National Council of Churches in New Zealand is founded.

The Council for Evangelization and Revival is founded in Zürich, Switzerland.

The first Base Ecclesial Communities are formed in Brazil to promote grassroots evangelism among the poor.

Thomas R. Kelly writes *A Testament of Devotion*.

H. Richard Niebuhr writes *The Meaning of Revelation* and *The Nature and Destiny of Man*.

Colin Gunton (1941–2003), an English theologian and leader of the Trinitarian movement, is born.

1942 The Martyrs of New Guinea die after being betrayed to Japanese invaders.

Wycliffe Bible Translators and the Summer Institute of Linguistics takes its current dual structure as a Bible translation agency and a scientific and educational agency.

The British Council of Churches is founded.

Ling Liang Worldwide Evangelistic Mission Association is founded in Shanghai to send Chinese missionaries to the uttermost parts of the world.

The New Tribes Mission begins in the United States to evangelize primitive tribes around the world.

C.S. Lewis writes *The Screwtape Letters*.

Richard Foster, an American Quaker theologian and writer, is born.

Lloyd Douglas publishes *The Robe*, a novel about the Roman soldier at Jesus's crucifixion.

1943 Pope Pius XII issues the encyclical *Divino Affiant Spiritu* ("Inspired by the Divine Spirit"). It sanctions modern principles of exegesis for interpreting the Bible. He also issues *Mystici Corporis* ("The Mystical Body of Christ").

The National Association of Evangelicals is formed when 147 people meet in Saint Louis.

The worker-priest movement begins in France but dissolves in 1959.

In Britain, Methodists lead the Christian Commando Campaigns from 1943 to 1947.

The National Religious Broadcasters of North America is formed as official broadcasting arm of the National Association of Evangelicals.

The Global Outreach Mission is founded in Buffalo.

The Conservative Baptist Foreign Mission Society is formed in Wheaton, Illinois.

Chiara Lubich founds Focolare, a movement of small communites that promote peace and unity.

1944 Ronald Knox's translation of the Latin Vulgate is published.

Torrey Johnson and Billy Graham found Youth for Christ International, an evangelism organization focusing on young people. The first Youth for Christ rally is held in Brantford, Ontario, under the leadership of Paul Guinness.

The Canadian Council of Churches is founded.

1945 Gerrit Verkuyl is editor in chief of a new translation of the New Testament, Zondervan's New Berkeley Version in Modern English. In 1959, the entire Bible is published as the Modern Language Bible.

The Nag Hammadi library, a collection of 13 Coptic papyrus codices from the first and second centuries, is found near Nag Hammadi, Egypt. The collection contains a manuscript of *The Gospel of Truth* and other Gnostic writings. It sheds new light on the diversity of early Christianity.

The United Pentecostal Church is formed through the merger of the Pentecostal Assemblies of Jesus Christ and the Pentecostal Church, Inc. It is a "oneness" church, baptizing only in the name of Jesus. It also has a demanding code of behavior.

Dietrich Bonhoeffer, a German Lutheran pastor and writer, is executed by the Nazis.

Mission Aviation Fellowship is founded to provide air transportation for missionaries working in remote areas.

The Evangelical Foreign Missions Association is formed as an association of Evangelical missions organizations.

The Church of England publishes the archbishops' report, *Towards the Conversion of England.*

1946 The American Standard Version is produced by 52 American scholars.

Frances Xavier Cabrini becomes the first American citizen to be declared a saint.

The first Urbana Student Missions Convention is held to foster an interest in Evangelical foreign missions among college and university students.

The African Orthodox Church (an independent Kenyan body) is accepted into communion by the Greek Orthodox patriarchate of Alexandria.

The Australian Council of Churches begins.

The Revised Standard Version of the New Testament is published in America. It is commissioned by the International Council of Religious Education. The Old Testament is completed in 1952.

The international radio station IKOR begins broadcasting in the Netherlands.

The Conference of Bible Societies at Haywards Heath in the United Kingdom creates the United Bible Societies (UBS) as a federation and fellowship of 13 autonomous Bible societies from Europe and North America.

The World Literature Crusade begins in Canada for radio outreach and expands into systematic tract distribution through Every Home Crusades.

Egede Institute of Missionary Study and Research is founded in Oslo to promote scholarly research in missiology.

Association Misionera Evangelica Nacional (AMEN, or the National Evangelical Missionary Association) begins as a home mission movement in Peru.

Emil Brunner writes *Dogmatics*, volume 1: *The Christian Doctrine of God*. Volume 2 follows in 1950 and volume 3 in 1960.

1947   Fuller Theological Seminary is founded in Pasadena, California. John Ockenga becomes its first president, establishing himself as one of the leaders of the New Evangelical movement.

The Oral Roberts Evangelistic Association begins a revival ministry founded on healing and Pentecostal gifts of the spirit. It becomes one of the most successful and lucrative independent ministries of the post-WWII period. It includes a foreign missions program.

The German Evangelical Lutheran Synod of Missouri, Ohio, and Other States changes its name to the Lutheran Church–Missouri Synod.

The Nobel Peace Prize is awarded to the British and Irish Friends Service Council and the American Friends Service Committee.

Carl F.H. Henry writes *The Uneasy Conscience of Modern Fundamentalism*.

The Dead Sea Scrolls are discovered by two Bedouin shepherd boys looking for a stray animal on the cliffs near Qumran and the Dead Sea.

The fifth meeting of the International Missionary Council at Whitby, Toronto, Canada, includes 112 delegates from 40 countries.

The World Council of Churches (still in formation) sponsors the Conference on Evangelism in Geneva, Switzerland.

The Church of South India is inaugurated by the merger of Methodists and Anglicans with Reformed and Congregationalist bodies.

The second World Conference of Christian Youth is held in Oslo, Norway.

Southern Baptist evangelist Billy Graham begins his global ministry. By 1976, he has preached face-to-face to more than 50 million people in 229 crusades with a million and a half inquirers.

The Lutheran World Federation is founded. Its first assembly is at Lund, Sweden. Two years later it forms the LWF Commission on World Missions.

The first Pentecostal World Conference is held in Zürich, Switzerland, including 100 people from 20 countries.

Andrew Gih begins the Evangelize China Fellowship in Shanghai.
The World Revival Prayer League is founded in Japan.

1948   The last edition of the *Index of Forbidden Books* is issued.

Thomas Merton writes *The Seven Storey Mountain*.

The World Council of Churches is officially formed after a delay of
   seven years caused by World War II. The first assembly of the World
   Council of Churches is held in Amsterdam and includes 147 church
   familes from 44 countries, 351 delegates, and 238 alternates. Its
   theme is "Man's Disorder and God's Design."

Radio Vatican broadcasts in 19 languages.

The Byzantine-Rite Uniate Catholic Church of Romania is declared dissolved by a few priests, who rejoin the Romanian Orthodox Church.

The eighth Lambeth Conference includes 329 bishops.

International radio stations begin in the Philippines (FEBC) and Costa
   Rica (TIFC).

Far East Broadcasting, an American corporation, opens radio DZAS in
   the Philippines.

Youth for Christ International convenes the first World Congress on
   World Evangelization at Beatenberg, Switzerland. It is led by Billy
   Graham.

The International Council of Christian Churches is founded as an anti-
   ecumenical and fundamentalist alternative to the World Council of
   Churches.

Christian Crusade magazine (published by Christian Echoes National
   Ministry) begins in Tulsa, Oklahoma. In 1953 it creates a plan to send
   one million Scripture portions in hydrogen-filled balloons into Eastern Europe.

Rudolf Bultmann writes *Theology of the New Testament*.

A.W. Tozer writes *The Pursuit of God*.

1949   Dietrich Bonhoeffer writes *Ethics*.

Thomas Merton writes *Seeds of Contemplation*.

Fulton J. Sheen writes *Peace of Soul*.

Reinhold Niebuhr writes *Faith and History*.

Howard Thurman writes *Jesus and the Disinherited*.

The T.L. Osborn Evangelistic Association, later called T.L. Osborn Ministries International, is founded for mass evangelism, utilizing native
   workers.

World Gospel Crusades is founded for mass evangelization through
   print and broadcast media.

Survey Application Trust produces the first *World Christian Handbook*, edited by Kenneth Grubb, with church membership statistics by denomination for every country.

Cursillos de Cristianidad is begun in Spain by Bishop J. Hervas as a crash course on Christianity, including three-day retreats. The movement spreads to Latin America, the United States, and Britain.

The second Pentecostal World Conference is held in Paris.

The World Council of Churches publishes *The Evangelization of Man in Modern Mass Society*, a study of surveys done in Ceylon, Finland, France, Germany, Holland, India, Latin America, Scotland, and America.

The Burma Christian Council is formed.

After the Communist victory, China expels foreign missionaries—5496 Catholics, 3745 Protestants, and 198 Anglicans—over the next three years.

Billy Graham holds his first major crusade in Los Angeles, with 441,000 attenders and 5700 inquirers.

The Japanese Evangelical Missionary Society is formed in America and Tokyo to send Japanese abroad.

Kirchentag begins in Germany as an annual evangelistic mass event.

Organized churches are present in all the countries of the world except Afghanistan, Saudi Arabia, and Tibet.

The first Latin American Evangelical Conference convenes in Buenos Aires, Argentina.

1950 Pope Pius XII issues *Humani Generis* ("The Human Race"). It includes a nuanced response to evolution.

The Billy Graham Evangelistic Center is formed.

The Evangelical Free Church of America is formed from the merger of the Evangelical Free Church of America (Swedish) and the Evangelical Free Church Association (Danish and Norwegian).

The National Council of Churches is formed.

Pope Pius XII defines the Assumption of the Blessed Virgin Mary—the doctrine that Mary was taken, body and soul, into heaven at the end of her earthly life.

Mother Teresa founds the Missionaries of Charity. Originally under the auspices of the archdiocese of Calcutta, it is later recognized as a pontifical congregation under the jurisdiction of Rome. Members take a fourth vow, pledging service to the poor. Within the next 45 years, the order spreads to 80 countries.

In Hungary, 53 Catholic religious orders and congregations are forcibly dissolved.

"Guiana for God," a one-year evangelistic campaign in British Guiana promoted by the Christian Council, includes Roman Catholic, Protestant, and Anglican workers.

The first assembly of the World Council of Christian Education and Sunday School Association is held in Toronto, Canada.

The Haiti Inland Mission sponsors the Haiti Great Commission Crusades—ten crusades from 1950 to 1960.

Help Open Paths to Evangelize (HOPE) is founded.

Bob Pierce forms World Vision. By 2000 it becomes one of the largest philanthropic organizations in the world, working in more than 90 countries and effectively using computers and new technology.

The Baptist Bible Fellowship International is founded.

Worldwide Missions International begins in Nigeria.

Paul Ramsey writes *Basic Christian Ethics*.

Simone Weil writes *Waiting for God*.

1951

Paul Tillich completes the first volume of his *Systematic Theology*. He completes the three-volume work in 1963.

An archeological dig at the ruins of Qumran uncover an ancient Essene monastery. The ruins date from three periods: the seventh and eighth century BC, 135–31 BC, and 1 BC to AD 68.

Bill Bright begins Campus Crusade for Christ International at the University of California–Los Angeles.

The first International Patristic Conference is held.

The World Evangelical Fellowship is formed at Zeist, Netherlands.

T.Y. Wu initiates the Three-Self Patriotic Movement in China to encourage self-governance, self-support, and self-propagation in churches and to assure the government that the churches would be patriotic.

The Evangelical Alliance of Costa Rica is formed.

Methodist churches in Cuba conduct a two-week campaign called "Cuba for Christ." More than 2000 people make first-time decisions for Christ.

The first World Congress of the Lay Apostolate aims to mobilize all Catholics to reach the lost.

Hans Urs von Balthasar writes *Anxiety and the Christian*.

Thomas Merton writes *Ascent to Truth*.

H. Richard Niebuhr writes *Christ and Culture*.

Salvador Dali paints *Christ of Saint John of the Cross*.

Henri Matisse's Chapel of the Rosary is consecrated in Venice, France.

1952 The Full Gospel Businessmen's Fellowship International is founded by
dairy magnate Demos Shakarian in Los Angeles.

The International Missionary Council meets in Willingen, Netherlands.

Charles K. Williams publishes the New Testament: A New Translation
in Plain English.

The third World Conference of Christian Youth is held at Travancore,
India.

The third World Conference on Faith and Order is held at Lund,
Sweden.

The Sixth Meeting of International Missionary Council is held at Willingen, Germany, with 190 delegates.

The third Pentecostal World Conference convenes in London.

W.E. Allen launches the Worldwide Revival Movement in Ireland.

The Billy Graham Evangelistic Association founds World Wide Pictures
to make Christian motion pictures.

Norman Vincent Peale writes *The Power of Positive Thinking*.

1953 The Worldwide Evangelization Crusade begins work in Java, Indonesia,
and founds the Batu Bible School.

The World Committee for Christian Broadcasting is founded. In 1968,
it becomes the World Association for Christian Communication.

The Jesus Family, an indigenous Pentecostal movement in China begun
1927, is virtually obliterated by Communists.

1954 The second Assembly of the World Council of Churches meets in Evan-
ston, Illinois, under the heading "Christ the Hope of the World" with
502 delegates.

The fifth Kirchentag is held in Lepizig (East Germany), drawing
650,000 people for the closing rally.

International radio stations begin in the Paynesville area east of central
Monrovia (ELWA) and Tangier, Morocco (TWR).

The World Conference on Missionary Radio is formed in America.

J. Raymond Knighton begins Medical Assistance Programs International in Chicago as an interdenominational Evangelical service
agency providing medical assistance. MAP International moves to
Georgia in 1985.

World Missionary Evangelism begins as a nondenominational service
agency in Dallas, Texas.

The New Life League World Missionary Society begins in Waco, Texas.

Pope Pius XII dissolves the worker-priest movement.

1955   Francis August Schaeffer founds L'Abri, a study center in the Swiss Alps
where he offers a Christian critique of modern culture.

Radio IBRA is established by Swedish Pentecostals and begins broadcasting in Tangier in 20 languages.

The fourth Pentecostal World Conference is held in Stockholm, Sweden.

Midnight Call Missionary Work is founded in Zurich, Switzerland.

Pierre Teilhard de Chardin writes *The Phenomenon of Man*.

Billy Graham writes *The Secret of Happiness*.

Max Lucado, an American pastor and writer, is born.

Le Corbusier's Notre Dame du Haut is completed in Ronchamp,
France.

1956   The Presbyterian Church begins to ordain women.

The Methodist Church grants women full clergy rights.

Jim Elliot is martyred while serving as a missionary to the Aucas of
Ecuador.

The Charismatic (neo-Pentecostal) renewal begins among Episcopal
and Protestant churches and then becomes part of a worldwide
movement.

Belgian Charismatic cardinal Léon Suenens publishes *The Gospel to
Every Creature* on evangelism.

Hans Urs von Balthasar writes *Science, Religion and Christianity*.

Henri de Lubac writes *The Discovery of God*.

1957   Scott Walker Hahn, an American Catholic scholar, is born.

The Congregational Christian Church merges with the the Evangelical
and Reformed Church to form the United Church of Christ.

The National Patriotic Catholic Association is formed in China. It
opposes the Vatican.

The Conference of European Churches is formed at Liselund, Denmark.

The Conference of World Confessional Families is founded.

The East Asia Christian Conference is founded at Parapat, Sumatra, in
western Indonesia.

The Assemblies of God unveils the Global Conquest program "for the
rapid evangelization of the world." In 1967 its name is changed to the
Good News Crusades.

Anglican clergyman G.S. Ingram launches the Nights of Prayer for
Worldwide Renewal.

Send the Light (later Operation Mobilization) is founded as an interdenominational youth agency sending short-term missionary workers.

Pierre Teilhard de Chardin writes *The Divine Milieu*.

Martin Cyril D'Arcy writes *The Meeting of Love and Knowledge*.
Bernard J.F. Lonergan writes *Insight: A Study of Human Understanding*.
Watchman Nee writes *The Normal Christian Life*.
Karl Rahner writes *On the Theology of Death*.

1958 The International Missionary Council meets in Ghana.

The Amplified Bible is published.

J.B. Phillips, a vicar of the Church of England, completes The New Testament in Modern English, revising and republishing it in 1961 and 1972. It is a lively and idiomatic translation that at times approaches paraphrase.

The Lutheran Church founds the Congregation of the Servants of Christ, a distinctly Lutheran monastic order, in Michigan.

The fifth Pentecostal World Conference is held in Toronto, Canada.

The Federation of Evangelical Churches in Argentina (FAIE) is founded.

Abuna Basilios becomes the first Ethiopian-born patriarch of the Ethiopian Orthodox Church.

The Charismatic (neo-Pentecostal) renewal spreads to Brazil among Baptist pastors.

The ninth Lambeth Conference is attended by 310 bishops.

The final assembly of the International Missionary Council in Accra, Ghana, draws 215 delegates.

The Theological Education Fund is established in Ghana.

The first All-African Christian Conference is held at Ibadan, Nigeria.

In New York City, 253,922 people attend the Jehovah's Witnesses "Divine Will" international convention, and 7136 people are baptized.

The Christian Peace movement begins in Prague.

Elisabeth Elliot writes *Shadow of the Almighty: The Life and Testament of Jim Elliot*.

1959 The Persecution of Russian churches continues under the Krushchev regime until 1964.

The first assembly of the Conference of European Churches is held in Nyborg, Denmark.

Southern Baptists develop a long-term emphasis on "Sharing Christ Around the World" and approve its slogan, "Bold Mission."

The first nationwide Evangelism in Depth campaign is organized in Nicaragua. Later it spreads to Latin America and Japan and becomes incorporated into evangelization strategies.

1960 David R. Wilkerson, a Pentecostal minister, founds Teen Challenge, a ministry to inner-city young people, especially gang members. He writes the story two years later in *The Cross and the Switchblade*, which is made into a movie in 1970.

The archbishop of Canterbury, Geoffrey Francis Fisher, visits Pope John XXIII. He receives the first formal reception of any archbishop of Canterbury since the Reformation.

At the International Foreign Missions Association Congress on World Mission in Chicago, conservative Evangelicals reaffirm "The Evangelization of the World in this Generation."

Pope John XXIII establishes the Secretariat for Christian Unity in preparation for the Second Vatican Council.

The Congress on World Missions meets in Chicago.

Baptist International Missions is founded.

Loren Cunningham begins Youth With a Mission, an Evangelical-Charismatic sending agency. In 20 years it becomes the world's largest evangelistic agency.

1961 The New World Translation of the Holy Scriptures by Nathan H. Knorr and Frederick W. Franz is published by the Watch Tower Bible and Tract Society.

The World Council of Churches and the International Missionary Council meet in New Delhi. The Russian Orthodox Church joins the World Council of Churches.

The New English Bible is published. In 1989 it is significantly revised and republished as the Revised English Bible.

The first English-speaking Cursillo, a Roman Catholic spiritual growth movement, is held.

The American Unitarian Association merges with the Universalist Church of America to form the Unitarian Universalist Association.

The International Missionary Council merges with the World Council of Churches.

Hans Küng writes *The Council, Reform and Reunion*.

The third assembly of the World Council of Churches convenes in New Delhi, India. It absorbs the International Missionary Council to form the Division of World Mission and Evangelism. The Division launches the Joint Action for Mission but meets resistance from confessional and institutional structures of churches and missionary agencies.

The second Latin American Evangelical Conference meets in Lima, Peru.

The World Radio Missionary Fellowship inaugurates HCJB-TV (Quito, Ecuador), a pioneer missionary telecaster.

The sixth Pentecostal World Conference is held in Jerusalem.

World Missionary Press is founded in New Paris, Indiana.

The first Christian television station is opened in Virginia Beach, Virginia, by M.G. "Pat" Robertson.

The sixth International Student Missionary Convention meets in Urbana, Illinois.

1962 The Second Vatican Council (the Twenty-First Ecumenical Council) convenes.

- It officially restores the catechumenate.
- It increases lay participation in the Mass.
- It approves vernacular liturgy. Latin is no longer the sole language of liturgy in the Roman Catholic Church.
- It revises the Breviary and changes its name to Liturgy of the Hours.
- It declares that Mary "participates in the mediation of Christ in a unique and singular manner."

Six Soviet churches join the World Council of Churches (1962–1965).

The Haggai Institute for Advanced Leadership Training begins courses in Singapore to train missionary leaders from the Third World.

New Life for All, a ten-year evangelistic campaign, begins in Nigeria. It later spreads to other African countries.

Thomas Merton writes *New Seeds of Contemplation*.

George Huntston Williams writes *The Radical Reformation*.

Coventry Cathedral in West Midlands, England, is consecrated. It includes *Christ in Glory*, a tapestry by Graham Sutherland, and the sculpture *Saint Michael's Victory over the Devil* by Jacob Epstein.

1963 The Commission of World Mission and Evangelism meets in Mexico City.

The New Testament of the New American Standard Bible is published. The Old Testament is added in 1971.

The Roman Catholic Church approves the practice of cremation.

The second meeting of the Commission on World Mission and Evangelism is held in Mexico City.

The Lutheran World Federation opens RVOG (Radio Voice of the Gospel) in Addis Ababa, Ethiopia.

The fourth World Conference on Faith and Order is held in Montreal, Canada.

The All Africa Conference of Churches (AACC) begins in Kampala, Uganda.

American Evangelicals form the International Christian Broadcasters.

Missiologist Donald McGavran begins *Church Growth Bulletin*, renamed in 1979 as *Global Church Growth*.

Evangelical Missions Quarterly is founded.

Markings, Dag Hammarskjöld's 36-year diary, is published two years after his death.

Martin Luther King Jr. writes *Strength to Love*.

C.S. Lewis writes *Letters to Malcolm: Chiefly on Prayer*.

Kallistos Ware writes *The Orthodox Church*.

John L. Sherrill writes *They Speak with Other Tongues*.

1964 The seventh Pentecostal World Conference is held in Helsinki, Finland.

The Provisional Commission for Latin American Evangelical Unity is founded at Montevideo, Uruguay.

The pope begins international travel, visiting the Holy Land and Bombay (1964), New York City and the United Nations (1965), Fatima, Constantinople, and Ephesus (1967), Bogotá (1968), Geneva and Kampala (1969), and the Far East and Australia (1970).

Pope Paul VI and Athenagoras I of Constantinople meet in Jerusalem. It is the first meeting of a pope and an ecumenical patriarch in 900 years.

Pope Paul VI forms a Secretariat for Non-Christians, later renamed the Pontifical Council for Interreligious Dialogue. The next year, he creates a new Secretariat (later a Pontifical Council) for Dialogue with Non-Believers.

Egyptian bishop Antonios the Syrian (later Pope Shenouda III of the Coptic Orthodox Church of Alexandria) begins the evangelistic newspaper *Al Keraza* (*Spreading of the Word*).

The Fiji Council of Churches is founded.

TWR (Trans World Radio) opens a transmitter on the island of Bonaire, becoming the first superpower missionary radio station.

1965 The Roman Catholic Congregation of Rites permits the laity to receive the cup at Communion. Communion by intinction (dipping the consecrated bread into the consecrated wine before consuming it) is also permitted.

Mutual excommunications between the Eastern and Western churches are canceled by Pope Paul VI and Ecumenical patriarch Athenagoras I.

Pope Paul VI issues *Nostra Aetate* ("In Our Times"). Section 4 of this Vatican II document acknowledges Judaism's place in Christianity's spiritual foundations and denounces anti-Semitism. In *Mysterium Fidei* ("The Mystery of Faith"), Pope Paul VI reasserts the doctrine of transubstantiation.

The Oriental Orthodox Churches Conference in Addis Ababa is the first conference of heads of the Armenian, Coptic, Ethiopian, and Syrian churches.

The Division of World Mission and Evangelism holds a consultation at Yaoundé, Cameroon. "The Evangelization of West Africa Today" is preceded by a four-month survey.

Mass revivals begin in Indonesia, producing 2.5 million Protestant and Catholic converts within 15 years.

Universities Mission to Central Africa and Society for Propagation of the Gospel in Foreign Parts merge to form United Society for the Propagation of the Gospel.

1966 Robert Bratcher completes Good News for Modern Man: The New Testament in Today's English Version. He is the editor of the Old Testament in 1976, which is called Good News Bible: The Bible in Today's English Version. It is revised with inclusive language in 1992.

The (Catholic) Jerusalem Bible is released.

The Roman Catholic Church announces that no new editions of the *Index of Prohibited Books* will be published. Existing editions are declared to be no longer binding. The penalty of excommunication for reading listed books is lifted.

Official Roman Catholic observers attend the third assembly of the World Council of Churches.

The National Association of Evangelicals of Bolivia (ANDEB) is formed.

The Christian Council of Botswana begins.

The Evangelical Congress on the Church's Worldwide Mission meets in Wheaton, Illinois.

Burma expels 250 Protestant and Anglican foreign missionaries.

The two-year "Christ for All" national campaign in Zaire begins.

The World Congress on Evangelism meets in Berlin under the banner "One race, one gospel, one task." It is attended by 1200 delegates from 100 countries.

In the Great Proletarian Cultural Revolution in China , more than 11 million Red Guards suppress all churches and temples, destroying churches and Scriptures.

The total elimination of religion begins in Albania as the world's first atheist state.

The World Conference on Church and Society meets in Geneva, considering "Christians in the technical and social revolutions of our time."

The first Assembly of Pacific Conference of Churches meets in Lifou, Loyalty Islands province, New Caledonia.

The Evangelical Congress on the Church's Worldwide Mission meets in

Wheaton, Illinois, and signs the Wheaton Declaration, "covenanting together for the evangelization of the world in this generation."

The World Congress on Evangelism is held in Berlin.

World Vision founds Missions Advanced Research and Communication Center as a research and publication agency, using the tools of technology for advancing the gospel.

Shūsaku Endō writes *Silence*.

Agnes White Sanford writes *Healing Gifts of the Spirit*.

1967 The Catholic Charismatic Renewal movement begins at Duquesne University in Pittsburgh.

The Roman Catholic Church simplifies the indulgence system. Occasions for obtaining indulgences are limited, and time equivalents are dropped.

The Far East Broadcasting Associates (from the United Kingdom) open FEBA in Seychelles, a 155-island nation in the Indian Ocean.

The Macedonian Orthodox Church unilaterally declares full independence from the Serbian Orthodox Church.

The Sacred Congregation of Propaganda (Rome) is renamed the Sacred Congregation for the Evangelization of Peoples.

Guinea expels foreign missionaries except for 26 from the Christian Missionary Alliance.

The International Congress on Religion, Architecture, and the Visual Arts meets in New York.

The first Synod of Bishops meets in Rome, addressing dangers to the faith, canon law, and liturgy.

The eighth Pentecostal World Conference is held in Rio de Janeiro, Brazil.

The Solomon Islands Christian Association is founded.

The International Correspondence Institute is founded by the Assemblies of God, offering Bible courses by mail.

Millions attend the Crusade for World Revival in Seoul, Korea.

Pope Paul VI issues *Populorum Progressio* ("On the Development of Peoples"), stressing that the economy of the world should serve mankind and not just the few.

1968 Pope Paul VI issues *Humanae Vitae* ("On Human Life"), condemning all forms of birth control except the rhythm method.

The Wesleyan Methodist Church and the Pilgrim Holiness Church unite to form the Wesleyan Church, a Holiness denomination with Methodist roots.

The fourth assembly of the World Council of Churches is held in Uppsala, Sweden.

The Jesus movement, a youth-oriented Christian counterculture movement, begins. Members refer to themselves as "Jesus people" or "Jesus freaks."

The Roman Catholic second general conference of CELAM (the Latin American Episcopal Council) is held at Medellin, Colombia.

The tenth Lambeth Conference is the first not to take place in Lambeth Palace (because it could not accommodate the 459 Anglican bishops). Meetings are held at Church House, Westminister.

Major schisms occur in Pakistan among Presbyterians, Methodists, and Anglicans, influenced by the International Communion of Charismatic Churches.

The fourth assembly of the World Council of Churches is held in Uppsala, Sweden, under the banner "Behold, I make all things new." Its attendance is 2741, including 704 delegates and 750 press.

The West African Congress on Evangelism is held at the University of Ibadan, Nigeria.

The Southeast Asia/South Pacific Congress on Evangelism meets in Singapore and includes 1100 delegates from 24 nations.

1969 William Barclay publishes his New Testament commentaries, which include his own translation. The 17-volume series is later fully updated and republished as the New Daily Study Bible series.

The Association of Evangelical Lutheran Churches is formed.

The Anglican state church is disestablished in Barbados.

The third Latin American Evangelical Conference (CELA III) is held in Buenos Aires, Argentina.

Jehovah's Witnesses hold a series of five-day "Peace on Earth International Assemblies" in 13 cities around the world with 840,572 attenders.

Pope Paul VI becomes the first pope to visit the World Council of Churches in Geneva.

The first Latin American Congress on Evangelism (CLADE I) is held in Bogota, Colombia, proclaiming "Action in Christ for a Continent in Crisis." It is attended by 920 delegates from 25 countries.

The second assembly of the All Africa Conference of Churches is held in Abidjan, Ivory Coast.

More than 5000 delegates attend the first American Congress on Evangelism in Minneapolis with the theme "Much Is Given—Much Is Required."

African independent church movements now include more than 5800 denominations. They have 17 million adherents and are growing by 960,000 each year.

Pope Paul VI visits Kampala, Uganda, and canonizes 22 Catholic martyrs in Namugongo.

An extraordinary Synod of Bishops in Rome establishes relations between the Holy See and Episcopal Conferences.

A National Congress on Evangelism is held in Kinshasa, Congo.

Pentecostal evangelist Jimmy Swaggart launches his radio ministry, *Camp Meeting Hour*, followed three years later by a television ministry, following God's directive to carry out the Great Commission by means of radio and television. Twenty years later the ministry collapses because of a sex scandal.

The World Evangelism Foundation is founded in Texas by Baptist missionaries to promote partnership evangelism.

1970 The New American Bible is the first Roman Catholic translation directly from Hebrew (Old Testament) and Greek (New Testament) into modern English. Its translators referred neither to previous translations nor to the Latin.

Pope Paul VI makes Teresa of Avila and Catherine of Siena doctors of the church. They are the first women to be so named.

Altar rails are no longer required in Roman Catholic churches.

The World Alliance of Reformed Churches is formed in Nairobi, Kenya. Its purpose is to create harmony among Reformed, Presbyterian, and Congregationalist churches, to discuss theological issues, and to do relief work.

The shepherding movement begins, mainly in Charismatic churches. It emphasizes spiritual guidance for every member of a congregation through a hierarchy of elders. Christian Growth Ministries is one of the key organizations.

The Lutheran Church begins to ordain women.

The Billy Graham Center is founded on the Wheaton College Graduate School campus to collect and archive information about missions and evangelism.

Roman Catholic priests worldwide are no longer required to wear the tonsure (cap). For some time, the custom has not been required in the United States, England, or other places where it is not a recognized symbol of priesthood.

The Church of Pakistan is founded.

The Pontifical Commission for the Pastoral Care of Migrants and Tourists is formed in the Vatican.

Thailand holds its first Congress on Evangelism east of Bangkok.

The Church of North India is inaugurated through the merger of Anglican, Baptist, Brethren, Disciples of Christ, Methodist, and United churches.

The Orthodox Church in America is granted autocephalous (independent) status by the Moscow patriarchate.

The World Council of Churches allocates its first grants to 19 antiracist organizations throughout the world for humanitarian work.

Sodoin Dendo (total saturation evangelism) mass campaigns begin in various areas of Japan.

The Federation of Protestant Churches and Missions in Cameroon is formed.

The All India Congress on Evangelism meets in Deolali, Maharashtra, India.

The Euro '70 Crusade is largest evangelistic campaign in Europe, using radio and TV. Attendance reaches 839,000.

The All Philippines Congress on Evangelism meets in Cainta, Rizal, Philippines.

Fourteen conservative Evangelical German Lutheran theologians promulgate the Frankfurt Declaration on Mission.

The Canadian Congress on Evangelism meets in Ottawa.

The first World Conference on Religion and Peace is held in Kyoto, Japan, with 1600 delegates from 22 world religions.

The ninth Pentecostal World Conference is held in Dallas, Texas.

The circulation of subsidized Scriptures doubles from 80 million worldwide in 1966 to 173 million in 1970.

The Oberammergau Passion Play draws 530,000 attenders in Bavaria. It has been repeated every ten years since 1634.

From Samoa, Pope Paul VI sends out his Missionary Message to the World, urging the spread of the gospel.

Hal Lindsay's *The Late Great Planet Earth* inspires widespread interest in eschatology and conversions among its ten million readers.

The evangelistic ship *Logos* begins missionary voyages, visiting large ports with books and other evangelistic tools. In 1988 the ship is lost at sea. In 1977 its sister ship, *Doulos*, joins the endeavor.

Anthony Bloom writes *Beginning to Pray*.

Jacques Ellul writes *Prayer and Modern Man*.

1971   The Living Bible, Kenneth Taylor's paraphrase of the Scriptures, is published with its distinctive green padded cover. It began with Living Letters in 1962. The New Testament was completed in 1967.

Pimen I becomes patriarch of the Russian Orthodox Church.

Jesus Christ, Superstar, a play by Andrew Lloyd Weber and Tim Rice, opens on Broadway in New York.

The vernacular Mass becomes obligatory in the Roman Catholic Church by direction of Pope Paul VI.

A Congress on Evangelism is held in Taipei, Taiwan.

The second Synod of Bishops in Rome addresses the priesthood and justice in the modern world.

Zaire (now the Democratic Republic of the Congo) officially recognizes three churches—the Roman Catholic Church, the Church of Jesus Christ on Earth, and the Evangelical Church in Zambia. (The Greek Orthodox Church is added in 1972.) More than 500 indigenous churches are deprived of legal recognition.

The European Congress on Evangelism in Amsterdam includes 1064 participants from 36 European nations.

The first Ecumenical Pentecostal Meeting is held in Augsburg, Germany, for Catholics and Protestants.

The World Assembly of the World Council of Christian Education meets in Lima, Peru.

The Roman Catholic Church holds an international catechetical congress in Rome.

The World Evangelization Strategy Consultation meets in White Sulphur Springs, Georgia.

Corrie ten Boom writes *The Hiding Place.*

1972 The World Council of Christian Education is integrated into the World Council of Churches.

The World Conference of the Commission on World Mission and Evangelism is held in Bangkok, Thailand, under the banner "Salvation Today."

Ireland abolishes the "special position" of the Catholic Church.

The three-volume history of Catholic Missions, *Sacrae Congregationis de Propaganda Fide Memoria Rerum,* is published, spanning from 1622 to 1972.

Explo '72, the first Campus Crusade for Christ Training Congress on Evangelism, is held in Dallas, Texas. Daily attendance is 80,000 during the week and 200,000 for the final day.

The International Catholic Charismatic Renewal Office is founded in Ann Arbor, Michigan.

Josh McDowell writes *Evidence That Demands a Verdict.*

1973 The New International Version New Testament is published. The Old

Testament is added in 1978. The version undergoes a minor revision in 1984 and an update in 2011.

Gustavo Gutierrez writes *A Theology of Liberation*.

Jews for Jesus is incorporated by Moishe Rosen as an evangelical mission to Jews.

The Conservative Presbyterian Church in America splits from the Presbyterian Church in the United States (Southern Presbyterians) over biblical authority, women's ordinations, and potential union with the Northern Presbyterians.

Lutheran and Reformed churches adopt a concord at Leuenberg, Switzerland. They move toward agreement on Christology, predestination, the Eucharist, and justification. Several Methodist churches have since joined the concord.

The third Latin American Catholic Charismatic Leaders Conference includes 250 delegates from 25 countries. It is held in Aguas Buenas, Puerto Rico.

The Caribbean Conference of Churches is founded in Kingston, Jamaica.

Uganda bans 28 Christian denominations, resulting in some coming under the wing of the Anglican Church. Others go underground.

The Key '73 evangelistic campaign covers America.

Finland holds a congress on evangelism.

SPRE-E '73 youth rallies are held at Earl's Court in the United Kingdom.

At the largest preaching service in history, 1.1 million people hear Billy Graham in Seoul, Korea, during one of the five days of the crusade.

The All Asia Mission Consultation is held in Seoul, Korea.

The tenth Pentecostal World Conference is held in Seoul, Korea, under the banner "Anointed to Preach."

The tenth InterVarsity Missionary Convention in Chicago is called Urbana '73. Attendance is 17,000.

The Presbyterian Church launches Mission to the World.

The first annual Summer Institute of World Mission is held in Seoul, Korea.

Global Missionary Evangelism is begun in Pensacola, Florida.

Paul and Jan Crouch launch the Trinity Broadcasting Network in Southern California as a Pentecostal television station "to get the gospel to every living human being on planet Earth."

The World Film Crusade is founded in Florida.

1974   The first International Congress on World Evangelism in Lausanne,

Switzerland, is attended by 2700 representatives of 150 countries. The steering committee was headed by Billy Graham. The Lausanne Covenant was drafted by a committee headed by John Stott. By 1980, the congress develops into the Lausanne Movement, directed by the Lausanne Committee for World Evangelization.

Jim Bakker, a South Carolina evangelist, founds the PTL (Praise the Lord) television ministry.

The first Vineyard church begins when Ken Gulliksen brings together two small Bible studies in Los Angeles. In 1977 Gulliksen turned over the leadership of the Vinyard churchs to John Wimber.

The *Graduale Romanum*, the official Vatican collection of chant melodies, is revised in response to the changes mandated by the Second Vatican Council.

The first plenary assembly of the Federation of Asian Bishops' Conferences is held in Taipei with the theme "Evangelization in Modern-Day Asia."

The third assembly of the All Africa Conference of Churches is held in Lusaka, Zambia, proclaiming, "Living No Longer for Ourselves, but for Christ."

The first Japanese Congress on Evangelism is held in Kyoto.

The first Iberian Congress on Evangelism is held in Madrid, Spain.

The second Training Congress on Evangelism (Campus Crusade for Christ) in Seoul, Korea, is called Explo '74. Attendance includes 323,419 residents for one week, with evening meetings reaching 800,000 daily. One rally draws a new world record of 1.5 million people. It is the biggest Christian conference in history.

The third Synod of Bishops in Rome meets with the theme "The Evangelization of the Modern World."

The Discipline a Whole Nation (DAWN) Conference in the Philippines plans for seven million more churches by 2000.

The Presbyterian Order for World Evangelism begins in Pasadena, California, as a support agency.

E. Glenn Hinson writes *A Serious Call to a Contemplative Lifestyle*.

Annie Dillard writes *Pilgrim at Tinker Creek*.

1975   The General Synod of the Anglican Church finds the ordination of women to be theologically unobjectionable.

The first American-born saint, Elizabeth Ann Bayley Seton, is canonized.

The fifth assembly of the World Council of Churches is held in Nairobi. Its theme is "Jesus Christ Frees and Unites."

The Asia Missions Association forms in Seoul, Korea, and promulgates the Seoul Declaration on Christian Mission.

Pope Paul VI's *Evangelii Nuntiandi* ("Evangelization in the Modern World") becomes the major Catholic statement on evangelization.

Luis Palau reaches 75 million Latin Americans on radio and TV in a three-week mission in Nicaragua.

Foreign missionaries are expelled from Cambodia and later from Vietnam.

A Brazilian congress on evangelism is held in Rio de Janeiro.

The thirteenth meeting of Baptist World Alliance is in Stockholm.

The fourth International Christian Television Festival is held in Brighton, England, sponsored by the World Association for Christian Communication and the International Catholic Association for Radio and Television.

Pope Paul VI addresses 10,000 pilgrims in Saint Peter's Basilica in Rome at the International Catholic Charismatic Conference.

Campus Crusade for Christ sponsors Here's Life, America, a two-year, multimillion-dollar evangelistic media campaign in more than 200 major cities.

The Consultation of United Churches is held in Toronto, Canada.

Nigeria holds its first National Congress on Evangelization with 800 participants.

The fifth International Congress of Christian Physicians convenes in Singapore. Other meetings had been held in Amsterdam (1963), Oxford (1966), Oslo (1969), and Toronto (1972).

The second World Conference on the Holy Spirit is held in Jerusalem.

The Full Gospel World Mission Association is established in Seoul, Korea.

New Life International begins as an evangelical Charismatic service agency in Fresno, California. In 1984 it is renamed Total World Evangelization Vision.

The Genesis Project is begun to produce the entire Bible on film in 33 years.

Henri J.M. Nouwen writes *Reaching Out*.

Sojourners is founded in Washington, DC, to promote social justice.

1976 Karl Rahner writes *Foundations of Christian Faith*.

Gabriel Olasoji World Evangelism, founded in Ibadan, Nigeria, holds crusades in 25 nations.

The US Center for World Mission is founded in Pasadena, California.

David Yonggi Cho begins Church Growth International seminars in Seoul.

The first Chinese Congress on World Evangelization meets in Hong Kong.

The Lausanne Intercession Advisory Group sets Pentecost Sunday as an annual day of prayer for world evangelization.

Argentinian Mario Marino becomes the first Latin Native American to be consecrated as an Anglican bishop.

The first Pan-orthodox Pre-conciliar Conference is held in Pregny-Chambésy, Switzerland.

The first World Congress of Fundamentalists is held in Edinburgh, Scotland, with 2000 in attendance.

One million Catholics participate in the forty-first International Eucharistic Congress in Philadelphia, Pennsylvania.

The eleventh Pentecostal World Conference is held in Albert Hall, London, with the theme "The Spirit of Truth."

The Pan-African Christian Leadership Assembly meets in Nairobi with 700 delegates.

More than 1.3 billion people hear the Christmas address by Pope Paul VI over radio and TV.

The Episcopal Church General Convention passes legislation allowing women's ordination. The previously ordained 15 women priests are accepted.

Pope Paul VI suspends Marcel Lefebvre, leader of the Priestly Fraternity of Saint Pius X, from priestly duty. His Catholic traditionalist movement continues.

Morton T. Kelsey writes *The Other Side of Silence: A Guide to Christian Meditation*.

Hans Küng writes *On Being a Christian*.

1977   The fifth Latin American Catholic Charismatic Renewal Leaders Conference in Caracas, Venezuela, draws leaders from almost all Latin American countries.

The second National Evangelical Anglican Congress is held at Nottingham University in England. The first congress was at Keele University in Staffordshire, England, in 1967.

The first Conference of the Charismatic Renewal in the Christian Churches meets in Kansas City. It is ecumenical, embracing all Pentecostal traditions. As many as 50,000 attend.

The fourth Synod of Bishops meets in Rome with the theme "Catechetic in Our Time," dealing with evangelization of children and youth.

The World Conference on Audio-Visuals and Evangelization is held in Munich, Germany.

Campus Crusade for Christ launches Here's Life, World, a saturation and total mobilization evangelization campaign. It includes more than 100 countries and every continent.

Five hundred million people hear or see Rex Humbard's one-hour Christmas Eve gospel service, broadcast on radio and TV from Jerusalem in seven languages simultaneously.

In Burma (the Republic of the Union of Myanmar), 6200 converts are baptized in the largest single baptismal service in recent Christian history. It is held by the Kachin Baptist Convention, an evangelical denomination.

1978 The one-year-old International Council on Biblical Inerrancy develops the Chicago Statement on Biblical Inerrancy, providing evangelicals with a clear statement of the doctrine.

Jim Jones, a former San Francisco minister, commits a mass-murder of his followers at Jonestown, Guyana, and takes his own life as well.

The World Methodist Council begins a four-year plan of global evangelism.

The Congress on Evangelism for Malaysia and Singapore includes 300 leaders.

The International Conference on the Charismatic Renewal in the Catholic Church is held in Dublin with the theme "You Shall Be My Witnesses," drawing 15,000 participants.

The eighth International Convention on Missionary Medicine is held in Wheaton, Illinois.

The eleventh Lambeth Conference meets in Canterbury, England, with the theme "Today's Church in Today's World." It includes 420 Anglican bishops.

The second Nigeria National Congress on Evangelization meets in the ancient city of Ife, northeast of Lagos. It has 1000 participants.

The National Christian Leadership Assembly meets in Rhodesia.

Pope Paul VI dies and is succeeded by John Paul I. On his death 34 days later, cardinals elect the first non-Italian pope in 450 years—John Paul II.

The Latin American Council of Churches is created at Oaxtepec, Mexico, with 340 representatives.

The World Congress of Mission and Migration meets in Rome.

The Asian Leadership Conference on Evangelism meets in Singapore with the theme "Together Obeying Christ for Asia's Harvest." It includes 280.

The International Conference on the Charismatic Renewal in the Catholic Church meets in Dublin, led by Cardinal Suenens.

Richard J. Foster writes *The Celebration of Discipline*.

1979 Churches reopen in China.

The Church of England supplements *The Book of Common Prayer* with the *Alternative Services Book*. It reflects the modern study of historical liturgical development.

The Evangelical Council for Financial Accountability is formed as a self-regulatory evangelical agency.

The Protestant Episcopal Church in the United States of America changes its name to the Episcopal Church in the United States of America.

Mother Teresa is awarded the Nobel Peace Prize.

The third General Conference of the Latin American Episcopal Council is held in Puebla, Mexico, with the theme "Evangelization in Latin America Now and in the Future."

More than 10,000 pilgrims attend the International Charismatic Pilgrimage to Lourdes on the centennial of the shrine.

The twelfth Pentecostal World Conference is held in Vancouver, Canada, with the theme "The Holy Spirit in the Last Days."

The second Latin American Congress on Evangelization is held in Huampari, Lima, Peru, with 266 delegates from 21 countries.

The first Norwegian Conference on World Evangelization is held in Drammen, Norway.

Sharing of Ministries Abroad (SOMA), an Anglican renewal agency, holds its first international conference in Singapore.

Campus Crusade for Christ produces *Jesus*, a film dubbed in nearly 300 languages and eventually seen by billions of people.

Billy Graham calls for 120,000 missionaries by 2000 at InterVarsity's Urbana conference.

1980 Marjorie Matthews is the first woman elected to the episcopacy of the Methodist Church.

Robert Schuller builds the Crystal Cathedral.

Óscar Arnulfo Romero, archbishop of Salvador, is assassinated while celebrating Mass. He was a leading proponent of liberation theology and an opponent of the Revolutionary Government Junta of El Salvador.

The Lutheran Church–Missouri Synod becomes the first denomination to urge its members to become organ donors.

The seventh General Assembly of the World Evangelical Fellowship is held in High Leigh, United Kingdom, and includes delegates from 50 countries.

The World Evangelization Crusade in Seoul, Korea, has a combined attendance of 16.5 million, including the largest single meeting in Christian history (2.7 million).

The fifth Synod of Bishops in Rome focuses on the Catholic family.

The United States Festival of World Evangelization draws 50,000 participants.

The International Congress on Evangelization and Atheism meets at Pontifical Urbaniana University in Rome.

The World Consultation on Frontier Missions meets in Edinburgh with the theme "A Church for Every People by the Year 2000" and includes 270 delegates.

The first World Missionary Conference on Mission and Evangelism is held in Melbourne, Australia, with the theme "Thy Kingdom Come."

The Consultation on World Evangelization meets in Pattaya, Bangkok, Thailand. It is themed "How Shall They Hear?" and includes 875 delegates.

Basil Pennington writes *Centering Prayer*.

1981 The fourth assembly of the All Africa Conference of Churches meets in Nairobi with the theme "Following the Light of Jesus Christ."

The Chinese Congress on World Evangelization meets in Singapore.

The World Evangelization Strategy Work Group is formed by the Baptist World Alliance.

Ed and Gaye Wheat write *Intended for Pleasure*.

1982 The thireenth Pentecostal World Conference is held in Nairobi, Kenya.

World Satellite Evangelism begins in Tulsa, Oklahoma, to reach closed countries. It forms a global media task force in 50 nations.

The Institute on World Evangelism is established in Atlanta, Georgia, by the World Evangelism Committee of the World Methodist Council.

Robert A. Schuller writes *Self-Esteem: The New Reformation*.

The Dutch Reformed Mission Church drafts the Confession of Belhar as an "outcry of faith" against apartheid. It is officially accepted in 1986.

Bruce Metzger supervises a committee that produces the Reader's Digest Bible, which contains 60 percent of the original.

The New King James Version, conceived by Arthur L. Farstad, is published.

The World Council of Churches publishes *Baptism, Eucharist, and Ministry*, a statement of essential doctrine that all member denominations can supposedly accept.

The Sudan Interior Mission unites with the Andes Evangelical Mission to form SIM International, one of the largest evangelical foreign missions agencies.

1983 The 1918 *Codex Juris Canonici* (*Code of Canon Law*) is completely revised, taking into account the theological impact of the Second Vatican Council. Excommunication is redefined as a "medicinal" censure rather than a lifelong penalty.

The National Council of Churches releases an inclusive-language lectionary. It is based on the Revised Standard Version of the Bible but contains inclusive language and references to God as Father and Mother.

Elizabeth Schüssler Fiorenza writes *In Memory of Her*, a reconstruction, based on New Testament texts, of the role women played in the life of the early Christian community.

Pope John Paul II makes the first-ever papal visit to a Lutheran church to celebrate the five hundredth anniversary of the birth of Martin Luther.

The American Northern and Southern Presbyterian Churches are reunited.

Imprimaturs are mandated by Roman Catholic canon law. Translations of Scripture, theological textbooks, liturgical books, and catechisms must be approved by the bishop of the author or publisher's diocese. The imprimatur is a license that guarantees that the material does not conflict with official Catholic teaching.

The sixth assembly of the World Council of Churches is held in Vancouver. Its theme is "Jesus Christ, the Life of the World."

The World Baptist Congress on Urban Evangelism is held in Niterói, Brazil.

In Amsterdam, the first International Conference for Itinerant Evangelists is attended by 3800 evangelists from 132 nations.

Lumen 2000 is launched as a Catholic global television evangelism agency based in Dallas and Vatican City.

The Committee on the Holy Spirit and Frontier Missions is formed in California.

New Focus is founded in San Bernardino, California, to promote evangelism during sports events, especially the Olympic games.

Gustavo Gutiérrez writes *We Drink from Our Own Wells*.

Desmond Tutu publishes *Hope and Suffering: Sermons and Speeches*.

1984 Under a revised concordat, Roman Catholicism is no longer the state religion in Italy.

1985 The Youth Congress on World Evangelization meets in Stuttgart, Germany.

The Interchurch Consultation on Future Trends in Christian World Mission meets in Maryknoll, New York, to discuss unfinished tasks of world evangelization.

The International Consultation on Missions is convened in Jos, Nigeria.

Maranatha Campus Ministries unveils World Ambassadors, a plan to evangelize foreign non-Christian students in the United States.

The Global Network of Centers for World Mission is formed with 30 members.

Campus Crusade for Christ holds Explo '85, a global Christian training teleconference.

The Association of International Mission Services is formed with 75 member agencies.

Max Lucado writes *No Wonder They Call Him the Savior*.

Jaroslav Pelikan writes *Jesus Through the Centuries*.

Robert Webber writes *Worship Is a Verb*.

1986 The Church of England allows women to become deacons.

The Intercontinental Broadcasting Network begins in Virginia Beach, Virginia.

The Assemblies of God unveils plans to reach all world cities by 2000.

The International Conference for Equipping Evangelists is held in Sacramento, California.

The second International Conference for Itinerant Evangelists meets in Amsterdam.

The Presbyterian Church announces the Decade of Evangelism, 1990–2000.

The US Society for Frontier Missiology is founded in Colorado Springs, Colorado.

Walter Brueggemann writes *Praying the Psalms*.

John Piper writes *Desiring God: Meditations of a Christian Hedonist*.

John Wimber writes *Power Evangelism*.

Gary Smalley and John Trent write *The Blessing*.

Desmond Tutu becomes the first black Anglican archbishop of Cape Town.

1987 The Vatican releases "Instruction on Respect for Human Life in Its Origin and on the Dignity of Procreation," one of the most comprehensive discussions issued by a church organization on bioethics.

The Presbyterian Church in the United States of America merges with the Presbyterian Church in the United States to form the Presbyterian Church (USA).

Jim Bakker, head of the PTL Ministry, resigns in the midst of a sexual and financial scandal. Jerry Falwell takes over.

Pope John Paul II creates Evangelization 2000, a new Roman office to plan for the Decade of Evangelization.

The International Conference of Evangelical Bible Societies is founded with ten member agencies.

The World Literature Crusade changes its name to Every Home for Christ.

The North American General Congress on the Holy Spirit and World Evangelization meets in New Orleans.

Adopt-a-People begins. Its mission is to link North American churches and mission agencies with unreached people groups.

The Worldwide Prayer Crusade is initiated by the Vatican.

The International Global Missions Conference in Dallas is attended by 20 mission agencies.

The Decade of Harvest is inaugurated by the Assemblies of God to reach all human beings by 2000. A similar program, Decade of Destiny, is launched by the Church of God (Cleveland).

Advance Ministries, a mission-sending agency serving independent Charismatic churches, is begun with Mennonite support.

Frank Peretti writes *This Present Darkness*.

1988 Tadao Ando's Church on the Water is completed in Japan.

The Evangelical Lutheran Church in America (ELCA) is formed through the merger of the Lutheran Church in America, the American Lutheran Church, and the Association of Evangelical Lutheran Churches.

Carbon-dating tests on the Shroud of Turin place its origins in the thirteenth or fourteenth century.

Jimmy Swaggart is removed from the Assemblies of God ministry after he admits to having sex with a prostitute. He loses 69 percent of his TV viewers and 72 percent of his college enrollment.

The World Wesleyan Conference on Witness and Evangelism is held on the two hundred fiftieth anniversary of John Wesley's conversion.

Dallas Willard writes *The Spirit of the Disciplines*.

1989 The Episcopal Church consecrates its first woman bishop, Barbara C. Harris.

The Revised English Bible and the New Revised Standard Version are released.

The Global Consultation on World Evangelization meets in Singapore.

The second World Conference on World Mission and Evangelism meets in San Antonio, Texas.

The second International Conference on World Evangelization (Lausanne II) is convened in Manila.

Patrick M. Morley writes *The Man in the Mirror*.

1990   Henry T. Blackaby and Claude V. King write *Experiencing God*.

Philip Yancey writes *Disappointment with God*.

Pope John Paul II issues *Redemptoris Missio* ("The Mission of the Redeemer") on the permanent validity of the church's missionary mandate.

Bill McCartney and Dave Wardell found the Promise Keepers, which provides training and support for Christian men.

The Washington National Cathedral is completed 83 years after the foundation stone was laid.

The Decade of Universal Evangelization begins with around-the-world prayer events.

Pope John Paul II lays the foundation stone of the Basilica of our Lady of Peace, the largest church in the world, at Yamoussoukro, Ivory Coast.

The post-Soviet Russian government restores religious freedom.

1991   The seventh assembly of the World Council of Churches is held in Canberra, Australia. Its theme is "Come, Holy Spirit, Renew the Whole Creation."

The Global Congress of Charismatic Leaders for World Evangelization is held in Brighton.

The Pan-Orthodox Ecumenical Council meets for the first time since 787.

Tentmakers International Exchange holds its second international conference in London.

The Quadrennial World Assembly of the International Fellowship of Evangelical Students is held in Wheaton, Illinois, on the theme "The Cross of Jesus."

Pope John Paul II and 1.3 million students attend the sixth World Youth Day in Katowice, Poland.

Neil Anderson writes *Released from Bondage*.

1992 *The Catechism of the Catholic Church*, the first "universal catechism" in almost four centuries, is issued. It is a reference work for Catholic bishops seeking to include the teachings of Vatican II in their catechesis.

The Evangelical Lutheran Church in America, the Presbyterian Church (USA), the Reformed Church in America, and the United Church of Christ declare that they are in full communion with one another.

April Ulring Larson becomes the first female Lutheran bishop.

The third Latin American Congress on Evangelization is held in Quito, Ecuador.

The sixteenth triennial Pentecostal World Conference convenes in Oslo, Norway, attended by 12,500 people.

The World Council of Churches holds the fifth Conference on Faith and Order in Santiago de Compostela, Spain.

John Stott writes *The Contemporary Christian*.

Henri Nouwen writes *The Return of the Prodigal Son*.

The General Synod of the Church of England approves the ordination of women.

1993 David Koresh's Branch Davidians commit suicide by setting fire to their compound in Waco, Texas, after a 51-day standoff with federal law enforcement personnel.

Pope John Paul II issues *Veritatis Splendor* ("The Splendor of Truth"), addressing fundamental questions of the church's moral teaching.

1994 The Vatican officially recognizes the State of Israel.

Randy Clark's revival meetings at a Toronto Vineyard church produce ecstatic experiences—crying, falling, uncontrollable laughing, and shaking—that participants attribute to the Holy Spirit. The church draws more than 1.2 million people for nightly meetings during the next four years.

The World Holy Spirit Conference convenes in Seoul, Korea.

The first world conference of the World Assemblies of God Fellowship is held in Seoul, Korea.

Max Lucado writes *When God Whispers Your Name*.

Mark Noll writes *The Scandal of the Evangelical Mind*.

The Seven Promises of a Promise Keeper includes chapters by many leading Evangelicals.

1995 Thirty-two African-American churches in the Southern United States are bombed or burned in the worst outbreak of arson since the Civil rights movement.

Revival erupts in the Brownsville Assembly of God Church in Pensacola, Florida.

Tim LaHaye and Jerry Jenkins begin the Left Behind series.

Pope John Paul II issues *Evangelium Vitae* ("The Gospel of Life"), on the value and inviolability of human life, and *Ut Unum Sint* ("That They May Be One"), a commitment to ecumenism.

1996   Since 1990, 340 monasteries, 10,000 parish churches, and 14 seminaries have opened in Russia.

The third World Missionary Conference on World Mission and Evangelism is held in Salvador, Brazil.

Kathleen Norris writes *The Cloister Walk*.

John Updike writes *In the Beauty of the Lilies*.

Henri J. M. Nouwen writes *Bread for the Journey*.

Andrew Walls writes *The Missionary Movement in Christian History*.

Forrest Church writes *God and Other Famous Liberals*.

Miroslav Volf writes *Exclusion and Embrace*.

1997   Promise Keepers holds a mass rally for national repentance in Washington, DC, attended by 1.5 million men.

Pope John Paul II visits Cuba.

Ten million believers in 150 countries join March for Jesus.

Mark Noll writes *Seasons of Grace*.

Billy Graham writes *Just as I Am: The Autobiography of Billy Graham*.

Jim Cymbala writes *Fresh Wind, Fresh Fire*.

1998   The World Conference on Intercession, Spiritual Warfare, and Evangelism is held in Guatemala City.

The first National Conference on Fasting and Prayer is held in Houston, Texas, attended by 1.8 million.

Lee Strobel writes *The Case for Christ*.

John Paul II issues *Fides et Ratio* ("Faith and Reason"), addressing the relationship between them.

Dallas Willard writes *The Divine Conspiracy*.

1999   The World Conference on Deliverance: Equipping the Church for Revival is held in Colorado Springs.

The First International Consultation on Discipleship is held in Eastbourne, England.

Anne Lamott writes *Traveling Mercies: Some Thoughts on Faith.*
The Joint Declaration on the Doctrine of Justification is signed by Catholic and Lutheran churches.

The Dawn of the Third Millennium

THE STATUS OF THE CHRISTIAN CHURCH

Sixty-six generations after Christ, 70 percent of the world is evangelized, and the population is 32.9 percent Christian. The church is 55 percent nonwhite, and printed Scriptures are available in 1911 languages.

SIGNIFICANT EVENTS AND INFLUENCES

- In 2033 the Christian church will complete an important benchmark—its first 2000 years. It provides a coign of vantage from which to assess the status of the church and the task ahead.
- There were more than two billion Christians in the world in 2010. This is the number from which everything in this book flows. Christianity can be understood only in terms of the fact that it touches this many people.
- The percentage of Christians in the global population has decreased slightly in the past 30 years. This is partly due to the greater birthrate of non-Christians. However, Christians make up more than 50 percent of the literate population of the world. In all countries, Christians are more literate than non-Christians. More than 60 percent of Muslims and 45 percent of Hindus are illiterate.
- More than 18 billion human beings have lived on earth as Christians since AD 33. Every day the number of Christians grows by 72,900. Of these, 24,000 are added in Africa, 21,000 in South America, 19,400 in Asia, 5000 in North America, 2200 in Europe, and 800 in Oceania. Christianity became a predominantly nonwhite religion in the 1990s. It has experienced massive losses in the Western world since the end of World War II.
- In most human institutions, futurists can extrapolate trends and chart the short-term future. But Christianity is not a human institution. If it were, it would have disappeared long ago. The rudder of the universal church is in the hands of the Holy Spirit, and its time lines are already set. There are no surprises in Christian history because it proceeds in a straight line and toward a set goal. The New Testament assures believers that the church militant and the suffering church of what Paul calls "the present age" will be replaced by the church triumphant, reunited with her Lord along with the hosts of believers. When the end is so clearly delineated, the ups and downs of the journey to that goal become less important.
- Numerically, Christianity, now the religion of one-third of humanity, has passed its cusp and may not be able to make great gains in the new century.

Further, it is in serious decline based on external indicators in almost all countries that constitute traditional Christendom, and this decline is expected to continue. During the past 2000 years, it was able to compensate serious losses in any one region by expanding into others. Thus when it lost its traditional home in the Middle East, it gained Europe through evangelization. When it lost Turkey and Central Asia, it gained the two continents of the New World. Finally, when in the modern age it lost Europe to Marxism, secularism, and humanism, it gained Africa, thus becoming a global religion incrementally. But the process cannot continue indefinitely after the gospel has reached "the uttermost parts of the earth." Further, resistance to the gospel is not merely from other religions but also from secular people in historically Christian countries. Missionary efforts tend to flag as fatigue sets in. The quality of Christian witness and experience has also tended to deteriorate in many countries, suffocated and smothered by the thorns and thistles of materialism. Even though statistics claim that there are more than two billion Christians, the percentage of committed believers may be as low as 25 percent.

- Church growth has always occurred in spurts. Long periods of dormancy are followed by quantum jumps. These leaps are invariably the result of divine intervention because the church alone has no directional compass or reserves of energy outside the Holy Spirit. Now that the entire inhabited world has access to the gospel, the next stage of Christian growth will be different from the past. The Christian church has been described as a pilgrim church, and it is not going to be permanently on earth. The next eschatological phase of Christian history will accelerate the pilgrimage of the church to its final destiny as the church triumphant.

CHRONOLOGY

2000 A new Cathedral of Christ the Savior is consecrated in Moscow.
Common Praise, the first full revision of *Hymns, Ancient and Modern*, is published.

2001 Pope John Paul II ends the Great Jubilee Year.
The Mennonite Church and the General Conference Mennonite Church merge to form the Mennonite Conference USA.

2002 Gene Robinson is consecrated as the first openly gay bishop of the Episcopal Church.

2003 Pope John Paul II issues the encyclical *Ecclesia de Eucharistia* ("The Church and the Eucharist"), a restatement of the Eucharistic doctrine.

2005 Pope John Paul II dies. Joseph Ratzinger is elected as Pope Benedict XVI. Roger Schutz, founder of the Taizé community, is murdered.

2006 Pope Benedict XVI issues the encyclical *Deus Caritas Est* ("God Is Love").

The ninth general assembly of the World Council of Churches meets in Brazil.

2013 Pope Benedict XVI steps down as pope, and Pope Francis becomes the first South American to be elected pope.

Pope Shenouda III, the Coptic patriarch, dies, and Pope Tawardos II is installed in his place.

Christian churches are burned and Christians massacred in Egypt and Syria.

2014 Pope Francis visits the Holy Land.

Appendixes

Appendix 1

Christian Literature

50–90   The New Testament

100–200   *Didache*

130   *Shepherd of Hermas*

150   *First Apology* and *Second Apology* by Justin Martyr

188   *Against Heresies* by Irenaeus

220   *On First Principles* by Origen

313   *On the Incarnation* by Athanasius

324   *Church History* by Eusebius Pamphili

379   *On the Christian Faith* by Ambrose

395   *The Great Catechism* by Gregory of Nyssa

397-398   *Confessions* by Augustine

400-428   *On the Trinity* by Augustine

405   The Vulgate by Jerome

413-426   *City of God* by Augustine

419   *Institutes of Monastic Life* by John Cassian

528   *The Rule of Benedict* by Benedict of Nursia

640   *The Ladder of Divine Ascent* by John Climacus

1030   *Spiritual Life* by Peter Damian

1126   *On the Necessity of Loving God* by Bernard of Clairvaux

1150   *Book of Sentences* by Peter Lombard

1265-1274   *Summa Theologica* by Thomas Aquinas

1320   *The Divine Comedy* by Dante Alighieri

1322   *The Little Flowers of St. Francis*

1346   *Adornment of the Spiritual Marriage* by Jan Van Ruysbroeck

1393   *Revelations of Divine Love* by Julian of Norwich

1395   *The Cloud of Unknowing* (Anonymous)

1418   *Of the Imitation of Christ* by Thomas à Kempis

1440   *On Learned Ignorance* by Nicholas of Cusa

1456   The Gutenberg Bible

1517   "95 Theses" by Martin Luther

1525   *The Bondage of the Will* by Martin Luther

1536   *Institutes of the Christian Religion* by John Calvin

1539   *Foundation of Christian Doctrine* by Menno Simons

1548   *Spiritual Exercises* by Ignatius of Loyola

1549   *The Book of Common Prayer*

1554   *Foxe's Book of Martyrs*

1587   *The Dark Night of the Soul* and *The Ascent of Mount Carmel* by John of the Cross

1588   *The Interior Castle* by Teresa of Avila

1609   *Introduction to the Devout Life* by Francis de Sales

1624   *Devotions upon Emergent Occasions* by John Donne

1650   *The Rule and Exercise of Holy Living and Holy Dying* by Jeremy Taylor; *The Saints' Everlasting Rest* by Richard Baxter

1667   *Paradise Lost* by John Milton

1670   *Pensées* by Blaise Pascal

1678–1684   *The Pilgrim's Progress* by John Bunyan

1682   *Discourses on the Existence and Attributes of God* by Stephen Charnock

1685   *A Short and Very Easy Method of Prayer* by Madame Guyon

1692   *The Practice of the Presence of God* by Brother Lawrence (Nicholas Herman)

1694   *Journal of George Fox*

1704 *Christian Perfection* by François Fenelon

1728 *A Serious Call to a Devout and Holy Life* by William Law

1739 *Journals* by John Wesley

1746 *A Treatise Concerning the Religious Affections* by Jonathan Edwards

1749 *The Diary of David Brainerd*

1766 *A Plain Account of Christian Perfection* by John Wesley

1835 *Lectures on Revivals of Religion* by Charles Grandison Finney

1843 *The Way of Holiness* by Phoebe Palmer

1847 *Purity of Heart Is to Will One Thing* by Søren Aaye Kierkegaard

1870 *The Christian's Secret of a Happy Life* by Hannah Whitall Smith

1871 *Systematic Theology* by Charles Hodge

1886 *Systematic Theology* by Augustus Hopkins Strong

1896 *In His Steps* by Charles Monroe Sheldon

1906 *The Quest of the Historical Jesus* by Albert Schweitzer

1908 *Orthodoxy* by Gilbert Keith Chesterton

1910 *The Fundamentals*

1918 *Poems* by Gerald Manley Hopkins

1919 *The Epistle to the Romans* by Karl Barth

1930 *Christus Victor* by Gustav Aulen

1932 *Church Dogmatics* by Karl Barth

1936 *Diary of a Country Priest* by Georges Bernanos

1937 *The Cost of Discipleship* and *Letters and Papers from Prison* by Dietrich Bonhoeffer

1942 *The Screwtape Letters* by C.S. Lewis

1948 *The Seven-Storey Mountain* by Thomas Merton; *Pursuit of God* by A.W. Tozer

1951 *Christ and Culture* by H. Reinhold Niebuhr

1952 *Mere Christianity* by C.S. Lewis

1957 *The Normal Christian Life* by Watchman Nee

1962 *New Seeds of Contemplation* by Thomas Merton

1963 *Markings* by Dag Hammarskjöld; *The Orthodox Church* by Timothy
         Kallistos Ware

1964 *They Speak with Other Tongues* by John L. Sherrill

1970 *The Late Great Planet Earth* by Hal Lindsay

1971 *The Hiding Place* by Corrie ten Boom

1972 *Evidence That Demands a Verdict* by Josh McDowell

1973 *Knowing God* by J.I. Packer

1974 *On Being a Christian* by Hans Küng

1975 *Reaching Out* by Henri J.M. Nouwen

1978 *The Celebration of Discipline* by Richard Foster

1981 *Godric* by Frederick Buechner

1986 *Desiring God* by John Piper

1988 *The Spirit of the Disciplines* by Dallas Willard

1990 *Experiencing God* by Henry T. Blackaby and Claude V. King

1995 Left Behind (Series) by Tim LaHaye and Jerry Jenkins

1996 *Exclusion and Embrace* by Miroslav Wolf

1999 *Traveling Mercies* by Anne Lamott

2002 *The Purpose-Driven Life* by Rick Warren

2005 *Christ Plays in Ten Thousand Places* by Eugene H. Peterson

Appendix 2

Christian Creeds

THE APOSTLES' CREED

I believe in God, the Father Almighty, Maker of heaven and earth.

And in Jesus Christ, his only Son, our Lord: who was conceived by the Holy Spirit, born of the Virgin Mary, suffered under Pontius Pilate, was crucified, died and buried. He descended to hell, on the third day he rose again from the dead. He ascended into heaven and sits at the right hand of God the Father Almighty. From thence he will come to judge the living and the dead.

I believe in the Holy Spirit, the holy catholic church, the communion of saints, the forgiveness of sins, the resurrection of the body and the life everlasting.

THE NICENE CREED

We believe in one God, the Father Almighty, Maker of all things visible and invisible.

And in one Lord Jesus Christ, the Son of God, begotten of the Father, that is, of the essence of the Father, God of God, Light of Light, very God of very God, begotten, not created, being of one substance with the Father, by whom all things were made, both in heaven and in earth; who for us men and for our salvation came down and was incarnate and was made man. He suffered, and the third day he rose again and ascended into heaven. From thence he will come to judge the living and the dead.

And in the Holy Spirit.

But those who say, "There was a time when he was not," and "He was not before he was made," and "He was made out of nothing," or "He is of another substance or essence," or "The Son of God is created," or "changeable," or "alterable"—they are condemned by the holy catholic and apostolic Church.

THE CREED OF CONSTANTINOPLE (381)

We believe in one God, the Father Almight, Maker of heaven and earth, of all things visible and invisible.

And in one Lord Jesus Christ, the only begotten Son of God, begotten of the Father before all time, Light of Light, very God of very God, begotten, not created, being of one substance with the Father, by whom all things were made, who for us men and for our salvation came down from heaven, and was incarnate by the Holy Spirit of the Virgin Mary, and was made man. He was crucified for us under Pontius Pilate, and suffered and was buried, and rose on the third day, according to the Scriptures, and ascended into heaven, and sits on the right hand of the Father. From thence he will come again with glory to judge the living and the dead. His kingdom shall have no end.

And in the Holy Spirit, the Lord and giver of life, who proceeds from the Father, who is worshipped and glorified together with the Father and the Son, who spoke through the prophets.

And in one holy catholic and apostolic church. We acknowledge one baptism for the remission of sins; we look forward to the resurrection of the dead and the life of the world to come. Amen.

100 Most Consequential Events in Christian History

30 Jesus's crucifixion, resurrection, and ascension; Pentecost

35 martyrdom of Stephen; Paul is converted

40 first apostolic council in Jerusalem

65 martyrdom of Paul and Peter

70 destruction of Jerusalem by Titus

150 Justin Martyr's *First Apology*

196 Tertullian begins writing

205 Origen begins teaching and writing

270 Anthony the Great becomes a hermit in Egypt and begins Christian monasticism

312 conversion of Constantine

313 Edict of Milan

325 Council of Nicaea

328 Athanasius becomes bishop of Alexandria

367 Athanasius establishes the canon of the New Testament

385 triumph of Ambrose over the empress

387 conversion of Augustine

405 Jerome completes the Vulgate

432 Patrick begins evangelization of Ireland

461 Council of Chalcedon—some Eastern Churches break from the West

540 Benedict writes his monastic rule

563 Columba establishes a mission community on Iona

590 Gregory the Great elected pope

625   Alopen becomes the first Nestorian missionary to each China

716   Boniface sets out as missionary

731   publication of Bede's *Ecclesiastical History*

732   Battle of Tours

800   coronation of Charlemagne

863   Cyril and Methodius embark on mission to the Slavs

909   monastery at Cluny

988   conversion of Vladimir, Prince of Russia

1054 East–West Schism

1093 Anselm becomes archbishop of Canterbury

1095 Crusades launched by Pope Urban II

1115 Bernard founds monastery at Clairvaux

1173 Waldensian movement begins

1206 Francis of Assisi begins ministry

1272 *Summa Theologica* by Thomas Aquina

1321 Dante completes *The Divine Comedy*

1373 Julian of Norwich receivers her revelations

1378 great papal schism

1380 Wycliffe's translation of English Bible

1415 Hus burned at the stake

1453 Constantinople falls to the Turks, and Hagia Sophia is converted into a mosque

1456 publication of Gutenberg Bible

1478 establishment of Spanish Inquisition

1492 Columbus discovers New World

1512 Michelangelo completes the Sistine Chapel ceiling

1517 Luther posts his 95 Theses

1521 Diet of Worms

1523 Zwingli leads the Swiss Reformation

1525 Tyndale publishes his New Testament

1525 Anabaptist Movement begins

1529 Colloquy at Marburg

1530 Augsburg Confession

1534 Act of Supremacy

1536 John Calvin's *Institutes of the Christian Religion*

1538 The Great Schism

1540 Society of Jesus (the Jesuits) is established

1545 Council of Trent

1549 *Book of Common Prayer*

1559 Knox returns to Scotland to lead the Reformation

1582 Pope Gregory introduces the Gregorian Calendar

1598 Edict of Nantes

1609 Baptism of John Smyth, founder of the Baptists

1611 King James Bible

1618 Synod of Dort

1620 Pilgrims sign the Mayflower Compact

1647 Westminster Confession

1648 George Fox founds the Society of Friends

1662 Rembrandt completes *The Return of the Prodigal Son*

1738 Conversion of John and Charles Wesley

1793 William Carey sails for India

1807 William Wilberforce spearheads abolition of slavery in Britain

1811 the Campbells begin the Disciples of Christ

1812 Adoniram and Ann Judson sail for India

1830 Charles Finney leads revival in New York

1830 John Nelson Darby helps start the Plymouth Brethren

1833 John Keble launches the Oxford Movement

1840 David Livingstone leaves for Africa

1854 Hudson Taylor arrives in China

1854 C.H. Spurgeon becomes a pastor in London

1855 D.L. Moody's conversion

1865 Hudson Taylor founds China Inland Mission

1869 Vatican I; Pope Pius IX proclaims papal infallibility

1878 William and Catherine Booth found the Salvation Army

1886 Student Volunteer Movement begins

1906 Azusa Street Revival breaks out, marking the beginning of modern Pentecostalism

1919 Karl Barth's *Epistle to the Romans*

1927 Calvary Episcopal Church in Pittsburgh launches first Christian radio station KDKA

1931 Radio Vatican is inaugurated by Pope Pius XI

1934 Cameron Townsend founds Wycliffe Bible Translators

1948 founding of the World Council of Churches

1949 Billy Graham holds his tent meeting (called Crusade) in Los Angeles

1949 Chinese People's Republic wipes out centuries of missionary work in China

1961 Pat Robertson launches first Christian television station CBN

1962 Vatican II

1963 Martin Luther King Jr. leads march on Washington

1968 Jesus People movement invigorates the church

1990 collapse of Communism in Russia and Eastern Europe

To learn more about Harvest House books and
to read sample chapters, log on to our website:

www.harvesthousepublishers.com

HARVEST HOUSE PUBLISHERS
EUGENE, OREGON